Challenges of CAFTA

Challenges of CAFTA

Maximizing the Benefits for Central America

Carlos Felipe Jaramillo
Daniel Lederman
Maurizio Bussolo
David Gould
Andrew Mason

THE WORLD BANK

1818 H Street NW
Washington DC 20433
Telephone: 202-473-1000
Internet: www.worldbank.org
E-mail: feedback@worldbank.org

1 2 3 4 09 08 07 06

ISBN-10: 0-8213-6444-8
ISBN-13: 978-0-8213-6444-4
eISBN: 0-8213-6445-6
DOI: 10.1596/978-0-8213-6444-4

Library of Congress Cataloging-in-Publication Data

Jaramillo, C. Felipe, 1962-
Challenges of CAFTA: maximizing the benefits for Central America / C. Felipe Jaramillo, Daniel Lederman.
p. cm. -- (Directions in development)
Includes bibliographical references and index.
ISBN-13: 978-0-8213-6444-4
ISBN-10: 0-8213-6444-8
1. CAFTA (Free trade agreement) (2005). 2. Free trade--Central America. 3. Central America--Commerce. I. Lederman, Daniel, 1968-. II. Title. III. Directions in development (Washington, D.C.)

HF1782.J37 2006
382'.9172--dc22

2005058107

Cover design by Naylor Design, Inc.
Cover photo by Curt Carnemark/World Bank

Contents

Boxes

Figures

Tables

Foreword

The signing of the free trade agreement (FTA) among Costa Rica, the Dominican Republic (DR), El Salvador, Guatemala, Honduras, and Nicaragua with the United States (DR-CAFTA) may represent a landmark for the five Central American countries and the DR that decided to engage in a reciprocal FTA with their main trading partner, the United States, instead of relying on the hitherto discretional unilateral preferences received through the Caribbean Basin Initiative. Indeed, although the authors of this book caution that estimates of impact are "more art than science," they provide a body of evidence that strongly suggests important consumer, efficiency, and dynamic gains derived from the expanded and more certain market access. Dynamic gains, in terms of investment promotion and technological progress through the acquisition of foreign technologies and know-how (that will receive a push from the highest certainty in market access), as well as the pressures exerted on domestic firms and institutions to become more innovative and efficient, can be especially large. Moreover, in the case of the DR-CAFTA beneficiaries, the FTA with the United States presents perhaps the clearest option for enhancing Central America's economic and social prospects in an inevitably globalizing economy characterized by fast-growing economies with abundant unskilled labor (relative to skilled labor) and tough competition for niches in the U.S. market, especially but not exclusively in the apparel sector.

Furthermore, the decision to make the provisions of the agreement apply multilaterally among Central American countries and the DR will deepen subregional integration efforts and permit taking advantage of economies of scale that are key for countries like these with limited population and economic size. It could seem somewhat paradoxical that in the past years the major boost for subregional integration has come from successful trade negotiations with a third partner. However, a guaranteed joint access to the large U.S. market—by far the largest market for each country—gives much more value to economies of scale in production.

Notwithstanding these expected effects, the authors rightly emphasize that the real challenge is to pursue a complementary agenda that includes improving institutions (from a more efficient regulatory environment to the reduction of corruption), infrastructure, and education and innovation policies. Such improvements are in any case the backbone of a successful development strategy, but their value and urgency are enhanced with the signing of the FTA. Indeed, the positive effects of DR-CAFTA will be much larger for those countries that make the greatest advances in this agenda—and specifically make strides in removing current specific binding constraints to increased and more diversified exports. At the same time, such developmental actions will yield more benefits with expanded and more certain access to the large U.S. market. Hence, although not all potential gains from DR-CAFTA will be automatic, this book provides some clues to potential policy priorities that could be pursued by the various trade agreement beneficiaries to enhance the value of the agreement and their overall development. Each country needs to have an open but well-informed national dialogue about the long-term complementary agenda focusing on broader development challenges that seem inextricable from international trade and investment flows.

Of particular importance for Central American countries (perhaps with the exception of Costa Rica) is the process of adjustment that will affect primarily small rural producers of sensitive crops, although the authors' estimates suggest that the number of families who might be negatively affected does not exceed 3 percent of the national population in any of the countries involved. Whereas gradual tariff and quota phase-out periods and key exemptions (for example, for white corn) negotiated into the text of the agreement will help by providing time for net producers of sensitive crops to improve their productivity or shift to other crops or activities, complementary and well-targeted public programs for small producers in these sectors can provide larger social gains than will the gradual liberalization. Here again it is not clear that "one size fits all," and thus this book discusses various options for designing appropriate adjustment-assistance policies in each country.

Finally, only Costa Rica will face the need to make significant legislative changes to adapt policies and regulations to the commitments in the area of services under DR-CAFTA, specifically with respect to its telecommunications and insurance industries. Although such reforms are politically challenging, the reforms will permit the modernization, efficiency, and competitiveness of those key areas of the Costa Rican economy in which the country currently lags with respect to many of its subregional and global partners and competitors.

Guillermo Perry
Chief Economist, Latin America and Caribbean Region
May 2006

Acknowledgments

This study was led by Carlos Felipe Jaramillo, Lead Economist for the Central America Department, and Daniel Lederman, Senior Economist, Office of the Chief Economist. It included a core team comprising Maurizio Bussolo, Norbert Fiess, David Gould, Andrew Mason, and Ricardo Tejada. Key responsibilities for chapters were as follows: chapters 1, 2, 3, and 7—C. Felipe Jaramillo and Daniel Lederman; chapter 4—Maurizio Bussolo, David Gould, C. Felipe Jaramillo, and Daniel Lederman; chapter 5—C. Felipe Jaramillo, Daniel Lederman, and Andrew Mason; and chapter 6—Norbert Fiess, C. Felipe Jaramillo, and Daniel Lederman.

Excellent research assistance was provided by Ricardo Tejada (chapters 2, 3, and 4), Jorge Camacho (chapters 2 and 4), Ana Maria Menéndez (chapter 3), and Ana Cristina Torres (chapter 5). The peer reviewers were Antonella Bassani, José Manuel Salazar, and Jack Stein. In addition, the team benefited greatly from comments and conversations with colleagues, including Carlos Arce, Amparo Ballivian, Paulo Correa, Pablo Fajnzylber, Dante Ariel Mossi, Francisco Pichón, Helena Ribe, Manuel Sevilla, and Neeta Sirur.

Desktop publishing was done by Sonia C. Molina. Elena Serrano and Alejandra Viveros were responsible for developing the dissemination strategy, and Nicky Bowyer coordinated translation services. Rodrigo Jarque and Beatriz Prieto-Oramas provided proofreading and editing help.

The report, prepared under the stewardship of Jane Armitage, Country Director, and Guillermo Perry, Chief Economist, draws on the work of an extended team both within and outside the World Bank. Background papers were written by Amy Angel (*Fundación Salvadoreña para el Desarrollo Económico y Social* [FUSADES]) on agricultural quotas; Norbert Fiess (World Bank) on business cycle synchronization; Caroline Freund (World Bank) on reciprocity in free trade agreements, and with Bineswaree Bolaky (University of Maryland) on trade, regulations, and growth; Anabel González (consultant) on legal and institutional changes; Maria del Pilar Londoño-Kent and Paul Kent (consultants) on ports; José Marques (Synthesis) on impacts in El Salvador; Ricardo Monge (Costa Rican High Technology Advisory Committee) and Florencia Castro-Leal (World Bank) on impacts in Nicaragua; Ricardo Monge, Miguel Loría (World Bank), and Claudio González-Vega (Ohio State University) on impacts on agriculture; Caglar Ozden (World Bank) and Daniel Lederman (World Bank) on the Caribbean Basin Initiative versus the free trade agreement and other trade preferences; Caglar Ozden and Gunjan Sharma (University of Maryland) on textile and apparel trade; Claus C. Pörtner (University of Washington) on impacts in Guatemala; Andrés Rodríguez-Clare (Penn State University) on innovation and technology adoption; Sergio Schmukler (World Bank) on financial globalization; and J. Edward Taylor (University of California–Davis) on trade integration and rural economies.

Most important, this report reflects a long process of interactive research and policy dialogue, originally launched in San José, Costa Rica, at a round table with Central American ministers of trade in December 2002—one month before formal DR-CAFTA negotiations were launched. Preliminary findings of the study and background papers were discussed a month after the end of negotiations, at a regional conference (co-sponsored by the Department for International Development) in San Salvador, El Salvador, in February 2004. At that conference, stakeholders from all sectors of Central American societies were invited to participate. The report benefited from fruitful exchanges with a large number of citizens of all Central American nations, including government officials, civil society stakeholders, and representatives from other donor agencies. The authors would like to acknowledge especially valuable conversations with trade ministers Mario Arana, Norman Garcia, Miguel Lacayo, and Alberto Trejos, and with negotiators Enrique Ayala, Yolanda de Gavidia, Roberto Echandi, Anabel Gonzalez, and Fernando

Ocampo. Others who helped us with information and useful insights include Amy Angel (FUSADES-El Salvador), Diego Arias (Inter-American Development Bank [IADB]), Rebeca Grynspan (Economic Commission for Latin America and the Caribbean), Hans Peter Lankes (International Monetary Fund [IMF]), Jose Marques (Synthesis-El Salvador), Pablo Rodas (Association for Research and Social Studies-Guatemala), Ennio Rodríguez (Inter-American Development Bank [IADB]), Mary Ryckman (U.S. Trade Representative [USTR]), Jose Manuel Salazar-Xiriñachs (Organization of American States), Alfred Schipke (IMF), and Regina Vargo (USTR). The team would like to thank all of those people who gave generously of their time to meet with the team and share their thoughts.

About the Authors

Carlos Felipe Jaramillo is Macroeconomics Sector Manager for Turkey, South Caucasus, and Central Asia at the World Bank. When the book was written, he was Lead Economist for Central America at the World Bank. He holds Ph.D. and M.A. degrees in applied economics from Stanford University. His current research interests focus on the impact of trade on development and the challenges faced by former socialist economies.

Daniel Lederman is Senior Economist in the World Bank's Development Economics Research Group. He is also affiliated with the Office of the Chief Economist for Latin America and the Caribbean at the World Bank. He holds Ph.D. and M.A. degrees from Johns Hopkins University's School of Advanced International Studies. He is the author of numerous articles and books on Latin American development.

Maurizio Bussolo is Senior Economist in the Development Economics Prospects Group of the World Bank. He holds a Ph.D. in economics from the University of Warwick, United Kingdom. He has published articles on quantitative analyses of economic policy and development, including studies of the links among trade, growth, and poverty.

David Gould is the Lead Economist for Central America at the World Bank. He holds a Ph.D. in economics from the University of California, Los

Angeles. Prior to joining the World Bank, he was Director of Global Economic Analysis at The Institute of International Finance and was a senior economist with the Federal Reserve Bank of Dallas, Texas. He is the author of many academic articles and policy reports on macroeconomics and international trade.

Andrew Mason is Senior Economist with the Human Development Department of the World Bank's Latin America and the Caribbean Region. He holds a Ph.D. in applied economics from Stanford University and an M.A. in public policy from the John F. Kennedy School of Government, Harvard University. He is the author of numerous reports on social protection, poverty, and gender inequality in developing countries.

Acronyms

BCS	business cycle synchronization
CACM	Central American Common Market
CAFTA	Central American Free Trade Agreement
CARICOM	Caribbean Community
CAUCA	*Consejo Arancelario y Aduanero Centroamericano*
CBERA	Caribbean Basin Economic Recovery Act
CBI	Caribbean Basin Initiative
CCT	conditional cash transfer
CES	constant elasticity of substitution
CET	constant elasticity of transformation
CGE	computable general equilibrium
CINDE	*Coalición Costarricense de Iniciativas de Desarrollo*
CPI	Corruption Perceptions Index
DR	Dominican Republic
EHPM	*Encuesta de Hogares para Propósitos Múltiples*
EMNV	*Encuesta de Medición del Nivel de Vida*

ENCOVI	*Encuesta Nacional de Condiciones de Vida*
EPZ	export processing zone
EU	European Union
FDI	foreign direct investment
FIDE	*Fundación Iberoamericana para el Desarrollo*
FTA	free trade agreement
FTAA	Free Trade Area of the Americas
FUSADES	*Fundación Salvadoreña para el Desarrollo Económico y Social*
GATT	General Agreement on Tariffs and Trade
GDP	Gross Domestic Product
GSP	Generalized System of Preferences
HIPC	Heavily Indebted Poor Countries
IC	Investment Climate [Assessment]
ICS	Investment Climate Survey
ILO	International Labour Organization
INSAFORP	*Instituto Salvadoreño de Formación Profesional*
IPR	intellectual property rights
MERCOSUR	*Mercado Común del Sur*
MFN	most-favored nation
NAFTA	North American Free Trade Agreement
NGO	nongovernmental organization
OECD	Organisation for Economic Co-operation and Development
PPP	purchasing power parity
R&D	Research and Development
RIA	regional integration arrangement
RPS	*Red de Protección Social*
SAC	Central American Tariff Classification
SAM	Social Accounting Matrix
SAT	*Superintendencia de Administración Tributaria*
SPS	sanitary and phytosanitary
TFP	total factor productivity

TPL	tariff preference level
TRAINS	Trade Analysis and Information System
TRIMs	Trade-Related Investment Measures
TRIPS	Trade-Related Aspects of Intellectual Property Rights
TRQs	tariff-rate quotas
U.N.	United Nations
UNCOMTRADE	U.N. Commodity Trade Statistics Database
UPOV	International Union for the Protection of New Varieties of Plants
USTR	United States Trade Representative
VAT	value-added tax
VAR	vector autoregression
WBI	World Bank Institute
WTO	World Trade Organization

CHAPTER 1

Summary of Findings and Introduction

A central factor in determining the future of Central America will be the ratification and implementation of DR-CAFTA, the free trade agreement FTA) negotiated by Costa Rica, the Dominican Republic (DR), El Salvador, Guatemala, Honduras, and Nicaragua with the United States. This agreement is important not only because the United States is the major trading partner for these nations, but also because the treaty holds the potential of increasing trade and investment in the region. Those results, in turn, are key to promoting economic growth and improving the welfare of the people of Central America and the DR, including those living in poverty.

This book provides a preliminary assessment of DR-CAFTA, with particular attention to three key themes: (1) expected trade and nontrade benefits, (2) actions that Central American countries need to pursue to capitalize optimally on the new opportunities, and (3) identification of the population groups that may require assistance to adapt to a more competitive environment. The text focuses on the developing countries of Central America, namely, Costa Rica, El Salvador, Guatemala, Honduras, and Nicaragua.

Past experience demonstrates that predicting the precise effects of any free trade agreement is always difficult. However, this report draws upon a number of different approaches and methodologies to reach the conclusion that DR-CAFTA is likely to improve growth levels for the participating countries in Central America and the DR because of the expected positive effects on trade and investment levels. Greater trade levels will arise from the removal of virtually all tariff and quota barriers to trade among all parties, consolidating—and in some cases expanding—the preferential market access that Central American countries have enjoyed in U.S. markets through the Caribbean Basin Initiative (CBI) program. DR-CAFTA is also expected to deepen regional trade integration (and increase trade levels) among the Central American nations themselves and with the Dominican Republic. DR-CAFTA additionally should promote greater levels of foreign and domestic investment, by improving the certainty of these countries' market access to the United States, solidifying the broad economic reforms of recent years and spurring further reform efforts. Investors should respond positively to the modernization of key regulations in such areas as trade in services, government procurement, and intellectual property rights—including provisions for greater transparency in government regulations—which will be made more credible under DR-CAFTA commitments.

At the same time, the book's analysis of the gains from trade suggest that, as has been found with other trade agreements, these gains will depend on the ability of the Central American economies to successfully adjust to the changes that the agreement will bring (including changes in relative prices) and to handle effectively the ensuing restructuring of the economy. Hence, the magnitude of the benefits from DR-CAFTA will depend critically on the ability of the Central American economies to pursue a complementary policy agenda, because the agreement's benefits can lead to substantial developmental gains if the treaty is accompanied by parallel efforts in areas like trade facilitation (for example, ports, roads, and customs), institutional and regulatory reforms, and innovation and education.

The analysis presented in the book shows that the vast majority of the population in Central America is likely to experience welfare gains from implementation of DR-CAFTA, even in the short run. At the same time, the removal of trade barriers in sensitive agricultural crops could adversely affect a small share of the population living in rural areas in Central America. Although provisions in DR-CAFTA will allow for long timetables in reducing tariffs for most sensitive products, appropriate support programs may need to be designed. In addition, selective investments in education, rural infrastructure, rural finance, and technical assistance will be required to ensure that the rural poor have the means to take full advantage of the new opportunities arising out of DR-CAFTA.

The rest of this introductory chapter reviews the main findings of the other chapters in the order in which they appear. Chapter 2 places DR-CAFTA in the historical context of the economic reforms that Central American countries have been undertaking since the late 1980s. Chapter 3 provides a summary overview of the recently negotiated DR-CAFTA, with special attention on the extent to which the agreement's provisions would significantly change market access for Central American goods and services, and on how far they could be expected to consolidate prior reforms. Chapter 4 reviews various analyses that assess the potential impacts of DR-CAFTA on the developing countries of Central America. Chapter 5 focuses on the identification and quantification of populations potentially affected by the easing of trade restrictions in sensitive agricultural products and analyzes policy options to assist vulnerable groups. Chapter 6 reviews evidence related to key macroeconomic implications of DR-CAFTA, namely, the potential revenue losses that might be produced by the removal of import taxes and the treaty's possible effect on the patterns of business cycle synchronization. Chapter 7 reviews evidence from each Central American country in the areas of trade facilitation, institutional and regulatory reforms, and innovation and education to identify key priorities for the complementary agenda for DR-CAFTA.

Trade and Development in Central America since 1990: Is DR-CAFTA the End of the Road?

Chapter 2 provides a description of the wide-ranging unilateral and regional trade reforms that Central American nations have pursued since the late 1980s. Tariffs have been slashed and most nontariff barriers have been removed. Regional agreements have been revitalized and countries have engaged in the expansion of trade markets through the negotiation of bilateral trade agreements. The CBI preferences granted by the United States have also opened important opportunities, especially in the development of new *maquila* exports.

However, these impressive achievements in the area of trade policy have yielded mixed economic results. On the one hand, export volumes have increased and some diversification has occurred, as demonstrated by the appearance of new exports—including the impressive growth of *maquila* in most Central American countries and high-technology goods in Costa Rica. These are positive developments because, among other considerations, exporting sectors have been shown to provide higher wages and improved working conditions, compared to other areas of the economy.

On the other hand, although trade has made a significant contribution to growth in Central America since 1990, its impact has not been sufficient to raise aggregate growth rates enough to transform these countries' economies and radically reduce poverty rates. Nor have trade opportunities by themselves served to offset some of the constraints to progress in the region, such as the still inadequate progress in improving infrastructure, education, and governance, and the continuing vulnerabilities in areas of macroeconomic and financial management that continue to add to investors' uncertainties in some of the countries. Beyond this, the new *maquila* industries have only developed a limited degree of integration with the local economies, whereas textiles and apparel export prospects are still fragile because of the growing competition from Asian industries. Although the diversification of Central American countries' exports has increased, this tendency partly reflects negative trends during the period, such as the decline or stagnation in exports of traditional commodities like cotton, coffee, and bananas. Ironically, although Honduras has achieved the highest degree of trade openness relative to its level of income, it is also the country with the weakest record of growth in Central America since the early 1990s.

Why these mixed results? As noted earlier, trade policy is unfortunately not the only determinant of trade (or growth) outcomes. There are still many obstacles to further export growth and trade diversification in Central American nations, including poor infrastructure, weaknesses in labor skills, inflexible regulations, trade barriers in other markets, deficiencies in governance (for example, corruption, inefficient customs), and macrofiscal and financial market vulnerabilities.

DR-CAFTA certainly caps the decade and a half of reforms in Central America, particularly in the trade area. It offers a great opportunity to make further progress in fostering trade-led growth. But it should not be seen as a silver bullet. On the positive side, it is a potentially more useful tool than the combination seen so far of unilateral removal of trade barriers and trade preferences because it effectively guarantees long-term market access to the largest trading partner and locks in the reforms of recent years, thus boosting credibility and attracting investment. However, DR-CAFTA alone should not be expected to unleash radically higher levels of trade and growth for the same reasons that trade policies since the early 1990s have obtained only limited results. Countries will need to accompany DR-CAFTA implementation with policies to address key constraints and bottlenecks to reap the full social and economic results of this initiative. Chapter 4 will justify this point in greater detail, and chapter 7 will illustrate it by identifying certain country-specific elements of the complementary agenda.

The Content of DR-CAFTA: Implications for Market Access and Domestic Reforms

Chapter 3 offers an overview of the recently negotiated DR-CAFTA, concentrating on the extent to which the agreement's provisions would significantly change market access for Central American goods and services, and on how far they could be expected to consolidate prior reforms and/or spur further domestic reforms in Central American countries. The overall assessment presented in the chapter is that, on both fronts, the answers are broadly positive, suggesting that DR-CAFTA should be expected to have a positive impact on trade flows and investment.

On market access, DR-CAFTA would consolidate and expand the generous access to the U.S. market that Central Americans currently enjoy, while extending broadly reciprocal access for U.S. goods to their own markets. The benefits offered under the CBI would be locked in for Central American countries, and permanent duty-free access would be gained for some goods previously exempted from CBI preferences. Other significant results would include making flexible the rules of origin for textiles and apparel, as well as commitments to help producers meet sanitary and phytosanitary standards required for entry into the United States of nontraditional agricultural exports. DR-CAFTA also includes reciprocal commitments on access to service markets, which consolidate domestic reforms that opened most of these markets to private participation in recent years.

Central American countries also agreed to grant reciprocal tariff-free access to their markets to U.S. products. Certain sensitive agricultural crops would be subject to extended transition periods (up to 20 years) to allow for gradual adjustment and to respond to domestic sensitivities. Central American countries secured access to flexible safeguard mechanisms to prevent sudden surges in imports or declines in prices.

Commitments embedded in DR-CAFTA would gradually erode current protection levels for various products that have retained high protection in

Central American economies during earlier efforts at easing trade restrictions. The gradual decline expected in prices of basic food staples as a result should prove positive for the vast majority of Central Americans who are net consumers of such goods and whose welfare will be enhanced by lower prices. This said, not all sensitive products are included, in response to cultural and political factors, and these limitations—together with the agreement's still excessively restrictive rules of origin for the entry of textile products to the United States—represent barriers to trade that will continue to foster some inefficiencies in the deployment of domestic resources in both Central America and the United States.

On the questions related to domestic reforms, DR-CAFTA commitments promise to lock in a number of the policy and regulatory changes implemented in recent years for the opening of competition in previously protected sectors (for example, telecommunications, financial services, energy) and the modernization of key norms and procedures in areas such as government procurement, intellectual property rights, and the treatment of foreign investment by locking in current levels of access to investors (and bidders) from the United States.

Costa Rica is the only country that will be required to make significant legislative changes to adapt policies and regulations to its commitments under DR-CAFTA, allowing access to significant portions of its telecommunications and insurance markets. These reforms have been long postponed and should further foster the modernization, efficiency, and competitiveness of these areas of the Costa Rican economy.

Aside from consolidating and spurring further reforms, the treaty should strengthen commitments to upgrade enforcement levels of domestic legislation. This incentive to enforce national laws represents a significant challenge in areas like labor, environment, and intellectual property rights, which will require decisive efforts and resources to modernize and boost the capacity of public agencies. The net impact of these efforts should be positive because investment is likely to be attracted to environments with effective institutions. However, although DR-CAFTA will put pressure on the modernization of these institutions, it will not create such modernization by itself. Countries will need strong independent plans of action and sufficient dedication of implementation capacity and resources.

The agreement includes cooperation accords to boost standards and enforcement levels in areas such as labor, environment, and customs. It also offers proposals to develop further cooperation and "trade capacity building," which should aid in mobilizing human and financial resources required for key reforms and institutional actions necessary to implement the agreement and the broader developmental challenges.

Finally, a welcome side effect of the negotiation of DR-CAFTA has been the advancement of regional integration efforts. The decision to make the provisions of the agreement apply multilaterally among Central American countries and the Dominican Republic will deepen regional integration efforts and facilitate the creation of a Central American customs union.

Economic Effects of DR-CAFTA: More Art Than Science

Chapter 4 reviews various analyses undertaken to assess the potential impacts of DR-CAFTA on the developing countries of Central America. It begins by highlighting the point that standard theoretical treatments of the gains from trade indicate that such gains depend on an economy's capacity to change its productive structure. Otherwise, the gains are limited to the those on the consumption side, which allow domestic agents to consume a bundle of goods that is larger in economic value than the one without trade reforms. The gains from productive transformation can be substantially higher than the gains from enhanced consumption alone. These conclusions refer to static analyses of the gains from trade.

Regarding empirical analyses of the potential static gains from trade, the evidence reviewed in the chapter highlights two key complementary factors, namely, the infrastructure that affects international transport costs and the regulatory environment. There is strong evidence suggesting that exports to the U.S. market will benefit from the shift from unilateral preferences (CBI) to a free trade agreement, but it may be more important that international transport costs (freight, insurance) have a robust and large effect on the value of exports, regardless of the type of preferential treatment. Also, the evidence reviewed suggests that the gains from trade in terms of increases in gross domestic product (GDP) per capita are intermediated by the regulatory environment that determines how quickly firms and workers can change their sectors of operation and employment. Thus a complementary agenda to enhance the impact of DR-CAFTA should consider these factors, even when concerned about the static gains from trade.

Partial equilibrium analyses of the potential sectoral effects of DR-CAFTA suggest that the main short-term winners of the agreement would be concentrated in the apparel industries, abstracting from any impact of the elimination of world quotas in this sector. Nevertheless, these analyses suffer from an inability to capture the potential effects on sectors that are relatively small because the effects predicted by these models are proportional to the initial level of exports. In addition, they have difficulty dealing with technical issues, such as the restrictiveness of rules of origin. Furthermore, such partial equilibrium models do not consider the effects of the trade reforms in the economy as a whole because they do not consider intersector interactions through factor and goods markets.

Chapter 4 also presents the simulation results from a so-called computable general equilibrium (CGE) model for Nicaragua linked to household data. The simulation relates the macroeconomic results of the model to changes in the returns to unskilled labor, and in turn it relates these changes in returns to labor to poverty outcomes. Indeed, under a restrictive set of conditions (for example, segmented labor markets, lack of dynamic effects, full transmission of tariff reductions to relative producer prices, and no further unilateral trade reforms), DR-CAFTA could have an overall modest positive effect on Nicaragua's welfare (income per capita) but with a very small (positive) effect on poverty and the potential for poor rural households to be negatively affected. Thus, as with the other static analyses, these results further support the contention that DR-CAFTA might not be enough to reduce poverty, although the results must be interpreted with caution because they are obviously limited by key theoretical and empirical assumptions.

The rest of the chapter is dedicated to understanding the potential dynamic gains from DR-CAFTA. The first part covers evidence concerning the potential effect of free trade agreements—and trade more generally—on foreign investment, corruption, and innovation. Existing evidence suggests that foreign direct investment (FDI) responds to FTAs indirectly by enhancing the effect of exports and GDP on FDI. The evidence also indicates that trade might not have a direct effect on corruption, and thus we should not expect large dynamic gains from DR-CAFTA to come from the impact of international trade on the quality of public institutions. The process of democratic consolidation seems much more important, although certain aspects of DR-CAFTA that put pressure on governments to improve the enforcement of their own laws could also be helpful. The existing literature on innovation and economic discovery suggests a mixed picture. On the one hand, innovation efforts might not be related to the incidence of international trade. On the other hand, the probability of observing episodes of "economic discovery" seems to be positively correlated with overall export growth.

Chapter 4 also reviews the econometric challenges and results by investigating the empirical link between FTAs and subsequent economic growth in a large sample of countries. The main result is that the growth rate of GDP per capita is positively associated with a country's participation in FTAs. This finding is robust to the inclusion of an array of control variables and econometric methods. Unlike the evidence presented in previous work, the new evidence reviewed does not find that the annual increase in GDP growth of approximately 0.6 percent was sensitive to the type of partner in the FTA. In contrast, a previous empirical study using a different set of control variables and specifications of the empirical models, did find that access to larger markets has a larger effect on growth than FTAs with smaller partners. In any case, there seems to be substantial evidence that FTAs might help accelerate the pace of economic development, at least for the first five years subsequent to implementation. In the long run, the steady-state level of income will be determined by a plethora of other factors and, as economies get richer, their pace of growth will tend to decline. Consequently, there does not seem to be a silver bullet, and DR-CAFTA is unlikely to be the solution to all development challenges faced by Central America.

The evidence reviewed should make clear that ex ante analyses of the potential effects of DR-CAFTA (and trade reforms in general) remain an art rather than a science because the results are highly sensitive to theoretical assumptions and empirical methods. Chapters 5, 6, and 7 provide more guidance regarding the "complementary agenda," which includes policies that can help DR-CAFTA beneficiaries overcome the challenges posed by the adjustment process as well as the long-term challenge of economic development in the context of DR-CAFTA.

Policy Approaches to Managing the Economic Transition: Ensuring That Poor People Can Benefit from DR-CAFTA

Although the vast majority of people in Central America are expected to benefit from DR-CAFTA in the medium to long term, there are at least some people who are at risk of bearing the costs of trade-related economic adjustment in the short to medium term. Specifically, although the Central American economies are already relatively open, as a result of unilateral efforts at lowering barriers to trade undertaken in the 1990s (chapter 2), a handful of sensitive agricultural commodities (for example, maize, beans, dairy, and poultry) still have significant levels of protection. Chapter 5 focuses on quantifying the size of the potentially affected population and the magnitude of the possible effects. It additionally examines alternative policy approaches on how to best assist vulnerable groups to ensure that they can benefit from emerging opportunities arising out of DR-CAFTA.

Given current levels of protection, the introduction of more trade competition for sensitive agricultural commodities under DR-CAFTA can be expected to lead to lower domestic prices for sensitive commodities in each country—in some cases, significantly lower prices. For this reason, DR-CAFTA includes a wide range of provisions (described in chapter 3) for dealing with the easing of trade restrictions on sensitive goods, including grace periods for initiating the removal of tariffs, extended phase-out periods for tariffs, interim quotas and/or phase-downs of tariff-rate quotas, as well as special safeguard measures to protect local farmers from undue harm. Indeed, the agreement includes extended timetables for reducing protection on sensitive agricultural crops. For some commodities, phase-out periods are as long as 20 years, and white maize, an important staple crop produced by the poor farmers, was exempted from the commitments to eliminate tariffs, at least for a few countries. These provisions in themselves represent important protections for producers of sensitive crops, giving them an extended timeframe over which to undertake the necessary economic adjustments.

Given this situation, what might policymakers expect to be the impacts of removing barriers to trade in sensitive agricultural commodities under the DR-CAFTA? Three new empirical studies using nationally representative household survey data from El Salvador, Guatemala, and Nicaragua help shed light on this and related policy issues. All three studies applied a comparable *net consumer-net producer* framework to assess the likely first-order impacts on household welfare of eliminating quotas and reducing to zero tariffs on several sensitive agricultural products, including maize, beans, milk, poultry meat, bovine meat, apples, pork, wheat, and rice. Despite the phasing out of trade protection negotiated under DR-CAFTA, these analyses examine expected impacts *as if* all tariffs and quotas were going to be removed completely and immediately under the treaty. The approach provides useful insights into the first-order impacts of introducing in the markets more competition for sensitive commodities. It also provides a useful baseline from which to examine policy options—including some important policy trade-offs implicit in the gradual approach to easing trade barriers negotiated under the agreement.

This analysis on El Salvador, Guatemala, and Nicaragua indicates that the vast majority of households in these countries stand to gain from the price changes associated with removing trade barriers for the sensitive agricultural commodities. More specifically, 90 percent of Nicaraguan households, 84 percent of Guatemalan households, and 68 percent of Salvadoran households were found to be *net consumers* of the basket of sensitive agricultural commodities and, as such, can be expected to benefit from DR-CAFTA-related price changes. Only about 9 percent of Nicaraguan households, 16 percent of Guatemalan households, and 5 percent of Salvadoran households were found to be *net producers* of the basket of sensitive commodities and thus would be expected to experience welfare losses. For El Salvador, a further 27 percent of households were estimated to remain unaffected because of their essentially negligible gains or losses. Even though potential losers are thus relatively small minorities, appropriate attention needs to be paid to ensure that anticipated losses do not harm the poorest and most vulnerable groups, and targeted programs aimed at those people who may suffer significant welfare losses may be justified.

Although DR-CAFTA has built into it considerable grace periods and extended phase-out periods for eliminating tariffs and quotas that provide reasonable protection to producers of sensitive crops over a prolonged adjustment period, this approach is not without its own economic and social trade-offs. Whereas phasing of reforms provides producers an extended period to make the necessary economic adjustments, for that same extended time period it also deprives consumers of the benefits associated with lower prices for important agricultural staples. In this context, an alternative (and some people might argue more efficient) approach might involve a shorter period of removal of trade barriers for the sensitive commodities, coupled with transfers targeted to those adversely affected by DR-CAFTA in the short term. In principle, a shorter liberalization period combined with targeted transfers is more efficient economically than phased removal of barriers because consumers do not have to wait as long as 20 years to reap the full benefits of lower prices. Coupling well-targeted transfer programs with quick easing of trade restrictions could thus enhance households' welfare in the short term on the consumption side while providing producers with a reasonable period of support to make the economic transition.

Regardless of whether the DR-CAFTA countries in Central America choose to pursue this alternative approach, it is important to understand the broad options that policymakers can use to mitigate potential income losses arising from declines in commodity prices if extended phase-outs and safeguards are deemed insufficient. Those options are (1) "decoupled" income support payments to farmers of sensitive crops (as, for example, in Mexico's PROCAMPO program); (2) technical assistance programs for farmers of sensitive crops; (3) conditional cash transfers (CCTs) to rural families that make investments in their children's education, health, and nutrition; and (4) provision of public goods (for example, economic infrastructure, basic education, rural financial services, technical assistance) directed to households and/or regions that are expected to be particularly affected by DR-CAFTA.

These options can be viewed from two different perspectives. The first considers the institutional sophistication required to implement support programs, recognizing that different approaches will tax to different degrees the implementation capacity of Central American countries. This criterion recognizes that effective programs will require, inter alia, a viable method of targeting vulnerable populations, a minimum degree of know-how among the civil servants of the implementing public sector agency, the creation of new government organizations (or transformation of old ones), and a minimum amount of independence to ensure the application of technical criteria and to avoid political interference. The second perspective is related to whether the program provides incentives (or other support) for broad production diversification, including strengthening the capacity of families to exploit new income opportunities for off-farm and/or nonagricultural activities—which may be critical to ensure greater economic mobility among poor households.

The classification is useful to assess the requirements and objectives that may be relevant in each country because the choice of which type of support program would be more appropriate should be made on the basis of country-specific factors. Decoupled transfers require relatively low institutional sophistication but offer few incentives for farmers to seek new income opportunities, as demonstrated by the PROCAMPO experience in Mexico. Technical assistance programs place a greater burden on the capacities of government agencies, while within agriculture they give incentives for productive diversification (or upgrading). Public goods programs require less institutional sophistication by relying on existing institutions for program delivery, while creating conditions for rural inhabitants to diversify economic activities—although programs of this type may require a strong regional concentration of potentially affected poor households to make economic sense. CCTs require relatively sophisticated new institutional capacity (especially in countries where programs of this type are not currently being implemented, such as Costa Rica, El Salvador, and Guatemala), although by strengthening families' human capital, they offer broad support for production diversification.

Macroeconomic Policy Implications of DR-CAFTA

Chapter 6 reviews evidence related to two macroeconomic policy issues. The first concerns the potential revenue losses that might be produced by DR-CAFTA's removal of import taxes. The other topic is related to the treaty's potential effect on the patterns of business cycle synchronization (BCS) that could be affected by changes in the structure of international trade.

The fiscal losses that DR-CAFTA is likely to create need to be compensated in all Central American countries to avoid further deterioration of public finances. At present, all Central American countries except Guatemala exhibit relatively high debt indicators and require tight fiscal stances to maintain or decrease indebtedness. However, relatively small losses in the first years of the agreement allow for some flexibility in timing the fiscal response in several countries—particularly because time may be needed for adequate political conditions to emerge.

A more comprehensive fiscal response to DR-CAFTA requires efforts to raise revenues above and beyond fiscal losses because some of the key measures needed to optimize its effect require increases in public investments (for example,, infrastructure, education, institutional strengthening, and transitional adjustment programs). Although some of these expenditures may be temporary and could arguably be financed by greater indebtedness, this may be difficult in practice as a result of high current debt levels.

The fiscal response to DR-CAFTA should be adapted to the fiscal situation of each country. For the cases of El Salvador and Guatemala, where tax revenue ratios are low (below 13 percent of GDP), the ideal fiscal response would be actions that go significantly beyond recovering direct losses, to finance additional social and infrastructure investments that are needed to boost growth and that are made more urgent and productive by the opportunities of DR-CAFTA. In Costa Rica, where the tax ratio is higher but still short of the level needed to guarantee debt sustainability, the ideal response should also involve going beyond compensation for the relatively low projected losses, making improvements in the efficiency and allocation of public expenditures as well as attracting private financing to fund some of the most significant infrastructure needs. Honduras and Nicaragua, which have benefited recently from the Heavily Indebted Poor Countries (HIPC) Initiative, will likely require additional fiscal revenues, improvements in expenditure efficiency, and attraction of private financing to respond to the opportunities of DR-CAFTA. In all countries, an essential element of efforts to improve fiscal performance should include the institutional strengthening of tax agencies and their collection capacity, as well as the elimination of exonerations from value-added and income taxes.

DR-CAFTA implementation should also be used to deepen regional coordination efforts in the realm of tax policy. Going forward, a regional coordination agenda should include gradual harmonization of value-added and excise tax rates, fiscal incentives for foreign investors, information exchange for tax enforcement efforts, double taxation treaties, and transference prices.

Regarding the prospects for macroeconomic policy coordination among Central American countries and perhaps with the United States, business cycle synchronization within Central America is quite low compared to that of the North American Free Trade Agreement (NAFTA) and the European Union (EU), but not when compared to the Common Market of the South (MERCOSUR). In fact, synchronization in Central America is highest between Costa Rica and El Salvador, El Salvador and Guatemala, El Salvador and Nicaragua, and Honduras and Nicaragua. Costa Rica and Honduras have a higher degree of co-movement with the United States than with any other Central American country, but synchronization with the United States is still below the levels among NAFTA partners and even MERCOSUR members.

Furthermore, unlike NAFTA, the EU, and MERCOSUR, trade in Central America is not predominantly intraregional. The United States is by far Central America's most important trading partner. With the exception of Costa Rica, there is virtually no evidence of intra-industry trade between Central America and the United States. The level of intra-industry trade within Central America is comparable to that of MERCOSUR members, but below the levels of NAFTA partners (Canada and the United States) and the EU (Germany and France). Finally, the degree of business cycle synchronization seems only weakly related to trade intensity and trade structure (intra-industry trade), although the relationship between intra-industry trade and synchronization is slightly stronger, which is consistent with existing international evidence. As such, the gain in synchronization through trade expansion could be modest.

In sum, at present neither Central America's trade structure nor its degree of business cycle synchronization makes a compelling case for macroeconomic coordination within Central America or between Central America and the United States. Clearly, trade integration is a dynamic process and as trade intensities and compositions of trade flows change, so will business cycle patterns. To fully assess the consequences of closer trade integration for the conduct of macroeconomic policies, information about the future evolution of trade structures in DR-CAFTA is needed. If trade becomes more intra-industry (vertically or horizontally), business cycles are expected to become more similar and the independence of macroeconomic policy will be less of a concern. If trade integration takes the form of higher inter-industry trade, however, then business cycles are likely to diverge from current levels of synchronization and the ability to conduct independent macroeconomic policies will grow more important. In the meantime, other factors that are not directly related to the structure of international trade will remain more important considerations for the design of macroeconomic policies over the business cycle in Central America. One important consideration, for example, is the extent of dollarization of financial assets and liabilities. Hence, the macrofiscal agenda in the light of DR-CAFTA should remain focused on fiscal consolidation, at least in the short run.

Priorities for the Complementary Agenda: Obtaining the Payoff from DR-CAFTA

Chapter 7 reviews recent evidence in the areas of trade facilitation, institutional and regulatory reforms, and innovation and education to identify key priorities for the complementary agenda for DR-CAFTA. The main challenges identified for Costa Rica include improving road quality, enhancing port and customs efficiency, boosting financial depth, and improving the quality and coverage of secondary education. For El Salvador, priorities focus around increasing road quality, reducing shipping costs, and tackling governance challenges, as well as improving the quality and coverage of secondary education. Both countries need to devote more public resources to research and development (with monitoring and evaluation efforts put in place to assess results over time), strengthen public-private partnerships for innovation, and enhance their institutional capacity to enforce intellectual property rights laws. In addition to tackling weaknesses in the areas identified for Costa Rica and El Salvador, Guatemala also needs to continue to build on recent accomplishments in improving customs administration, coverage and quality of primary education, and road density, as well as devoting some attention to fostering the development of new export products.

The challenges for Honduras and Nicaragua are likely to encompass a broader set of policy issues because they face more limitations as a result of their lower development levels. Both countries need to address governance and to work on improving the coverage and quality of primary education, improving the operational efficiency of ports, and increasing the quality of roads and their density. They also need to improve their capacity to absorb knowledge from abroad, strengthen institutions in charge of innovation policy, and increase linkages between public research and development programs and the needs of the private sector. Honduras also needs to upgrade customs administration and reduce the costs and time required to establish new business ventures.

All Central American countries share a regional economic agenda that needs to focus urgently on achieving a customs union, which is critical to reduce transaction costs to trade within the region. In addition, efforts should be deepened to coordinate the development of infrastructure that benefits from a regional perspective, including major road networks, and the development of ports. Mechanisms to formulate a common regional trade policy need to be strengthened to ensure coherence of future bilateral, regional, and global commitments with the new framework provided by DR-CAFTA. In addition, improved coordination of key regulatory policies (for example, financial supervision, competition, fiscal incentives) may be needed to establish the basis of a deeper and more integrated regional market in the future.

All of the elements of the complementary agenda mentioned here are also components of the broader agenda to boost economic growth in the region. Recent analytical work produced by the World Bank to prioritize actions for broad-based growth in the nations of Central America has highlighted the high return that would be obtained from improvements in the areas of infrastructure, education, and governance (for example, see World Bank 2005a, 2005b, 2004b). DR-CAFTA enhances the social return to these actions and makes them more urgent. It is hoped that this important agreement serves as a useful tool to rally support for consolidating policy reforms of recent years and pushing forward with new energy in the areas in which weaknesses remain so as to boost the pace of growth and poverty reduction across Central America.

CHAPTER 2

Trade and Development in Central America since 1990

Is DR-CAFTA the End of the Road?

Negotiations for a free trade agreement (FTA) between the United States and the nations of Central America followed a long process of trade and other policy reforms undertaken in the region since the late 1980s. Whereas reforms were associated with an initial growth spurt, the slowdown in most of the economies of the region in the late 1990s and early 2000s has yielded some disappointment. In some quarters DR-CAFTA has been received as the missing piece of the puzzle to jump-start economic activity in Central America, and others see the treaty as an opportunity for improving growth that requires complementary policies to obtain its promise.

This chapter provides the background for DR-CAFTA. To understand the regional context, the chapter provides a broad review of the progress in trade liberalization and integration policies that have taken place in Central America since the early 1990s, and the results obtained in the areas of trade flows, trade diversification, and economic growth. The analysis of the potential effects of DR-CAFTA for Central American economies is left for a later chapter.

The next section summarizes the most significant changes in Central American trade policy since 1990. The third section reviews the results obtained in trade performance and provides an analysis of its impact on growth. The fourth section presents a summary and some thoughts on the results that can be expected from DR-CAFTA for the Central American economies.

Trade Policies in Central America, 1990–2003

Over the past decade and a half, Central American countries have put in place ambitious reforms aimed at invigorating economic activity by shifting away from the inward-looking pattern of development to one that is more reliant on market forces and private initiative. The reforms have included trade liberalization, privatization of infrastructure services, removal of exchange controls, opening up to FDI, and efforts to boost the efficiency of government programs.

Trade and related reforms included unilateral liberalization of trade barriers; removal of exchange controls; opening up to foreign investment flows; and increased participation in global, regional, and bilateral trade agreements. To encourage trade flows, these policies were complemented with more flexible foreign exchange arrangements and selected actions in other fronts (for example, improved infrastructure and customs reform).

Tariff and Nontariff Barriers

Central American countries began to reduce tariffs unilaterally in the late 1980s or early 1990s. By the mid-1990s, average tariff levels in Central America were among the lowest in the Latin America and Caribbean region. For the five DR-CAFTA members, average import duties fell from 45.0 percent in 1985 to 14.1 percent in 1990 and to 7.1 percent by 1999 (see table 2.1). By 1999, Costa Rica exhibited the lowest average tariff at 3.3 percent and Nicaragua the highest at 10.9 percent.

The reduction of tariff levels has also been accompanied by a reduction in tariff dispersion levels. This process has been aided by harmonization efforts in the context of the Central American Common Market (CACM) to gradually converge to a four-tier common tariff ranging between 0 and 15 percent for most goods imported into the region.[1] Within the region, El Salvador stands out as having the most parsimonious tariff structure, with only five tariff levels (0, 5, 10, 15, and 20 percent) and dispersion levels among the lowest in Latin America and the Caribbean. At the other extreme, despite boasting a low average tariff, Costa Rica exhibits a relatively high dis-

Table 2.1. Average Tariffs, 1985–2000

Country	*1985*	*1990*	*1995*	*1999–2000 weighted*	*1999–2000 unweighted*
Costa Rica	53.0	16.4	11.2	3.3	6.0
El Salvador	23.0	16.0	10.2	5.7	7.0
Guatemala	50.0	16.0	12.0	7.6	6.9
Honduras	n.a.	41.9[a]	9.7	8.1	6.5
Nicaragua	54.0	8.0	10.7	10.9	5.1
Average	45.0	14.1	10.8	7.1	6.3

Sources: Lora 2001; IADB 2002.
n.a. = not applicable.
a. Data for 1989.

persion because of the persistence of a number of additional tariff levels beyond 20 percent.[2]

Most countries still exhibit a few tariff peaks (for example, ad valorem rates over 20 percent), protecting sensitive areas of the economy. Although the list varies across countries, sensitive goods typically include maize, poultry meat, rice, sugar, and dairy products. The continued protection afforded to these products has been explained by the strength of small, highly organized producer groups coupled with urban sympathy to some farming groups who may have difficulties in facing international competition (Monge, Loría, and González-Vega 2003; Arce and Jaramillo 2005).

To complement the reduction of tariffs, Central American nations also removed most nontariff barriers, which had been widely used prior to the reforms. As a result, prohibitions and quantitative restrictions are today mostly limited to sanitary or technical standards. However, specific complaints of the use of nontariff barriers—often using phytozoosanitary arguments—continue to be reported with some regularity.[3] In addition, some countries continue to require importers to purchase part of the local crop of some sensitive commodities before issuing import permits.[4]

Export Promotion

As part of the trade reforms of the early 1990s, Central American countries also restructured their approach to promoting exports. Direct fiscal subsidies gradually gave way to the recognition that the removal of traditional import protection eliminated their anti-export bias. Incentives to attract and facilitate the development of export ventures were granted through export processing zone (EPZ) regimes that exempted firms from import, sales, and income taxes. Most countries in the region also introduced regimes that allowed for the tax-free importation of inputs (raw materials, semiprocessed goods, machinery, and equipment) for use in the production of export goods and services. In conjunction with trade preferences granted by the United States, these measures facilitated the expansion of exports throughout the region since the late 1980s.

Integration Initiatives

In addition to unilateral liberalization efforts, trade developments in Central America were significantly influenced by other trade initiatives in the 1990s, including the active pursuit by Central American nations of multiple trade negotiations in what has been termed a three-tiered strategy (Salazar-Xiriñachs 2002). At the global level, all countries participated actively in the Uruguay Round (1986–1994) and those that were not already members joined the General Agreement on Tariffs and Trade (GATT)-WTO. At the regional levels, Central American countries revitalized the CACM under new principles (see below) and participated actively in the negotiations for the Free Trade Area of the Americas (FTAA). At the bilateral level, all countries actively engaged in negotiations of bilateral or subregional FTAs to expand markets and attract investment.

Costa Rica pioneered bilateral FTA negotiations, first with Mexico (1995), followed by agreements with Chile (2000), the Dominican Republic and the Caribbean Community (CARICOM) (2000), and Canada (2002). CACM members jointly negotiated FTAs with the Dominican Republic (1998), Chile (2001), and Panama (2002) and are currently participating in talks to establish the FTAA. The Northern Triangle (El Salvador, Guatemala, and Honduras) subscribed an FTA with Mexico in 2000.[5] This strategy of "open regionalism" has been the subject of some controversy (see IADB 2002, ch. 2). On the one hand, it has created a multiplicity of agreements (the so-called spaghetti bowl of trading arrangements) that may have high administration costs and can lead to confusion about application as well as information costs. On the other hand, these agreements have opened new trading opportunities, improved the capacity of national trading teams to participate in regional and global negotiations, and may have served as building blocks to reach negotiations with the large market represented by the United States. In any case, the literature suggests that these agreements are useful inasmuch as they do not generate trade diversion or hamper efforts for broader global negotiations.

The revitalization of the CACM also merits mention because it is responsible for a resurgence of intraregional trade in recent years. The CACM was created in 1961 as the first regional trade agreement in Latin America and the Caribbean under the inward-looking strategy of industrialization as a customs union, but with some exceptions to the common external tariff system and relatively low barriers to intraregional trade and high barriers to imports from the rest of the world. Beginning in the late 1960s, the CACM faced growing obstacles to its consolidation and suffered from the macroeconomic and political upheavals of the 1980s. The CACM was restructured and relaunched in the 1990s with a lower common external tariff structure and deeper integration disciplines in areas such as investment, intellectual property, and technical standards (Salazar-Xiriñachs et al. 2001). Revitalization occurred through the 1991 Tegucigalpa Protocol and the 1993 Guatemala Protocol aimed at eliminating the remaining trade barriers, working toward a customs union (without exemptions), and promoting integration in nontrade areas. Trade negotiations spurred by these protocols led to rapid progress in reducing trade barriers among members and in harmonizing tariffs toward extraregional partners. Lower trade barriers as a result of the new version of the CACM have yielded an impressive resurgence of intraregional trade, which has grown at rates that are more than double those of extraregional trade between 1990 and 2004. Whereas intraregional trade averaged only 21 percent of all trade in Central America in 1990, by 2004 these flows had increased to 38 percent.

Despite the progress made, there are some issues that need to be tackled to meet the trade liberalization objectives of the CACM. Intraregional trade still faces tariff and nontariff barriers in products such as nonroasted coffee, cane sugar, wheat flour, and ethyl alcohol. The CACM requires further progress in harmonizing external tariffs. As of early 2004, 8 percent of tariff lines required harmonization, including inconsistencies arising from differences in bilateral agreements that were not negotiated jointly by the five CACM members. Also, some rules of origins that are part of existing bilateral trade agreements signed by CACM members need to be brought to the same level of formality as the rules of origin of the DR-CAFTA.

Aside from trade, Central American countries have embarked on deeper regional integration efforts. The new regional integration agenda has included macroeconomic, political, legal, social, territorial, and environmental agreements. Many of the nontrade commitments, however, have had few practical consequences, and regional institutions in other areas are still weak. Clearly, trade stands out as the area where most substantive achievements have been made. A noteworthy development of the past decade is the significant growth of cross-border investment within the region, which has gone hand in hand with greater regional trade flows. The expansion of intraregional FDI flows (highlighted by investments in the financial sector and retailing from El Salvador and other countries) has been changing private-sector relationships and may be heralding the beginning of a deeper phase of integration.

Caribbean Basin Initiative

Since 1983 Central American countries have enjoyed trade preferences offered by the United States under the Caribbean Basin Initiative (CBI). This initiative allows duty-free access to the U.S. market for a substantial number of products. In 1986 the coverage was extended to include apparel assembled from fabric formed and cut in the United States, a key factor behind the birth of the *maquila* production of apparel in the region. In 2000 the U.S. Trade and Development Act extended the benefits of the CBI by granting trade concessions similar to those enjoyed by Mexico under the North American Free Trade Agreement (NAFTA) for apparel, and lowered tariffs for other products previously excluded from the initiative (for example, footwear, canned tuna, petroleum products, watches, and leather goods), granting duty-free access to almost 75 percent of all Central American exports to the United States.

The new access provisions approved in 2000 permitted the incorporation of more value added from the region in textile exports. In particular, it eliminated duties and quotas from apparel cut and assembled in the region from U.S.-made fabric, whereas tariffs previously were levied on the value added and products could not be cut in the region. New provisions also allowed for duty-free entry of items made from knit fabric made in the region from U.S. yarn, although subject to an annual quota. In addition, opportunities for greater regional value added were granted by allowing for some finishing processes to be performed in the region (that is, dyeing, permanent pressing, and printing) as well as for the use of some inputs (that is, findings and trimmings) not of U.S. origin.

The CBI has brought considerable benefits for trade expansion to Central American nations.[6] All these nations have become significant exporters of apparel to the United States, with the largest export volumes coming from

Honduras, El Salvador, and Guatemala—with Honduras achieving substantially greater exports over the others as a result, inter alia, of its logistical advantages in accessing East Coast destinations from the relevant urban center (that is, San Pedro Sula). Success in terms of exports of textiles and apparel (see figure 2.1) has come despite rules of origin restrictions that have limited the development of greater linkages with the local economy as well as greater flexibility in the sourcing of inputs.[7] Besides textiles and apparel, Central American countries have used CBI preferences to export traditional export goods (bananas, coffee, sugar) free of duty and to develop a number of growing nontraditional agricultural exports and some light manufactures. However, studies on the remaining hurdles to further expansion of exports despite CBI preferences reveal the continued existence of nontariff barriers for agricultural products in the United States (for example, sanitary and phytosanitary restrictions, standards, labeling), complex rules of origin for some sectors such as textiles, and the high costs of transport and the lack of economies of scale (Monge, Loría, and González-Vega 2003).

Figure 2.1. Textiles and Apparel Imports into the United States, 1990–2002

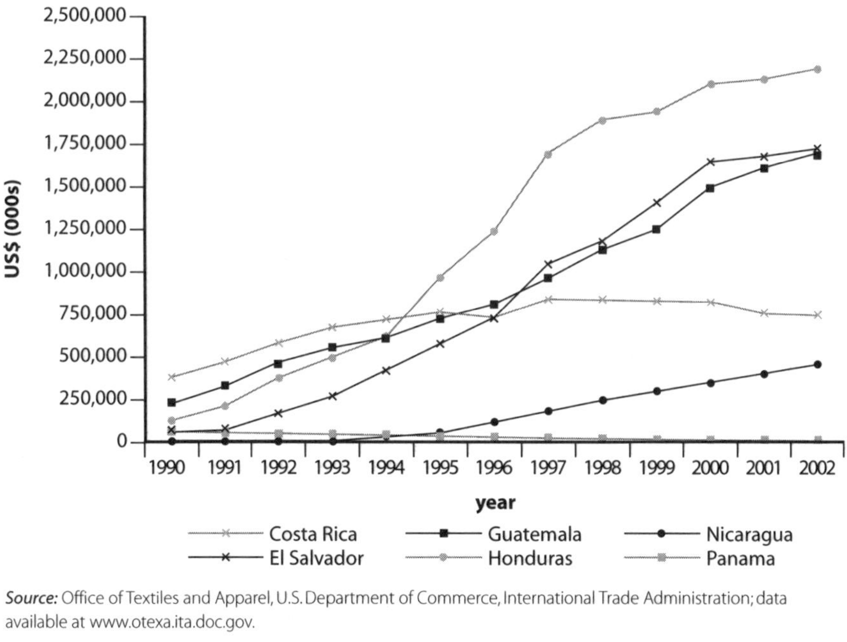

Source: Office of Textiles and Apparel, U.S. Department of Commerce, International Trade Administration; data available at www.otexa.ita.doc.gov.

Results of Trade Policies: Trade and Growth Outcomes

The ultimate test of the success of trade policies is significant growth and diversification of trade flows. However, simple assessments using these criteria are problematic as improvements in trade are usually determined also by a number of different policy and exogenous issues. Nevertheless, in this section we attempt a preliminary assessment of trade policies by examining recent trends in trade flows, trade diversification, and growth in Central America. The evidence on growth is also reviewed in an attempt to evaluate if trade policies of recent years may have contributed to overall economic performance since the early 1990s.

Trade Openness

Table 2.2 displays a common measure of trade flows (also known as trade openness, defined as exports plus imports as a share of GDP) for Central American countries and other Latin American and Caribbean countries for 1990–91 and 2000–01.[8] The figures indicate that in the early 1990s, trade volumes in the region (47 percent on average for the five DR-CAFTA countries) were somewhat lower than the Latin American and Caribbean average (51 percent). However, the figures for the early 2000s indicate that Central America led the region in the growth of trade volumes, along with Mexico. Between the early 1990s and the early 2000s, the Central American average grew by 29 percentage points to 76 percent. Expansion of trade volumes was most impressive for Honduras (62 percentage points) and Nicaragua (40 points); it was less but still quite significant for El Salvador (17 points), Costa Rica (14 points), and Guatemala (13 points).[9]

Between 1991 and 2001, growth in trade volumes in all countries of Central America was larger for imports (16.9 percentage points for the Central America average) than exports (10.2 percentage points) (see table 2.3). The disparity results mostly from the resumption of capital flows (including FDI, aid, and public and private indebtedness) that allowed for the financing of larger trade deficits than was possible in the 1980s. For countries such as El Salvador, Guatemala, and Honduras, the significant secular growth in remittances has also contributed to financing trade-account deficits. On the export side, growth can be explained in great part by the surge in *maquila* exports (mainly textiles and apparel) and the development of nontraditional agricultural exports (particularly in Costa Rica, Guatemala, and Honduras). Traditional exports have stagnated (coffee, bananas, sugar) or declined (cot-

Table 2.2. Trade Openness[a]
percent of GDP

Country	*1990–1*	*2000–1*	*Change*
Central America			
Costa Rica	0.56	0.70	0.14
El Salvador	0.42	0.59	0.17
Guatemala	0.38	0.51	0.13
Honduras	0.68	1.30	0.62
Nicaragua	0.32	0.72	0.40
Average, Central America	0.47	0.76	0.29
Other Latin American and Caribbean countries			
Argentina	0.14	0.22	0.08
Bolivia	0.48	0.43	–0.05
Brazil	0.16	0.25	0.10
Chile	0.64	0.65	0.01
Colombia	0.35	0.40	0.05
Dominican Republic	0.71	0.63	–0.08
Ecuador	0.61	0.69	0.09
Haiti	0.40	0.43	0.03
Jamaica	1.06	0.97	–0.09
Mexico	0.37	0.61	0.24
Panama	0.73	0.70	–0.03
Paraguay	0.71	0.59	–0.12
Peru	0.28	0.33	0.05
Suriname	0.47	0.94	0.47
Trinidad and Tobago	0.75	1.02	0.28
Uruguay	0.40	0.39	–0.01
Venezuela, R. B. de	0.59	0.42	–0.16
Average, other Latin American and Caribbean countries	0.52	0.57	0.05
Average, Latin America and the Caribbean	0.51	0.62	0.11

Source: World Bank with data from central banks and private-sector sources.
a. Exports and imports of goods, including *maquila* (gross).

ton) as a result of heavy supply competition and slow demand growth, which have led to declining prices. Costa Rica's outstanding performance is related also to success in developing new manufacturing lines of export, including high-technology exports (for example, Intel microchips) and a wide array of other manufacturing products.

Table 2.3. Trade Openness, Exports and Imports[a]
percent of GDP

Country	*1991*	*2001*	*Change*
Guatemala	0.39	0.50	0.11
Exports	0.18	0.19	0.01
Imports	0.21	0.31	0.10
El Salvador	0.42	0.57	0.15
Exports	0.14	0.21	0.07
Imports	0.29	0.36	0.08
Honduras	0.69	1.28	0.59
Exports	0.34	0.58	0.24
Imports	0.35	0.69	0.34
Nicaragua	0.32	0.71	0.39
Exports	0.09	0.24	0.15
Imports	0.23	0.47	0.24
Costa Rica	0.59	0.70	0.12
Exports	0.27	0.30	0.04
Imports	0.32	0.40	0.08
Central America average	0.48	0.75	0.27
Exports	0.20	0.31	0.10
Imports	0.28	0.45	0.17
Mexico	0.36	0.67	0.31
Exports	0.16	0.33	0.16
Imports	0.19	0.34	0.15

Source: World Bank with data from central banks and private-sector sources.
a. Exports and imports of goods, including *maquila* (gross).

Although trade volumes have grown impressively in Central America since the early 1990s, there seems to be scope for further trade increases in the future. To evaluate this potential, it is useful to compare their trade outcomes with those of other economies with similar levels of economic development. Figure 2.2 shows the results of a simple benchmarking exercise of trade openness indicators for a sample of 124 countries by per capita income, controlling for factors that may affect trade but are unrelated to government policies (that is, area, population, access to coast, oil exports).[10] In this light, the positive performance of trade since 1990 can be reinterpreted as catching up from significant initial deficits, relative to international norms. By 2001 Honduras was the only Central American country that performed beyond international comparators, resulting in great part from the huge success of *maquila* exports. For the remaining countries, only Nicaragua managed to cut the deficit significantly since 1990, although the other countries are among the top in Latin America in terms of progress achieved on this front.[11] However, the fact that most of the countries continued to exhibit shortfalls in relation to international comparators by the early 2000s is a likely result of continued constraints in transportation costs, port bottlenecks, and other behind-the-border weaknesses.

Trade Diversification

Another important measure of the success of trade policies is the degree of export diversification. It is well known that countries that rely heavily on a few goods for its exports revenues are more vulnerable to swings in market conditions than are those that enjoy a diversified export basket. The importance of this point was highlighted in a study by Lederman and Maloney (2003b), which found that countries that exhibit a high concentration of exports in a few products tend to exhibit less growth.

The export basket for most Central American countries has undergone significant changes since 1990. A clear structural transformation is evident, with the share of traditional commodity exports declining in favor of light manu-

Figure 2.2. Trade Openness as a Percentage of GDP: Deviations from Predicted Values, by Level of Income

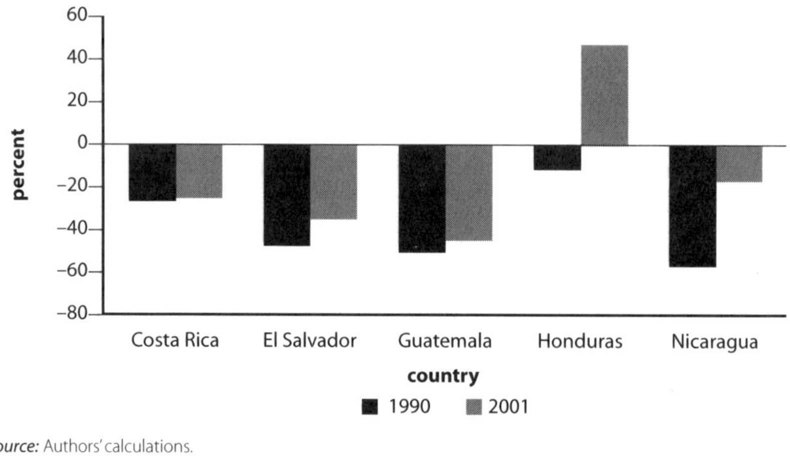

Source: Authors' calculations.

factures. The case of El Salvador is representative. Traditional exports fell from 50 percent of total exports in 1990 to 15 percent in 2002. In the same period, the shares of nontraditional exports and net *maquila* exports went from 48 percent to 58 percent and from 3 percent to 28 percent, respectively.

Despite the structural change in the composition of exports, conclusions about their diversification are not as sanguine. For El Salvador, Honduras, and, to a lesser extent, Nicaragua, the Herfindahl index of export revenue concentration (calculated with export revenue data at the two-digit level of disaggregation) deteriorates sharply from the early 1990s, as the concentration in a few traditional commodities has been replaced by a new concentration of exports in *maquila* manufactures (figure 2. 3). Results for Guatemala show unchanging diversification levels until the late 1990s, followed by increasing concentration levels in recent years. Costa Rica displays a diversification trend that ends abruptly in 1999, when the sudden surge in high-technology exports produces a new concentration trend.

It is interesting to note that if the analysis excludes *maquila* and high-technology products, strong diversification trends become evident for all countries except Nicaragua. This demonstrates that aside from the disproportionate success of *maquila* products and microprocessors—industries still not fully integrated into the local economies— exports in Central America have shown significant diversification, particularly into nontraditional agricultural goods, processed foods, and other light manufactures.

Growth

Table 2.4 presents growth figures for the five Central American countries, starting in 1990. Although there is substantial disparity in annual growth rates across countries, it is possible to detect three distinct phases. The first phase was characterized by relatively high growth rates between 1990 and 1995. The second phase was one of mixed results between 1996 and 1999. Poor economic results are more prevalent in the third phase, which starts around 2000. The only country that seems to deviate from the general trend is Nicaragua, which exhibited low growth until 1994 and a boom situation in 2000 induced by aid flows after Hurricane Mitch.

An important question is whether the expansion of trade flows described above had an influence on growth. Generally, correlations and scatter plots do not display a simple bivariate relationship between trade volumes (or growth in trade volumes) and economic growth. Figure 2. 4 illustrates this point with data from a large sample of countries. Can we conclude then that

Figure 2.3. Export Diversification Index, 1990–2001

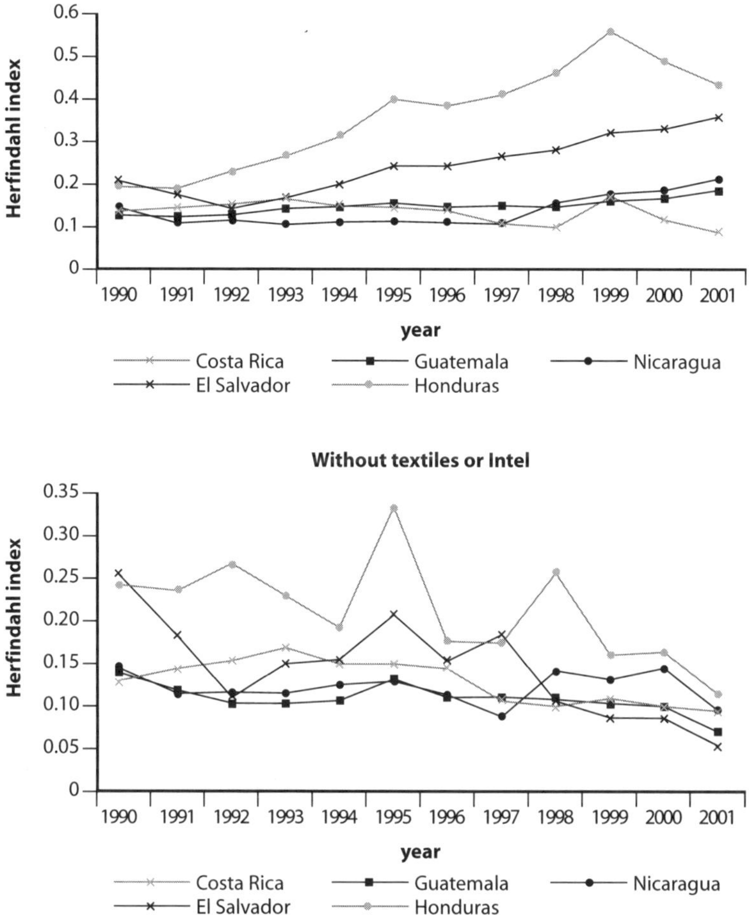

Source: Authors' calculations.

the positive trade results of recent years had no discernible impact on growth?

There are several reasons that explain why a simple bivariate empirical relationship between growth and trade is not obvious, and why the growth record of Central America was lackluster in the late 1990s despite progress in increasing trade flows throughout the decade. The first reason is that in addition to trade, a number of other important factors impinge on growth. For ex-

Table 2.4. GDP Growth, 1990–2004
percent

Year	*Costa Rica*	*El Salvador*	*Guatemala*	*Honduras*	*Nicaragua*	*Average*	*Average excluding Nicaragua*
1990	3.6	4.8	3.1	0.1	–0.1	2.3	2.9
1991	2.3	3.6	3.7	3.3	–0.2	2.5	3.2
1992	9.2	7.5	4.8	5.6	0.4	5.5	6.8
1993	7.4	7.4	3.9	6.2	–0.4	4.9	6.2
1994	4.7	6.0	4.0	–1.3	3.3	3.4	3.4
1995	3.9	6.4	4.9	4.1	4.3	4.7	4.8
1996	0.9	1.7	3.0	3.6	4.8	2.8	2.3
1997	5.6	4.2	4.4	5.0	5.1	4.9	4.8
1998	8.4	3.8	5.0	2.9	4.1	4.8	5.0
1999	8.2	3.4	3.8	–1.9	7.4	4.2	3.4
2000	1.8	2.2	3.6	5.7	12.8	5.2	3.3
2001	1.0	1.7	2.4	2.6	3.0	2.1	1.9
2002	2.9	2.1	2.2	2.5	1.0	2.2	2.5
2003	5.6	2.0	2.1	3.2	2.3	3.0	3.2
2004[a]	3.9	2.1	2.6	4.3	4.3	3.4	3.2

Source: Central banks of Central America and World Bank projections.
a. Projected.

Figure 2.4. Growth and Trade Openness, 1990s Average

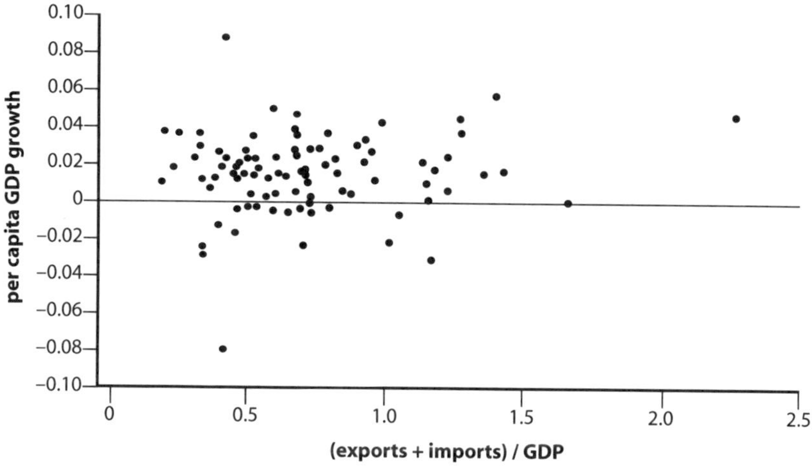

Source: Authors' calculations.

ample, in the endogenous growth literature, trade openness is one of the structural and institutional factors linked to growth, along with other public policies such as education, financial depth, government burden, public services and infrastructure, and governance. In addition to structural determinants, long-run growth performance is also a result of successful fiscal, monetary, and financial policies that contribute to a stable macroeconomic environment and avoid financial and balance of payments crises. External conditions (for example, terms of trade, external financing flows, and investor perceptions) also exert significant influence on economic developments.

Disentangling the effects of trade policies on growth from other effects (from structural, macroeconomic, and external conditions) is challenging. This is particularly difficult in Latin America during the 1990s because the region was hit by volatile capital flows that exerted an amplified impact on the short-run economic performance of regional economies as a result of weak macrofinancial policies. Loayza, Fajnzylber, and Calderón (2002) found that after controlling for cyclical and global factors, trade and other variables that capture the structural reforms of the 1990s had a significant effect on growth for a sample of 135 countries. This finding is consistent with many recent cross-country studies that have also confirmed a positive and significant relationship between trade openness and income growth (see, for example, Kraay 2003; Dollar and Kraay 2002).[12]

Table 2.5 displays the determinants of changes in growth for the Central American economies derived from the Loayza, Fajnzylber, and Calderón study of those economies in the 1990s. These results indicate that growing trade volumes in the 1990s contributed moderately to higher growth rates in all countries of Central America (ranging from 0.21 percentage points to 0.41 points annually, except for Honduras[13]), although not as much as in countries like Mexico, which saw large growth in trade volumes as a result of NAFTA and other factors. The results suggest that the progress registered in trade and other policy areas was not sufficient to compensate for weak performance in other areas (for example, financial depth in Costa Rica, Guatemala, and Honduras; education in Honduras; and business cycle factors in El Salvador, Guatemala, and Nicaragua).

A second important reason for the lack of a clear relationship between trade and growth is that liberalization policies need to be complemented for trade to exert its full positive effect on growth. Recent studies have shown that Mexico did not take full advantage of NAFTA because of lagging complementary actions. The states of the South of Mexico took little advantage because of a poorly trained workforce, infrastructural deficiencies (especially telecommunications), and weak institutions (Lederman, Maloney, and Servén 2005). These conclusions suggest that there are interactions between trade and other policies that are required for trade to be a significant engine of growth. A recent study by Bolaky and Freund (2003) found that trade has

Table 2.5. Explaining Changes in Growth, 1990s Versus 1980s
percentage points

	Costa Rica	El Salvador	Guatemala	Honduras	Nicaragua
Structural determinants					
Education	0.15	0.42	0.46	−0.10	0.48
Financial depth	−0.10	0.13	−0.06	−0.16	0.41
Trade openness	0.41	0.37	0.21	−0.07	0.30
Government burden	0.26	0.65	0.43	0.44	1.00
Infrastructure	0.35	0.63	0.41	0.60	0.37
Other	0.05	−0.11	−1.45	0.10	−0.72
Change in growth 1990s versus 1980s					
Predicted	1.13	2.09	2.44	0.82	1.84
Actual	3.80	4.14	3.05	0.84	4.40

Source: Adapted from Loayza, Fajnzylber, and Calderón 2002.

little impact on growth in economies with excessive business and labor regulations because these regulations prevent resources from moving into the most productive sectors following liberalization. Furthermore, in highly regulated economies, increased trade is more likely to occur in sectors in which comparative advantage is weak.

A third reason why increased trade openness does not always lead to higher growth is that the composition of exports is also relevant. Traditionally, much of the literature had assumed that export concentration in primary products was a "curse" of early developing countries. However, Lederman and Maloney (2003b) found that concentration in any type of goods, be it agricultural or manufacturing, has an empirically measurable deleterious effect on growth outcomes. This finding is of concern to Central American nations because the favorable export performance of the last decade and a half has not been accompanied by growing diversification levels, as shown earlier.

More technical reasons include the difficulty of measuring trade-policy stances and establishing causation. Also, obtaining summary measures of trade policy often involves aggregating tariff levels and nontariff barriers, with the latter being more technically difficult to establish. An often-quoted paper by Rodríguez and Rodrik (2000) shows that trade openness, usually measured by imports plus exports relative to GDP, is likely to be endogenous, making traditional inferences problematic.

Trade, Poverty, and Inequality

Fewer empirical studies have focused on the impact of trade on poverty and inequality. On the relationship between trade and poverty, a recent survey concluded that the empirical evidence broadly supports the view that trade liberalization reduces poverty in the long run and on average, as predicted by economic theory, that outcome is mainly the result of liberalization's effect on growth (Winters, McCulloch, and McKay 2004). This study also found that because trade policy is only one of many determinants of growth (and, by extension, of poverty reduction), greater trade should generally contribute positively to poverty reduction, but the ultimate outcomes are jointly determined by a host of additional factors.

The stronger empirical linkage between growth and poverty reduction has been documented in numerous studies. Using cross-country regression methods, Ravallion (2001) found that a 1 percent increase in mean income results, on average, in a fall of 2.5 percent in the proportion of people in absolute poverty. Kraay (2003) concluded that between 66 and 90 percent of the variation in medium-term changes in poverty can be explained by growth in average incomes. In a similar vein, Dollar and Kraay (2002) investigated the determinants of growth in incomes of the poorest quintile in a large sample of countries and found that it tracked growth in average incomes one-for-one. Although there have been some methodological challenges to cross-country studies, these findings are broadly consistent with those of country case studies (Winters, McCulloch, and McKay 2004). The broad empirical backing for growth as the key determinant of poverty reduction in recent decades is also consistent with the reduction of Central American poverty rates, which have tracked growth performance closely over the past decade and a half.

In contrast, the empirical evidence on the link between trade and inequality is more mixed. Some studies have found that increased openness increases summary measures of inequality, at least in low-income countries (Barro 2000; Lundberg and Squire 2003; Milanovic 2003; López 2004). Dollar and Kraay (2002), however, found no correlation between several measures of openness and income distribution. Kraay (2003) found some evidence of openness reducing inequality and poverty using a cross-country sample of household survey data, and he indicated that among the factors that may play a role in facilitating reductions in inequality are policies that support small farmers and small firms in taking advantage of new trade opportunities.

Because Central American countries made significant improvements in trade openness in the 1990s, recent trends in inequality indicators may suggest a relationship. Although the measurement of inequality and its comparison across time is fraught with numerous pitfalls, table 2.6 presents the evolution of inequality (Gini) indicators for selected Central American countries, with the average from a large sample of Latin American and Caribbean

Table 2.6. Evolution of Inequality in Latin America and the Caribbean
Gini coefficients

Country	*Early 1990s*	*Early 2000s*	*Change*
Costa Rica	43.9	44.6	0.7
El Salvador	50.5	51.8	1.3
Honduras	55.6	53.0	–2.6
Nicaragua	54.2	54.1	–0.1
Latin America and the Caribbean average (unweighted)	50.5	51.4	0.9
Latin America and the Caribbean average (weighted)	51.9	51.5	–0.4

Source: De Ferranti et al. 2003.

countries drawn from a recent Bank study that examined this issue in detail (De Ferranti, Perry, Fereira, and Walton 2004). The overall trend in Latin America and the Caribbean between the early 1990s and the early 2000s is ambiguous, as the unweighted average displays a slight deterioration and the weighted average shows an improvement. Results for Central America are equally ambiguous. Between the early 1990s and early 2000s, the level of inequality seems to have increased slightly for Costa Rica and El Salvador, remained essentially unchanged for Nicaragua, and decreased for Honduras. This evidence suggests that there is not a simple relationship between changes in trade openness and inequality in Central America, an unsurprising conclusion in economies in which structural changes, exogenous shocks (such as natural disasters or terms-of-trade swings), and business cycle variations respond to a wide host of factors beyond trade.

Summary and Conclusions

This chapter has provided a description of the wide-ranging unilateral and regional trade reforms that Central American nations have pursued since the late 1980s. Tariffs have been slashed and most nontariff barriers have been removed. Regional agreements have been revitalized and countries have engaged in the expansion of trade markets through the negotiation of bilateral trade agreements. The CBI preferences granted by the United States have also opened important opportunities, especially in the development of new *maquila* exports.

However impressive were the trade-policy achievements of the past decade, the economic results have been mixed. On the one hand, export volumes have increased, and some diversification has occurred, as demonstrated by the appearance of new exports—including the notable growth of *maquilas* in most Central American countries and of high-technology goods in Costa Rica. These are positive developments because, among other considerations, exporting sectors have been shown to provide higher wages and improved working conditions compared with other economic activities.

At the same time, although trade has made a significant contribution to growth in Central America since 1990, its impact has not been sufficient to lift aggregate growth rates enough to transform these countries' economies and radically reduce poverty rates. Nor have trade opportunities by themselves served to offset some of the constraints to progress in the region, such as the still inadequate progress in improving infrastructure, education, and governance, or continuing vulnerabilities in areas of macroeconomic and financial management that continue to add to investors' uncertainties in some of the countries. Beyond this, the new *maquila* industries have only developed a limited degree of integration with the local economies, and textile and apparel export prospects are still fragile because of the growing competition from Asia. Although the diversification of Central American countries' exports has increased, this tendency partly reflects negative trends during the period, such as the decline or stagnation in exports of traditional commodities such as cotton, coffee, and bananas. Ironically, although Honduras has achieved the highest degree of trade openness relative to its level of income, it is also the country with the weakest record of growth in Central America since the early 1990s.

As noted earlier, trade policy is unfortunately not the only determinant of trade (or growth) outcomes. There are still many obstacles to further export growth and trade diversification in Central American nations, including poor infrastructure, weaknesses in labor skills, inflexible regulations, trade barriers in other markets, deficiencies in governance (for example, corruption, inefficient customs), and macrofiscal and financial market vulnerabilities.

DR-CAFTA certainly caps the decade and a half of reforms in Central America, particularly in the trade area. It offers a great opportunity to make further progress in fostering trade-led growth. Yet it should not be seen as a silver bullet. On the positive side, it is a potentially more useful tool than the combination of unilateral removal of trade barriers and trade preferences seen so far because it effectively guarantees long-term market access to the largest trading partner and locks in the reforms of recent years, boosting credibility and attracting investment. Nevertheless, DR-CAFTA alone should not be expected to unleash radically higher levels of trade and growth, for the same reasons that trade policies since the early 1990s obtained only limited results. Countries will need to accompany DR-CAFTA implementation with policies to address key constraints and bottlenecks to reap the full social and economic results of this initiative, as will be justified in more detail in chapter 4 of this report and illustrated by the identification of certain country-specific elements of the complementary agenda in chapter 7.

Notes

1. This common tariff structure consists of rates of 0 percent for goods not produced in Central America, 5 percent for primary and capital goods produced in

Central America, 10 percent for intermediate and capital goods produced there, and 15 percent for final goods.

2. Costa Rica's tariff levels beyond 20 percent currently include 30, 35, 40, 45, 50, 65, and 150 percent.
3. Allegations of arbitrary use of nontariff barriers for sensitive agricultural products in some Central American countries have been common at the World Trade Organization (WTO) and other fora. Honduras, for example, has been accused in recent years of the arbitrary use of sanitary and phytosanitary measures in agriculture, particularly in reference to imports of poultry, dairy products, pork, feed grains, and rice.
4. Under these schemes, producers and processors negotiate a reference price for these products. When the domestic supply to these grains has been exhausted, a quota is introduced that allows processors to import these products at a preferential rate, often duty free.
5. In addition, El Salvador, Guatemala, Honduras, and Nicaragua are jointly negotiating an FTA with Canada. Those countries plus Costa Rica are in the early stages of FTA talks with the European Union. In addition to FTAs, several Central American countries have signed partial-scope trade agreements with Colombia and the República Bolivariana de Venezuela.
6. The expansion in trade and FDI associated with CBI preferences is also the result of complementary actions by Central American governments, including export promotion and investment attraction policies. The latter included the active role of specialized agencies (Coalición Costarricense de Iniciativas de Desarrollo [CINDE] in Costa Rica, Fundación Salvadoreña para el Desarrollo Económico y Social [FUSADES] in El Salvador, and Fundación Iberoamericana para el Desarrollo [FIDE] in Honduras) in designing incentives, policies, and promotional activities.
7. Rules of origin restrictions might explain why a significant share of apparel exports to the United States do not qualify for CBI duty-free treatment. In 2002 the shares of apparel exports that were able to enter duty free were 65 percent for Costa Rica, 63 percent for El Salvador, 73 percent for Honduras, and only 29 percent for Nicaragua (Lederman, Maloney, and Servén 2005).
8. Although trade openness has been used in the literature as a common proxy for trade policy, strictly speaking it is an outcome variable that reflects a broad array of policies and other structural features of an economy (that is, area, landlocked situation, oil exporter). The indicators of trade volume presented in this section include the best available information for all trade, including all imports and exports related to free trade zones and *maquila* activity.

9. One of the reasons for the apparent large trade openness (and gains) magnitudes as a share of GDP obtained for Honduras and Nicaragua is the potential underestimation of their GDP figures.
10. Accounting for the factors mentioned is done so that we do not unfairly attribute to trade policy what is merely the result of structural country characteristics. We follow here the corrections included in Loayza, Fajnzylber, and Calderón (2002).
11. The reductions in the deficits for Costa Rica, El Salvador, and Guatemala seem small by comparison to achievements in Honduras and Nicaragua, but the latter may be overestimated because of the undervaluation of GDP.
12. The positive relationship between trade and growth was challenged by Rodríguez and Rodrik (2000) on the grounds that trade openness may capture the effect of omitted variables. However, Warcziag (2001) identified a positive direct effect of liberal trade policies on economic growth. A recent study by Lederman and Maloney (2003c) also found that trade liberalization policies have a positive effect on growth.
13. The estimations presented in Loayza, Fajnzylber, and Calderón (2002) use trade openness data that net out *maquila* flows, as opposed to the figures reported in tables 2.2 and 2.3. This underestimates most significantly the trade gains achieved in the 1990s for Honduras as reported in figure 2. 2, resulting from the substantial growth in gross *maquila* export flows. Rough estimates suggest that the impact of greater trade openness on growth for this country after correcting for the underestimation yields results in the range of 0.2-0.4 per year, in line with those for the other Central American nations.

CHAPTER 3

The Content of DR-CAFTA

Implications for Market Access and Domestic Reforms

After more than a decade of market reforms and significant advances in trade reforms, five nations of Central America (Costa Rica, El Salvador, Guatemala, Honduras, and Nicaragua) embarked on negotiations for an FTA with the United States in early 2003. The outcome is DR-CAFTA, an agreement that was signed by the executive branches of all countries involved in August 2004, and as of April 2006 it had been ratified by the legislatures of all countries except Costa Rica.[1]

Although the FTA with the United States is not a guaranteed path to sustained economic growth and prosperity, past experience suggests that it may play a fruitful role in two critical areas: improved market access and domestic reforms. The former is important because lowering trade barriers expands markets and increases trade flows that help resource allocation, specialization, economies of scale, and technology transfer. FTAs have also proven useful as a means of furthering policy and regulatory reforms in key areas and of improving their credibility and permanence. For Central American nations, locking many of the reforms of recent years with an FTA that is costly to violate should generate a credibility effect that could boost investment levels.[2] Also, the FTA itself contains features that can have strong investment effects including trade liberalization, nondiscriminatory treatment of domestic and foreign investors, and removal of restrictions for private-sector participation in most sectors of the economy.

This chapter presents an overview of the contents of the DR-CAFTA. Although a detailed analysis of the text and its implications falls outside the scope of this chapter, the text does summarize the agreement's most significant provisions and it evaluates them from the point of view of their potential effect on market access, domestic regulations, and institutions. The chapter attempts to provide preliminary answers to these two sets of questions:

1. *Expansion of market access*: Does the DR-CAFTA contain commitments to provide permanent and stable market access at least similar to that available to Central American exporters under CBI?[3] Will it provide access to exports (that is, relaxing of tariff and nontariff barriers, making rules of origin flexible) beyond that available to Central American countries under CBI provisions? Will it also remove trade barriers in the few remaining protected subsectors in Central America that have proven resistant to past liberalization efforts? A positive answer to this set of questions is likely to signify that DR-CAFTA would have the potential to increase trade flows, improve domestic resource allocation, and boost investment in new exporting ventures from Central America.

2. *Domestic reforms*: Do commitments included in the DR-CAFTA agreement effectively extend, lock in, or both extend and lock in the policy and regulatory reforms of recent years in Central American countries? Do they require significant additional changes? Do they require greater efforts in the enforcement of current regulations? A positive answer to this set of questions would suggest that DR-CAFTA will signal a strong commitment by Central American countries to consolidate and extend recent policy and regulatory reforms, and commitment to their enforcement. Although some countries in the region have already locked in some reforms through other international agreements, DR-CAFTA offers a chance for a higher credibility level of commitment that should yield a higher investment response.

This chapter is thus a summary of key commitments found in the DR-CAFTA text and it deals with the topics of the agreement in the following order: market access in goods (agriculture, manufactures, textiles and apparel), trade in services and related matters, other disciplines (that is, investment protection, intellectual property rights, labor and environment, government procurement, and other provisions), and the regional application of commitments. The main conclusions are drawn at the end of the chapter.

Market Access for Goods

As a result of DR-CAFTA, duties affecting trade with the United States will be eliminated for virtually all goods. Because of strong sensitivities, some agricultural products were exempted from the eventual zero-duty status: sugar for entry into the United States, white maize into four Central American nations (El Salvador, Guatemala, Honduras, and Nicaragua), and potatoes and onions into Costa Rica. Whereas the bulk of tariffs will be removed upon implementation, some tariffs will be phased out gradually. Central America's number of products with gradual phase-outs is significantly higher than those of the United States.

Agriculture

DR-CAFTA commitments in agriculture include the reciprocal elimination of all tariffs, with the only exceptions as described above. For Central American countries, this will consolidate the current access allowed under CBI legislation for Central American products and will provide for some expansion of their zero-duty access to a few new products that had been kept outside the preferences.[4] DR-CAFTA also includes reciprocal commitments from Central American countries to consolidate access to their agricultural markets for U.S. exports, eliminate tariff peaks, and open farther those sensitive sectors that still enjoy restrictions to imports.

- *Market access.* DR-CAFTA commits parties to eliminate tariffs for virtually all tariff lines, through tariff reductions, expansion of zero-tariff quotas, and combinations of these two approaches. A separate schedule of commitments applies to each country, with El Salvador, Guatemala, Honduras, and Nicaragua excluding white maize from tariff reduction obligations[5] and Costa Rica excluding onions and potatoes.

- *Tariff elimination.* Tariffs are to be phased out according to specific schedules negotiated on a product- and country-specific basis (table 3.1). Tariffs will be reduced within one of the following timeframes: immediate, 5 years, 10 years, 12 years, or 15 years (18–20 years for poultry parts, rice,

Table 3.1. Tariff Reduction Schedule for Sensitive Agricultural Products

	Guatemala			*Honduras*			*El Salvador*			*Nicaragua*			*Costa Rica*		
Product	*IT (%)*	*PP (yrs)*	*GP (yrs)*	*IT (%)*	*PP (yrs)*	*GP (yrs)*	*IT (%)*	*PP (yrs)*	*GP (yrs)*	*IT (%)*	*PP (yrs)*	*GP (yrs)*	*IT (%)*	*PP (yrs)*	*GP (yrs)*
Beef[a]	–	10	0	15	15	6	15	15	0	15	15	3	15	15	4
Pork	15	15	0	15	15	0	40	15	6	15	15	0	47	15	6
Poultry (leg quarters)	164.4	18	10	164.4	18	0	164.4	18	10	164.4	18	10	151	17	10
Dairy products	15	20	10	15	20	10	40	20	10	40	20	10	66	20	10
Yellow maize	–	10	0	45	15	6	15	15	6	15	15	0	15	15	0
Beans	20	15	6	15	15	0	20	15	15	30	15	0	47	15	0
Fresh potatoes	15	15	0	15	15	0	15	12	0	15	15	0		Excluded	
Rice	29.2	18	10	45	18	10	40	18	10	63	18	10	36	20	10
Sorghum	0	0	0	15	15	0	15	15	0	20	15	6	15	15	0

Source: CEPAL 2004.

GP = grace period; IT = initial tariff level; n.a. = not available; PP = phase-out period; yrs = years.

a. Beef products other than prime and choice cuts.

and dairy products). Although most tariffs will be reduced in equal annual installments over the phase-out period, tariff reductions for specified sensitive products will be back-loaded, with no cuts in the initial years of the phase-out period and larger cuts in the later years of the period. Central American producers obtained longer time periods for tariff phase outs as well as a greater share of the back-loaded phase-out periods than did the United States.

- *Tariff-rate quotas.* For many sensitive products, immediate market access will be provided through the creation and gradual expansion of tariff-rate quotas (TRQs) (that is, zero-duty access for a specified quantity of imports). For example, Nicaragua will gradually increase TRQs affecting some sensitive U.S. products such as peanuts, peanut butter, beef, and dairy products. Table 3.2 examines the TRQs obtained by Central America. For cases in which initial quotas account for relatively small shares of recent import volumes, significant changes in local market conditions should not be expected. For a few cases in which quotas are near 100 percent of local volumes or above, detailed analysis of specific commodity markets that falls beyond the scope of this report would be required. Such analysis would need to take into account the structure of the market, whether duty-free quota imports have been allowed in recent years (as in the case of several grains in El Salvador and Nicaragua), and whether performance requirements (see below) would apply in that market. Most quotas were agreed to grow at rates between 2 percent and 5 percent, roughly at or below the rates of growth of the economies projected for the next decade.

- *Agricultural safeguard.* DR-CAFTA includes a special agricultural safeguard to provide temporary protection against import surges of selected sensitive products. The safeguard is activated automatically if import quantities surpass prespecified levels. If activated, an immediate tariff increase to pre-agreement (most-favored-nation [MFN]) levels is allowed in the early years of implementation, and to gradually declining levels for the later years. The agricultural safeguard cannot be in force for more than four years and can only be used once for most sensitive crops listed in the agreement during the transition period.[6]

- *Sanitary and phytosanitary measures.* The parties agree to apply the science-based disciplines of the WTO Agreement on Sanitary and Phytosanitary (SPS) Measures. An SPS working group will expedite resolution of

Table 3.2. Recent Imports (2003) Versus DR-CAFTA Quotas of Sensitive Agricultural Commodities

	Guatemala		*Honduras*		*El Salvador*		*Nicaragua*		*Costa Rica*	
Commodity	*Imports*	*Quota*	*Imports*	*Quota*	*Imports*	*Quota*	*Imports*	*Quota*	*Imports*	*Quota*
Beef	9.5	15.0	3.2	NQ	50.0	0.7	0.0	NQ	8.7	NQ
Pork	42.3	55.6	80.0	35.9	66.7	45.2	25.0	115.4	2.8	86.1
Poultry	18.7	21.3	7.5	84.0	1.3	33.0	1.8	12.7	2.5	34.5
Potatoes	7.7	NQ	110.5	0.0	233.3	NQ	57.1	NQ	24.4	NQ
Maize	59.4	87.3	65.3	84.4	63.8	98.2	7.3	182.5	4483.3	NQ
Rice	275.6	84.0	1372.0	102.1	320.6	15.7	34.8	110.9	41.1	56.9
Milk	83.7	1.8	19.0	3.2	53.9	1.9	12.9	487.7	4.6	48.5
Butter	100.0	10.7	25.0	12.3	100.0	5.4	0.0	196.0	0.0	41.4

Source: Faostat 2004 and authors' calculations.

NQ = no quota.

Note: Imports are presented as percentage of local production; quotas are presented as percentage of total imports. NQ = no quota.

Table 3.3. Sugar Imports to the United States from Central America

		Additional quotas	
Country	*Average imports 2000–2*	*Year 1*	*Year 15*
Guatemala	58.9	32.0	49.8
El Salvador	30.5	24.0	36.0
Nicaragua	17.8	22.0	28.2
Costa Rica	15.8	13.0	15.8
Honduras	9.6	8.0	10.2
Total	132.6	99.0	140.0

Source: USTR.

technical issues and contribute to the dissemination of the regulations and procedures applied in the United States but affecting agricultural and food products, which we believe can contribute to rural and national development in Central America. During negotiations, a working group on these matters aided Central Americans in resolving problems to meet standards required to enter the U.S. market, and commitments were made for the continuation of technical assistance from U.S. sanitary and agriculture agencies.[7]

- *Agricultural export subsidies.* Although much public attention was paid to large U.S. production and marketing subsidies during DR-CAFTA negotiations, no significant commitments were made by the United States in this area, consistent with its policy to negotiate this issue in the context of global trade talks at the WTO. DR-CAFTA includes the commitment by all parties not to subsidize exports to each other's market, except to compete with third-party export subsidies.

- *Performance requirements.* Imports of some sensitive products will be subject to performance requirements (for example, agreements by importers to purchase a share of the local crop during the phase-out period). This is the case for pork, rice, and white and yellow corn in El Salvador, and for rice in Costa Rica and Honduras.

- *Sugar.* Although excluded from the final tariff elimination commitment by the United States, DR-CAFTA includes a pledge to double the zero-tariff import quota of sugar from Central American nations, from 99,000 metric tons in the first year to about 140,000 metric tons over 15 years (table 3.3).[8] Although this keeps imports from the region below 1.7 percent of total U.S. consumption, it will provide greater revenues for Central American producers, who will be able to increase sales in the United States where import prices have been almost 200 percent above those prevailing elsewhere.[9] The new market access will mean that Central American countries will double the share of current production that is exported to the United States, from an average of less than 4 percent to about 8 percent.

Evaluation

In agriculture, DR-CAFTA provides significant gains in market access for all parties. It consolidates current CBI access to Central American exporters, introduces some flexibility to current nontariff barriers, and includes commitments to provide technical assistance in overcoming sanitary standards for nontraditional agricultural exports. The last commitment is important for Central American producers interested in exporting to the U.S. market because lack of adequate information about how producers can satisfy these standards has been identified as a major obstacle to new exports in the past (Monge, Loría, and González-Vega 2003).

DR-CAFTA will also commit Central American countries to gradually eliminate remaining protection in products that had proven resistant to liberalization efforts in the past. Our impression is that skillful negotiators on all sides achieved a delicate balance between pressures to prolong adjustment periods and provide safeguards for import-competing products and market access for Central America's nontraditional agriculture. A comparison of the treatment afforded to Central America's sensitive commodities with that granted in other U.S. free trade agreements suggests that DR-CAFTA beneficiaries may have obtained the highest tariffs and longest tariff phase-out periods. This outcome was perhaps partly due to agriculture's importance for Central America's economies, including employment (figure 3.1).[10] This treatment will benefit farmers and laborers engaged in the production of sensitive crops, but it will limit gains for consumers—including the majority of the poor—who will not see immediate declines in prices of key components of the food basket. Although the exemptions granted in sugar, maize, potatoes, and onions respond to strong political factors, they will impede trade and the most efficient deployment of resources in Central America and the United States.

From the point of view of domestic reforms in Central American nations, DR-CAFTA provisions generally lock in current agricultural trade policies, and in the future will provide for greater liberalization by setting deadlines and firm commitments to move to freer trade for the bulk of agricultural commodities.

Figure 3.1. Weighted Tariffs for Sensitive Agricultural Items, U.S. FTAs: NAFTA, Chile, and DR-CAFTA

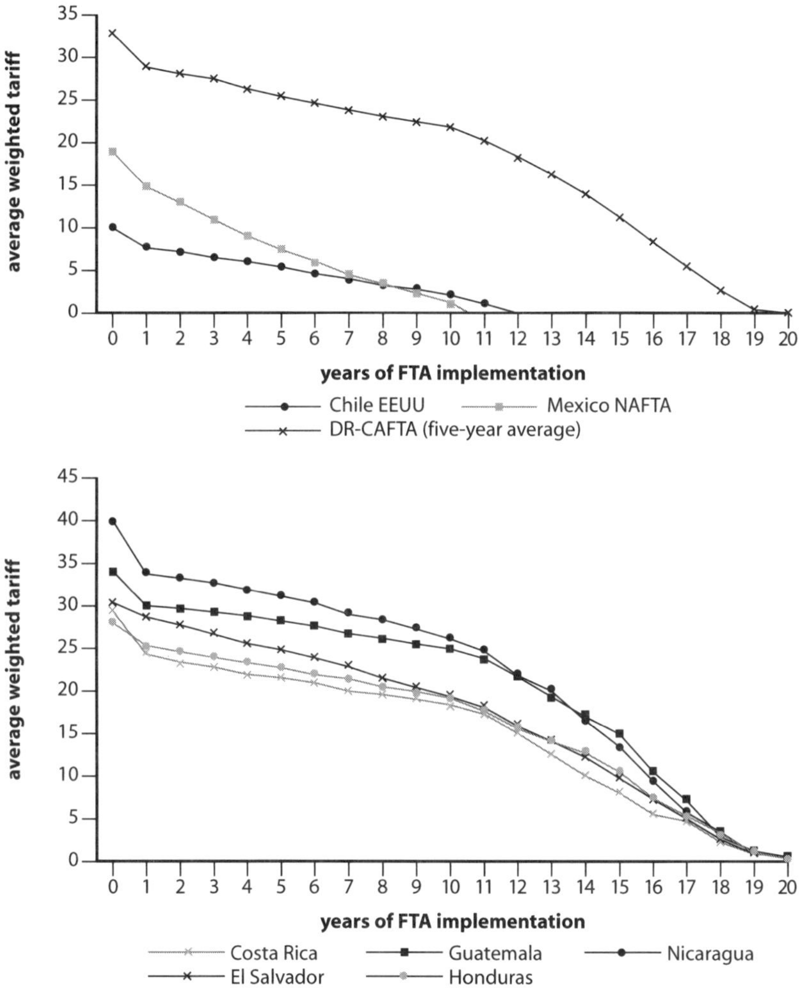

Source: Tejada and Jaramillo 2005.

Note: Tariffs weighted by each sensitive item's contribution to agricultural GDP.

On the issue of U.S. farm subsidies, it is unfortunate that no commitments were included in DR-CAFTA because it is well known that these types of policies continue to create significant distortions in some key global markets (World Bank 2002; Anderson 2004). World Bank studies have shown that the elimination of these interventions would be favorable for the reduction of poverty on a global scale, mainly because of the positive effect on the income of farmers and farm laborers in countries with large exporting potential in activities such as grains, oilseeds, cotton, and dairy products. However, these studies also warn that increasing food prices would represent welfare losses for consumers, and that food-importing countries with limited capacity to become exporters at low cost would lose from the removal of these subsidies (World Bank 2002). Argentina and Brazil would be among the most likely winners in Latin America, whereas net food importers such as the small island nations of the Caribbean and some Central American countries would stand to lose from this policy change (De Ferranti et al. 2005).

Manufactures

- *Market access.* Commitments to provide duty-free treatment to all manufactures imply a consolidation and some improvement over CBI benefits for Central American countries. Tariffs will be eliminated for a few products that had been explicitly excluded from CBI preferences, such as canned tuna, shoes, jewelry, and hooks.

- *Tariff elimination.* In contrast to agricultural goods, the vast majority of manufacturing tariffs will be eliminated upon DR-CAFTA's entry into force. There are some items that will undergo reductions in phase-out periods of 5 to 10 years. Once again, Central Americans placed more tariff lines in the gradual elimination categories, in response to considerations of so-called asymmetries between the United States and the developing countries of Central America. As a result, the United States will liberalize 99.8 percent of manufacturing products upon DR-CAFTA's entry into force, with only 19 Central American exports facing a 10-year gradual phase-out of U.S. tariffs. By contrast, about 80 percent of U.S. manufacturing exports will enter Central American countries duty free immediately. Whereas 9 percent will be subject to a 5-year phase out, 9 percent will be subject to a 10-year schedule and 4 percent will have a 12–15-year schedule. Transition periods were obtained by Central American negotiators for some sectors that requested time to prepare for competition with the United States (for example, beer, water, rum, and wheat flour) as well as for some items that generate significant fiscal revenues (such as imports of vehicles for Honduras).

- *Tariff-rate quotas.* Immediate market access for products included in phase-out categories is provided through the creation of tariff-rate quotas that grow in time.

- *Rules of origin.* A large number of manufacturing products are subject to special rules of origin. Although a careful evaluation of such provisions exceeds the scope of this chapter, DR-CAFTA takes, in general, a more flexible approach than NAFTA. (For example, in the case of steel products, the steel need not be produced in the region for the product to qualify for DR-CAFTA treatment.) Also, special provisions will allow for "co-production" arrangements in which different stages of inputs or final goods production can take place in Central American countries or the United States. The special case of textiles and apparel is treated separately because complex rules of origin requirements have been the instrument of choice to maintain trade restrictions.

- *Safeguards.* A safeguard provision is included to avoid the disruptive effects of sudden surges in imports. These safeguards can be invoked during the first 10 years of application of the treaty for manufactures (15 years for agricultural goods not subject to the special agricultural safeguard).[11] The safeguard can be invoked as long as total imports of the product surpass current import levels by at least 3 percent, reinstating current tariff levels temporally for up to 4 years.

- *Antidumping provisions.* DR-CAFTA allows countries to maintain their rights derived from the WTO's antidumping agreement. In addition, the United States vowed to continue to extend the preferential treatment afforded to Central American countries under CBI for antidumping investigations in the United States.

- *Dealer agreements.* DR-CAFTA includes commitments from four countries with existing dealer protection laws—Costa Rica, the Dominican Republic, El Salvador, and Honduras—to revise their legislation to eliminate compulsory exclusivity of distribution of imported products from the United States.[12]

Evaluation

DR-CAFTA consolidates and expands the access that Central American exporters enjoy under CBI preferences for manufactures. From the point of view of Central American reforms, DR-CAFTA provisions for manufactures lock in current trade policies and broaden them to apply to some sensitive items, after transition periods.

The elimination of all duties by all parties and the inclusion of products that had been excluded from CBI preferences should improve trade prospects and resource allocation. It is more difficult to evaluate the impact of the many sector-specific rules of origin. In some cases, these provisions are likely to continue to pose significant barriers to entry into the U.S. market, as has been shown by several World Bank studies, including *Lessons from NAFTA* (Lederman, Maloney, and Servén 2005). In other cases, Central American negotiators obtained special treatment that should facilitate trade. Given the importance and complexity of the textile and apparel provisions, a review of changes in rules of origin is included below.

*Textiles and Apparel (*Maquila*)*

In textiles and apparel, DR-CAFTA expands CBI treatment (as reflected in the Caribbean Basin Trade Partnership Act [CBTPA] of 2000, known also as "NAFTA Parity") by including some flexibility in the rules of origin that should allow zero-duty entry to the United States for a broader set of products. A number of features of DR-CAFTA will facilitate goods qualifying for duty-free treatment: unlimited use of regional inputs, flexible short-supply lists, accumulation of origin with regional partners, exceptions for specific types of apparel, and temporary quotas for goods that do not need to meet strict rules of origin for Costa Rica and Nicaragua.

- *Regional inputs.* DR-CAFTA provisions grant duty-free treatment to apparel made from regional (knit or woven) fabric using yarn produced in the region (known as the "yarn forward rule"). This treatment contrasts with the latest CBI legislation (CBTPA approved in 2000), which had only allowed duty-free and quota-free treatment for goods made in Central America from U.S. inputs, and duty-free entry for some goods that used regional fabrics and yarns but under quantitative restrictions.[13]

- *Accumulation.* The treaty allows for the accumulation of origin from Mexico and Canada as well as the Central American parties to the agreement. This means that inputs from these countries will count as domestic inputs (those from Mexico and Canada are subject to quantitative limits) for minimum content requirements.

- *Short supply.* A list of accepted short-supply inputs (those that can be sourced from third countries without losing zero-duty status) was expanded and the process to request inclusions of additional inputs to the list was streamlined.

- *Exceptions for selected products.* Less restrictive rules of origin were negotiated for selected products, such as bras, boxer shorts, pajamas and sleepwear, and textile luggage. For these products, the use of fabric made in third countries will be accepted as long as "substantial transformation" (that is, cutting and sewing) takes place in a Central American country.

- *De minimis rule.* The share of third-party content that may be allowed in garments (known as the "de minimis rule") was increased from the level currently applied under CBI (7 percent) to 10 percent in DR-CAFTA.

- *Temporary quotas.* Two Central American countries obtained temporary quotas (known as tariff preference levels, or TPLs) with less restrictive rules of origin. Nicaragua was awarded a temporary quota that exempts apparel exports from all rules of origin requirements.[14] The quota amount is for 100 million square meters equivalent (about 75 percent of its current use of third-party inputs); it will be in force for the first five years of the treaty, and eliminated gradually during the following five years. Costa Rica also obtained a two-year TPL for 500,000 squared meters equivalent for woolen apparel that would enter the United States free from rules of origin restrictions at a tariff level equivalent to 50 percent of the tariff applied for most-favored nations.[15]

In addition, liberalization commitments included in DR-CAFTA may be retroactive to January 1, 2004, only for textiles and apparel. This means that Central American exporters of these products will be able to obtain a refund for duties paid while DR-CAFTA was or is being ratified by legislatures. The purpose of this concession is for Central American countries to begin to capitalize on DR-CAFTA immediately, attracting new investments and allowing some time for the industry to prepare for the end of the global textile quota regime in early 2005.

Of particular interest to the *maquila* sector were the provisions related to export processing zones and duty drawbacks. DR-CAFTA provisions did not include commitments to change these instruments, aside from reinforcing the need to comply with WTO obligations. For the higher-income countries of Central America (Costa Rica, El Salvador, and Guatemala), WTO pledges will require that they dismantle fiscal subsidies implicit in export processing schemes starting in 2009.

Evaluation

DR-CAFTA provisions on textile products relax some of the current nontariff barriers implicit in rules of origin requirements that textile and apparel exports from Central America face under CBI. Under DR-CAFTA, Central American exporters will benefit from the world's most flexible set of market access conditions into the United States for this sector. Nevertheless, access conditions are still restrictive in comparison to those granted in virtually all other sectors of manufacturing.

The new rules have been seen as a potential boom to regional suppliers of fabrics, yarns, and other key inputs and may induce Central American exporters to forge new links with suppliers in Mexico and Canada. Given the dearth of regional supplies of textile inputs, DR-CAFTA provisions may help attract the establishment of textile mills in the region. Although all of this may favor exports of Central American apparel in the short run, it may also be extending implicitly the protection prevailing in U.S. markets to regional suppliers of inputs—a situation that may not be competitive in world markets and could be subject to future adjustment costs in a sector where global liberalization trends are likely to continue. In the short run, the retroactive nature of the agreement and making the rules of origin flexible should allow firms based in Central American countries to gain an edge in a more competitive environment in the U.S. market as a result of the end of global quotas in 2005. In the medium and long run, strong competition and the likely erosion of trade preferences imply that countries will need to increase their productivity and rely on a sound overall investment climate to attract further investment in this sector.

Trade in Services

In services DR-CAFTA breaks new ground in the relationship between Central American countries and the United States because current CBI legislation did not contain significant commitments in this area. In discussions and interviews with the authors of this report, policymakers and specialists from Central America have expressed optimism in the sense that these aspects of the treaty should boost the credibility of the reforms of recent years that opened provision of most services to private operators, including those from abroad.

DR-CAFTA includes commitments that apply to a long list of service sectors (exceptions are included in country-specific negative lists), including financial services, telecommunications, professional services, distribution, tourism, express delivery, computer and related services, audiovisual services and entertainment, energy, transport, construction and engineering, advertising, and environmental services. In addition, the agreement contains disciplines in the area of e-commerce, an area that most Central American countries had not included in previous FTAs. Although a thorough evaluation of the implications for each one of these sectors is beyond the scope of this chapter, this section provides a broad evaluation of implications for market access and domestic reform.

The commitments in services seek to eliminate discrimination against firms from partner countries in market access and in the application of domestic regulations. Because all Central American countries and the United States currently grant broad nondiscrimination status between domestic and foreign firms for access to most domestic service markets, as well as nondiscrimination in their regulations, DR-CAFTA consolidates the status quo by locking in the reforms undertaken in recent years to open sectors to private participation. Only for the notable case of Costa Rica, significant legislative reforms will be required to comply with obligations in the telecommunications and insurance markets (see box 3.1).

In addition, DR-CAFTA spells out strong commitments to transparency in regulatory processes. Regulatory authorities are required to use open and transparent administrative procedures, consult with interested parties before issuing regulations, allow for comment periods for proposed rules, provide advance notice before the entry into force of new regulations, and publish all regulations. Several of these rules have been applied in Central American countries, but some countries and some service sectors will require significant upgrading in the process of consultation and application of regulatory decisions. These improvements in the transparency of regulations in Central America, however, should contribute to strengthening the investment climate.

Service sector commitments include the following:

- *Financial services (banking, insurance, securities)*. Because of the complexities of the sector, a separate chapter in DR-CAFTA was negotiated to deal with financial services. The chapter centers on granting providers of these services nondiscriminatory rights to establish branches, subsidiaries, and *sociedades anónimas* while preserving the right of domestic regulators to apply prudential measures to ensure the security and stability of their financial systems. The chapter also includes provisions on transparency of

Box 3.1

Costa Rica's Commitments in Telecommunications and Insurance

Costa Rica did not open its telecommunications and insurance sectors to private competition in the 1990s, as did most other countries in Latin America, preferring to keep both sectors under the control of strong state-owned monopolies. An attempt to allow for competition in the provision of telecom services in the late 1990s was aborted as a result of strong public sentiment against the proposal. With DR-CAFTA, Costa Rica will commit to introduce competition to state agencies.

- *Telecommunications.* Costa Rica pledged to undertake a partial and gradual opening of its telecom sector, specifically in three areas—private network services, Internet services, and wireless phone services. The process of opening will need to comply with the principles of "universality" and "solidarity" in the supply of these services, meaning that plans must be designed to facilitate inclusion of rural and disadvantaged segments of the population. Costa Rica committed to approve legislation for the modernization and strengthening of the local telecom company (originally by December 2004, although approval has been delayed), and to have in place modern regulatory norms and a regulatory authority by January 1, 2006. Private network services will be open to competition by January 1, 2006, and wireless services by January 1, 2007.
- *Insurance.* Costa Rica also committed to allow private competition in its insurance market. The establishment of a modern regulatory framework, including a supervisory agency, is planned for 2007. The majority of the sector would be open by January 1, 2008, with universal access to private providers in all lines of insurance by January 1, 2011.

domestic regulatory regimes. U.S.-based firms also gained the possibility of offering cross-border services in areas such as financial information, data processing, and financial advisory services, and Central American mutual fund managers will be allowed to use foreign-based portfolio managers. For the case of insurance, Central American countries (except Costa Rica) committed to allowing access through branches within four years. In addition, Central American countries opened their markets to U.S.-based firms for the supply of insurance services on a cross-border basis for a limited number of risks (for example, reinsurance; reinsurance brokerage and marine, aviation, and transport insurance).

- *Telecommunications.* The agreement provides for nondiscriminatory access for users to public telecommunications networks, providing U.S. firms the right to interconnect at nondiscriminatory, cost-based rates (as in the Chile FTA). Commitments allow for current concession rights to private providers (such as Enitel in Nicaragua) to continue until their expiration.

- *Professional services (architects, engineers, accountants)*. An issue of debate during negotiations was temporary entry of professionals and procedures for assessing their qualifications.[16] Some Central American nations pledged to remove some local residency requirements for the exercise of some services. The agreement includes reciprocal recognition of domestic procedures and institutions that grant degrees and authorization to exercise a profession.

- *e-Commerce.* The agreement recognizes that services can be supplied through electronic means and binds the parties to uphold the nondiscriminatory treatment of digital products (software, music, videos, text), not to impose customs duties on digital products, and to cooperate on numerous policy areas related to e-commerce.

Other Provisions

The remainder of the legal agreements of DR-CAFTA focus on commitments on disciplines that cover a wide range of issues, most of which Central American countries had not included in previous trade agreements. In this section we provide summary observations of the content of each of these commitments and evaluate them briefly for their potential to strengthen the credibility of domestic regulations.

Investment Protection

DR-CAFTA grants reciprocal nondiscriminatory rights to investors from signatory parties to establish, acquire, and operate investments on an equal footing with local investors, unless specifically stated otherwise. The agreement's chapter deepens the commitments that Central American countries have made at the WTO and to one another in the area of investment protection. All forms of investment are protected under the agreement, including enterprises, debt, concessions, contracts, and intellectual property. Investors receive protection under DR-CAFTA for due process as well as the right to receive a fair market value for property in the event of an expropriation. The agreement also includes procedures for dispute settlement and explicit commitments to free and expeditious transfers of profits, subject to nondiscriminatory domestic regulations on the financial sector and the protection of creditor rights.

Evaluation

This chapter of DR-CAFTA locks in legal rights of U.S. investors that were already recognized by nondiscrimination norms throughout Central America; many of the rights had been locked in by bilateral investment treaties that some of the countries had signed with the United States in previous years, although some provisions remain controversial—see box 3.2. Nondiscrimination, stable rules, and compensation for expropriation are important, internationally recognized investor rights. The consolidation of these rights should send a strong signal of improvement in the investment climate.

Intellectual Property Rights

DR-CAFTA provisions in the intellectual property rights (IPR) chapter include commitments related to improving IPR protection and granting firms nondiscriminatory treatment. Three types of commitments are included. The first type is the obligation to ratify a number of international agreements dealing with trademarks, patents, satellite TV, newly developed plant varieties, and other IPR issues.[17] The second type of commitment is the establishment of minimum standards for protection in the areas of brands, geographical indications, Internet domains, authors' rights, satellite signals, and patents—including the extension of copyright protection from 50 years to 70 years. The third type is the application of procedures and resources for the enforcement of IPR, including the criminalization of end-user piracy. For

Box 3.2

Controversies in Protecting the Rights of Investors under FTAs

Some controversy has surrounded the chapters on investment protection in recent free trade agreements. Whereas there is consensus that attracting investment and providing stable rules for investors are positive steps, critics hold that treaties give foreign investors excessive privileges. However, Central American countries have already incorporated these commitments in other FTAs and bilateral investment treaties; hence, DR-CAFTA does not really impose "brand-new" obligations on Central American countries. Some of the key controversies in this front include the following:

- *Investors' rights and public interest.* Critics contend that FTAs extend rights to investors to use international arbitration panels to revoke local regulations, even if these regulations are enacted for legitimate public interest objectives, including public health, safety, and environmental protection. NAFTA's Chapter 11 has been criticized often in this vein. DR-CAFTA's Annex 10-C.4 (b) was drafted to address this issue by exempting most regulatory actions that are designed and applied to protect legitimate public welfare objectives, such as public health, safety, and the environment, from being deemed "indirect expropriations"—the source of most disputes in the NAFTA experience.
- *Dispute settlement.* Critics charge that the tribunals allowed under FTAs to resolve disputes enable investors to bypass domestic judiciary systems. However, the use of international panels has become commonplace for disputes with international investors because local judiciaries have often been perceived as more easily influenced by domestic concerns. In response to criticism, newer FTAs (including DR-CAFTA) are including the creation of an appellate body to review decisions of individual panels.
- *Performance requirements.* Investments provisions explicitly prohibit governments from imposing requirements on foreign investment, such as commitments to export certain volumes, minimum usage of local inputs, or compulsory technology transfer. Such requirements were commonplace in the past in many Latin American countries but were eliminated by the WTO's Agreement on Trade-Related Investment Measures (TRIMs), which eliminates most performance requirements in the area of goods. DR-CAFTA introduces the prohibition of some performance requirements in services.

continued on next page

Box 3.2, *continued*

- *Destabilizing capital flows.* The United States has pressed in its FTAs for provisions that limit the ability of governments to curtail the movement of short-term capital flows. This has been subject to debate because speculative short-term outflows have been linked in the past to certain types of balance of payments crises. Although the issue remains controversial, many studies suggest that monetary authorities should retain some powers to halt, even if temporarily, short-term debt or investment flows to prevent herding behavior and macroeconomic destabilization. This issue has not been a strong concern in Central America, where significant flows of short-term capital flows have not occurred.

the most part, commitments in this area imply obligations that apply generally, not merely to nationals of the signatory countries.

In the area of patents, significant obligations include the automatic extensions of patents in case of delays in processing of patenting submissions, as well as nondisclosure of confidential and sensitive information used for patent purposes (that is, test data and trade secrets) with terms of 5 years for pharmaceuticals and 10 years for chemicals. In the sensitive area of pharmaceuticals, DR-CAFTA preserves the rights of governments to use compulsory licenses and parallel imports for pharmaceuticals, on any grounds (as provided by the Trade-Related Aspects of Intellectual Property Rights [TRIPS] Agreement) including for public health emergencies such as HIV-AIDS. In addition, no obligations were developed in relation to the patenting of diagnostic, therapeutic, and surgical methods or for the recognition of patents for second uses of previously patented pharmaceutical products. As difficult as it is to ascertain the overall costs and benefits of these IPR reforms, our view is that the previous two provisions should help reduce the risk of rising prices for medicines to deal with pressing public health concerns.[18]

Evaluation

DR-CAFTA commitments in the area of IPR are similar to those included in other recent U.S. free trade agreements and, similarly, they go beyond several multilateral standards on intellectual property (Fink and Reichenmiller 2005). These commitments will lock in some recent upgrading to Central

American IPR legislation and will require significant modifications to legal frameworks, mainly through the adherence to a number of international treaties. Most important, DR-CAFTA will require more strict enforcement of IPR norms.

Enforcement of IPR might be important for two reasons. First, complaints and disputes with holders of IPR (such as television broadcasters; and owners of the content supplied on videos, on compact discs, and in books) could send negative signals to investors about overall respect for the rule of law in the country and thereby weaken the investment climate. Second, investors interested in development of important sectors (such as high technology, software, pharmaceuticals, and agrochemicals) will look for environments where their rights are protected when they consider new ventures.[19] With DR-CAFTA, noncompliance with IPR commitments will be subject to dispute settlement provisions that could lead eventually to monetary fines. Central American nations will need to improve their capacity to enforce IPR commitments, including substantial institutional strengthening of relevant agencies.

In controversial areas, such as the impact of more stringent standards (TRIPS-plus) for protecting pharmaceutical patents, no methodologies have been developed to evaluate the welfare impact of these types of commitments—especially if we consider gains from other aspects of the FTA. Although greater IPR protection usually entails restrictions on the sale and use of generic drugs during the life of the relevant patents, the treaty does provide flexibility for governments to bypass these protections, to guard public health through compulsory licensing and the option of parallel imports, as mentioned above.[20]

Labor and Environment

DR-CAFTA includes chapters on labor and environment, as mandated by the authorization given to the executive branch by the U.S. Congress. The inclusion of such provisions has generated heated public debate about whether they should be included in FTAs and whether they can be used effectively to improve standards in developing countries.[21]

DR-CAFTA commits all signatory countries to enforce current domestic labor and environmental laws and regulations. While respecting sovereign rights to modify its legislation in these areas, it bans the relaxation of labor or environmental regulations to encourage trade and investment. Obligations are subject to the dispute settlement provisions of the agreement and eventually could lead to monetary penalties (maximum of US$15 million), which would then be used by the offending party to strengthen its enforcement capacity.[22]

Parallel agreements establish a cooperative program to improve labor laws and enforcement, in league with the International Labour Organization (ILO). The office of the United States Trade Representative has announced programs to build the capacity of Central American nations to monitor and enforce labor rights through specialized consultations and targeted training programs in the areas of child labor, public awareness of worker rights, and labor inspection systems (USTR 2004). DR-CAFTA also includes an annex of labor cooperation that defines cooperation priorities and financing. The United States committed $6.7 million for the first year to support the improvement of DR-CAFTA countries' administrative capacity in labor matters.

The environmental chapter includes a cooperation agreement that provides a framework for capacity building (including strengthening the capacity to develop, implement, and enforce environmental laws) and establishes an Environmental Cooperation Commission. The agreement includes a commitment for frequent consultation mechanisms among the parties to evaluate compliance with DR-CAFTA obligations. The treaty goes beyond provisions included in recent treaties between the United States and Chile and the United States and Singapore in allowing for a public submissions process to ensure that views of civil society are considered; envisions benchmarking of environmental cooperation activities and input from international organizations in evaluating progress; and enhances the mutual support of DR-CAFTA and multilateral environmental agreements (USTR 2004). Furthermore, the agreement makes explicit reference to the right of member countries to protect and conserve genetic biodiversity.[23]

Evaluation

In effect, DR-CAFTA will lock in key features of current labor and environmental laws and regulations for the first time in most Central American countries through an international treaty.[24] The obligations under DR-CAFTA are unlikely to require significant changes in current legislation. They are likely, however, to prompt pressures to upgrade enforcement, particularly in exporting sectors. Although these sectors have been identified in the past as those in which labor and environmental regulations seem to be respected (Stern 2003), overall institutional strengthening is likely to improve enforcement efforts in all areas of the economy. This improvement should boost the investment climate by demonstrating a strong commitment to the rule of law. For *maquilas*, labor provisions will be critical in addressing past criticism related to cases of basic worker rights violations and should diminish pressure from sporadic international boycotts. Nonetheless, Central American countries probably will require resources and technical assistance to boost their enforcement of current norms, along the lines of the action plans included in the "White Book" drafted by trade and labor ministers and supported by the ILO and other international organizations.

Government Procurement and Corruption

DR-CAFTA includes commitments for reciprocal nondiscriminatory access of firms to public contracts, as well as commitments to improve transparency in procurement processes.[25] The agreement gives Central American firms access to markets for purchases by federal and state governments and U.S. firms gain access to bids on contracts from Central American government ministries, agencies, and departments. Low-value contracts are excluded and applicable thresholds vary by country. The agreement requires fair and transparent procurement procedures, such as advance notice of purchases and timely and effective bid review. In addition, strict guidelines are spelled out for situations in which governments can resort to procurement methods other than open bidding. Costa Rica will be able to keep its programs for bidding in favor of small and medium enterprises. DR-CAFTA commits signing parties to make bribery in government contracting a criminal offense.

Evaluation

DR-CAFTA locks in part of recent reforms of government procurement practices (see box 3.3). The importance of fair and transparent procedures in government procurement is self-evident. Despite substantial reforms in recent years, accusations of corruption and the lack of transparency in public purchases continue to plague Central American countries. DR-CAFTA will contribute to strengthening the trend toward transparent and efficient procurement methods. Consequently the treaty is likely to require some administrative process changes to boost transparency and reduce opportunities for corruption.

Customs

DR-CAFTA includes obligations aimed at strengthening, improving, and modernizing the operation of customs to facilitate trade among signatory

Box 3.3

DR-CAFTA and Government Procurement

DR-CAFTA requires that listed entities (for example, central government agencies, autonomous enterprises, and municipal governments) use specific procedures when the value of the procurement is above the agreed thresholds, and it commits governments to ensure the application of those procedures. The agreement contains basic disciplines on nondiscrimination, transparency, and due process. These disciplines specifically refer to publication of notice of intended procurement, time limits for the tendering process, tender documentation, technical specifications, requirements and conditions for suppliers' participation in procurement, tendering procedures, award of contracts, information on awards, and nondisclosure of information.

DR-CAFTA also establishes the obligation of the Central American governments to have operational a domestic review and challenge mechanism. This is an impartial authority that acts to preserve the supplier's opportunity to participate in procurement and to ensure that governments comply with their implementing measures. These measures require an effective procedure by which interested parties can bring complaints, initially, to the head of the procuring entity and, in the second instance, to the responsible manager in government for public procurement to take administrative remedies to correct violations of the regulations.

Furthermore, DR-CAFTA incorporates specific commitments on nondiscriminatory market access (that is, foreign suppliers of goods and services must be allowed the same treatment as domestic suppliers). The agreement's scope is limited to the entities listed in its annexes, including entities at the central, local, and decentralized levels when applying national budget funds. For example, in the case of Honduras the rules apply to 169 government entities:

Honduran Entities Subject to DR-CAFTA Requirements

Central level	*Municipalities*	*Other entities*
16	142	11

The agreement establishes that where the value of the procurement is estimated to equal or exceed agreed threshold levels, DR-CAFTA rules shall be applied. DR-CAFTA allows higher thresholds for the Central American countries for the first three years of the agreement; thereafter, all DR-CAFTA countries, including the United States, will have the same thresholds. For the specific case of Honduras, DR-CAFTA will require modifications in national legislation because all these thresholds differ substantially from those currently valid (see the table below).

DR-CAFTA also incorporates a provision for "ensuring integrity in procurement practices." This provision establishes that each party shall have and maintain systems that list each entity ineligible to participate in procurement because it has engaged in past fraudulent or other illegal actions. The agreement also provides for the exchange of this information with other DR-CAFTA members. To comply with this obligation, Central American countries will have to create a database of suppliers disqualified by national procuring entities.

DR-CAFTA's Thresholds for Goods and Services by Level of Administration
(US$)

Federal level	= > 58,550 = > 117,100[a]
Subfederal level	= > 477,000 = > 650,000[a]
Other entities	= > 250,000 = > 538,000[b]
For construction services, all levels	= > 6,725,000 => 8,000,000[a]

a. For Central American countries for a three-year period.
b. For specified U.S. entities.

Source: DR-CAFTA text and World Bank 2004a.

parties. Provisions seek to facilitate customs procedures and reduce room for discretion. The treaty includes rules of origin designed to be easier to administer. It also requires transparency, procedural certainty, and efficiency in administering customs procedures, including DR-CAFTA rules of origin. Central American countries committed to a list of actions within three years to accomplish goals such as Internet publication of all norms and regulations, the automation of the clearance procedures, the electronic presentation of certificates of origin, and the implementation of management and risk evaluation systems. All signatories also agreed to share information to combat illegal trans-shipment of goods. A program of technical assistance was agreed to support Central American countries in carrying out their commitments in this area.

Evaluation

Customs-related issues have posed significant barriers to trade in Central America because of their complex and lengthy procedures, inefficiencies, and opportunities for fraud and corruption. In many surveys conducted among private-sector firms, complaints against customs procedures and officials usually top the list. The clarifications and simplifications of some procedures with respect to verifying rules of origin are of value but unlikely to be enough to end deep-seated problems. Central American nations will need to push ahead with strong reforms (independent of DR-CAFTA) if they are to reap the full benefits of trade for development.

Dispute Settlement

The agreement provides for all core obligations to be subject to a bilateral dispute settlement panel with high standards for openness and transparency. It includes monetary penalties to enforce commercial, labor, and environmental obligations.

Evaluation

The dispute settlement section of any FTA is where key incentives are laid out for parties to get serious about complying with provisions and strengthening domestic norms and institutions. DR-CAFTA sets appropriately high standards for openness and transparency in settlement procedures. Although monetary penalties were included—a first for any FTA signed by Central American countries—the penalties would be used only after long consultation periods and tests for noncompliance. This reciprocal dispute settlement mechanism is a significant gain for Central American countries with respect to the CBI regime, in which no recourse was provided to counteract unilateral actions by the United States.

Trade Capacity Building

The agreement sets up a Committee on Trade Capacity Building for the first time in an FTA involving the United States or any of the Central American nations. Also planned is the creation of the Institute for Trade Capacity Building (in New Orleans, Louisiana), which will focus on developing capacity for support programs for small and medium enterprises. In addition, a coalition of U.S. companies came together to support the creation and strengthening of trade capacity in Central America.

Evaluation

Although it is too early to evaluate results of these provisions that have not been included in other U.S. free trade agreements, the committee could be of use in coordinating actions by donors, nongovernmental organizations (NGOs), and the private sector for the improvement of institutional capacity, adjustment to new liberalization commitments, and sensitive enforcement challenges.

Provisions to Deepen Regional Integration

Central American countries took a momentous step in making DR-CAFTA a treaty that would be applied multilaterally. Initially it was thought that the treaty would be so markedly different from the norms that have governed trade among members of the Central American Common Market—aside from including many areas that are not included in that agreement—that it would only apply bilaterally between the United States and each Central American partner, in what is known in the literature as the classic "hub-and-spoke" model. During negotiations, however, it was agreed that the treaty's commitments would be applied to trade and investment relations among all parties, including the Dominican Republic, as reflected in the agreement's Article 1.1. This important decision should have great impact in a number of areas, most significantly in deepening regional integration efforts.

The multilateral application of DR-CAFTA will qualify more goods for free trade among Central American countries than do current norms.[26] Under DR-CAFTA, all goods made with inputs from any of the parties to the agreement will qualify as meeting the rules of origin. In contrast, in the Central American Common Market regime input accumulation was not possible and inputs from the United States or the Dominican Republic could not count toward satisfying rules of origin. In addition, DR-CAFTA disciplines will allow free trade in goods produced in export processing zones, as long as they meet origin requirements. As pointed out by González (2005), firms will enjoy an expanded set of input sourcing options when producing for exports to DR-CAFTA members, thereby reducing the distortions that are created by the existence of multiple parallel FTAs. However, to avoid confusion, it may be important to modernize some of the existing Central American instruments that are not superseded by DR-CAFTA to ensure that they are consistent with the treaty and more up-to-date with recent international trends.

In addition, DR-CAFTA will not contribute to the "spaghetti bowl" syndrome associated with the administration of multiple treaties, which might be costly in terms of administering myriad sets of complex rules of origin. Instead, it is likely to foster an atmosphere conducive to finalizing steps for a customs union among CACM members, a task that requires only a few additional administrative steps to ensure that imports into the region can stop only once at the port of entry and then proceed to move freely across the region's borders.[27]

Multilateral application of DR-CAFTA also deepens other regional integration efforts. More than 40 years of history in such efforts has yielded a very advanced set of rules for trade in goods. But virtually no legal instruments exist for applying a common set of norms among these countries in other areas included in DR-CAFTA.[28] The agreement will provide modern rules and disciplines for relations among Central American countries and the Dominican Republic in the areas of trade in services, investment protection, and government procurement—including financial services, telecommunications, and e-commerce.[29] Moreover, it will allow the use of dispute settlement mechanisms in novel areas such as IPRs, labor, and environment. The new regional rules and disciplines are likely to strengthen regional ties and set the stage for even deeper integration efforts among Central American countries and the Dominican Republic in the future.

Conclusion

This chapter provides an overview of the recently negotiated DR-CAFTA, concentrating on the extent to which the agreement's provisions would significantly change market access for Central American goods and services, and on how far the provisions could be expected to consolidate prior reforms and/or spur further domestic reforms in Central American countries. The overall assessment presented in the chapter is that, on both fronts, the answers are broadly positive, suggesting that DR-CAFTA should be expected to have a positive impact on trade flows and investment.

Regarding market access, DR-CAFTA would consolidate and expand the generous access to U.S. markets that Central Americans currently enjoy, while extending broadly reciprocal access for U.S. goods to Central American and Dominican Republic markets. The benefits offered under the CBI would be locked in for Central American countries, and some additional permanent duty-free access would be obtained for goods previously exempted from CBI preferences. Other significant results would include making flexible the rules of origin for textiles and apparel, as well as commitments to help producers meet sanitary and phytosanitary standards required for the U.S. entry of promising nontraditional agricultural exports. DR-CAFTA also includes reciprocal commitments on access to service markets, which consolidate domestic reforms that opened most of these markets to private participation in recent years.

Central American countries also agreed to grant U.S. products reciprocal tariff-free access to their markets. Certain sensitive agricultural crops would be subject to extended transition periods (up to 20 years) to allow for gradual adjustment and to respond to domestic sensitivities. Central American countries secured access to flexible safeguard mechanisms to prevent sudden surges in imports or declines in prices.

Commitments embedded in DR-CAFTA would gradually erode current protection levels for various products that have retained high protection in Central American economies, during past efforts at easing trade restrictions. The gradual decline expected in prices of basic food staples as a result should prove positive for the vast majority of Central Americans who are net consumers of such goods and whose welfare will be increased by lower prices. This said, not all sensitive products are included, in response to cultural and political factors, and these limitations—together with the agreement's still excessively restrictive rules of origin for the entry of textile products to the United States—represent barriers to trade that will continue to foster some inefficiencies in the deployment of domestic resources both in Central America and the United States.

On the questions related to domestic reforms, DR-CAFTA commitments promise to lock in a number of the policy and regulatory changes implemented in recent years for the opening of competition in previously protected sectors (for example, telecommunications, financial services, and energy), and to modernize key norms and procedures in such areas as government procurement, IPR, and the treatment of foreign investment by locking in current levels of access from U.S. investors and bidders.

Costa Rica is the only country that will be required to make significant legislative changes to adapt policies and regulations to its commitments under DR-CAFTA, allowing access to significant portions of its telecommunications and insurance markets. These reforms have been long postponed and should further foster modernization, efficiency, and competitiveness of these areas of the Costa Rican economy.

Aside from consolidating and spurring further reforms, the treaty should strengthen commitments to upgrade enforcement levels of domestic legislation. This represents a significant challenge in areas like labor, environment, and IPR, which will require decisive efforts and resources to modernize and boost the capacity of public agencies. The net impact of these efforts should be positive because investment is likely to be attracted to environments with effective institutions. However, although DR-CAFTA will put pressure on the modernization of these institutions, it will not by itself create such modernization. Countries will need strong independent plans of action and sufficient dedication of implementation capacity and resources.

The agreement includes cooperation accords to boost standards and enforcement levels in areas such as labor, environment, and customs. It also offers proposals to develop further cooperation and trade capacity building that should aid in the mobilization of human and financial resources required for key reforms and institutional actions to implement the agreement and the broader developmental challenges.

Finally, a welcome side effect of the negotiation of DR-CAFTA has been the advancement of regional integration efforts. The decision to make the provisions of the agreement apply multilaterally among Central American countries and the Dominican Republic will deepen regional integration efforts and facilitate the creation of a Central American customs union.

Notes

1. As of this writing, DR-CAFTA has been formally ratified in El Salvador, Guatemala, and Honduras.
2. Trade agreements can effectively lock in domestic reforms if countries really value belonging to the agreement and if the credibility of the threat of action if rules are broken is high. From this point of view, a treaty with a developed country like the United States is apt to be most effective because large trade flows are at stake.
3. There is some question whether the benchmark to evaluate market access commitments should be the unilateral preferences under CBI or an alternative such as U.S. most-favored-nation tariffs or tariff binding levels at the WTO. If a country were not to ratify DR-CAFTA, it is likely that its market access would be less favorable in relation to the existing CBI preferences, as has been relayed in press accounts of statements by members of the U.S. Congress and officials of the executive branch.

4. Some of the goods that will now enjoy zero-tariff treatment under DR-CAFTA include canned tuna for Nicaragua; and products that contain up to 65 percent sugar, ethnic cheeses, fresh vegetables, snacks, fresh fruits, and melon for El Salvador. Nicaragua also obtained a peanut quota of 10,000 metric tons annually and 2,000 mt for peanut butter.
5. The exclusion of white maize was apparently motivated by the cultural importance and political sensitivity of the crop, according to press accounts and interviews with negotiators.
6. The treaty specifies that these safeguards expire after tariff protection is phased out but it allows for their extension, if all parties agree.
7. The United States is committed to resolve delays in food inspection procedures for meat and poultry products from Central America. Another example is the schedule that Honduras obtained from the United States for the resolution of sanitary issues that affect exports of poultry, dairy products, tomatoes, and peppers, as well as technical assistance to strengthen institutions in the sanitary and phytosanitary area. Nicaragua is receiving help in solving sanitary and phytosanitary problems for exports of cheese, papaya, pitahaya, peppers, and tomatoes. Costa Rica obtained guaranteed access of ornamental plants greater than 18 inches in height and more flexible sanitary treatment for some of its flower exports. Progress was also made in the recognition of Costa Rica's poultry inspection system. These changes are expected to have significant impact. For example, in the case of Costa Rica's ornamental plants, producers have estimated that simply exporting taller rather than shorter plants may increase their export earnings by 50 percent.
8. Costa Rica's quota includes 2,000 metric tons of organic sugar.
9. Article 3.15 of DR-CAFTA gives the United States the right to unilaterally compensate Central American exporters in lieu of allowing the quota obligations to enter duty free.
10. See Arce and Jaramillo (2005) for a discussion of the significance of sensitive agricultural activities in rural employment and in the value added of overall agricultural output. They found that sensitive crops are very heterogenous on both counts. Corn (especially, white corn) is important for employment in Guatemala, Honduras, and Nicaragua, but not too significant in Costa Rica or El Salvador. Beans are important in Honduras and Nicaragua, but of lesser relevance for employment and overall production elsewhere.
11. A special safeguard for the case of textiles and apparel is also contemplated, although its use is restricted to the first five years after the treaty's entry into force.
12. Dealer protection laws have been a long-standing source of friction between U.S. exporters and some Central American nations because they are perceived as

locking foreign companies into costly exclusive and permanent relationships with local distributors, regardless of the latter's performance. In some cases they have been used to ban imports of U.S. products when disputes have arisen with a local distributor, thus adding to perceived risks of trading in Central America.

13. Only knit apparel was allowed under the regional inputs quota.
14. Press reports and interviews with negotiators revealed that the quota obtained by Nicaragua was awarded because of the country's low level of economic development and the incipient status of its *maquila* industry.
15. This TPL could be extended beyond the original two years.
16. The issue of the temporary entry of business employees was discussed during the negotiations, but minimum annual visa numbers similar to those negotiated by the United States with Chile and Singapore were not agreed because of strong opposition to these provisions in the U.S. Congress.
17. Countries must adhere to the following treaties by the 2008 deadline: the International Treaty for Patent Cooperation, the Budapest Treaty on the International Recognition of the Deposit of Microorganisms for the Purposes of Patent Procedure, the agreement for the Brussels Convention Relating to the Distribution of Programme-Carrying Signals Transmitted by Satellite (1974), and the Trademark Law Treaty (1994). In addition, countries must make efforts to ratify the Patent Law Treaty (2000), Hague Agreement Concerning the International Deposit of Industrial Designs (1999), and the Protocol Relating to the Madrid Agreement Concerning the International Registration of Marks (1989). Regarding new plant varieties, countries are obligated to ratify the 1991 International Union for the Protection of New Varieties of Plants (UPOV) treaty.
18. The provisions protecting test data information for at least five years are perhaps the most ambiguous for us to evaluate a priori. On one hand, allowing the use of test data for domestic production of medicines can reduce the prices of products not yet available in the United States. On the other hand, there might be consumer and public health gains to be had from restricting access to information that could lead to the production of medicines not yet authorized. The existing empirical literature on IPR is not detailed enough to answer this type of question.
19. Fink and Maskus (2004) provided a comprehensive review of empirical evidence on the links among IPR, trade, FDI, and technology transfer.
20. Fink and Reichenmiller (2005) have highlighted the need to analyze further the difficulties that would be faced in granting compulsory licenses, related to regulatory permissions and test data exclusivity, as well as those associated with parallel imports.
21. Recent studies suggest that their inclusion is unnecessary because firms engaged in trade are those in which labor and environmental regulations tend to be followed (Stern 2003).

22. For monetary penalties to be required, noncompliance must have an effect on trade or investment, and several stages of consultation and dialogue with labor and environmental authorities must be exhausted before the dispute settlement rules can actually be activated. A contracting party will first need to require technical consultations in case of a complaint. If differences are not resolved at that level, consultations can be elevated to the Environmental Affairs Council. If the complaint is not resolved at this level, the dispute resolution mechanisms can be activated, calling for arbitration by experts. If the panel of experts agrees with the complaint, governments can face monetary penalties.
23. See article 15.1.5.a of DR-CAFTA, which states that signatory parties understand that there are no contradictions with adherence to the 1991 UPOV treaty and the rights of countries with respect to protection and conservation of genetic resources.
24. Costa Rica included a parallel agreement on labor in its FTA discussions with Canada. The agreement also commits Costa Rica to uphold its legislation and prohibits relaxation to favor trade or investment. A parallel environmental agreement was also included with similar commitments.
25. Commitments do not apply to purchases financed by loans and donations, hiring of public-sector employees, or sales of companies under liquidation.
26. Some of the arguments presented here draw from González's excellent analysis (2005) of the application of DR-CAFTA among Central American countries and the Dominican Republic.
27. Arrangements would need to be made during the transition period to free trade for different tariff phase-out periods and for the specific country commitments that were made for tariff rate quotas in sensitive goods.
28. Negotiations among Central American countries in recent years had yielded general texts for draft treaties on investment and services and on government procurement. Detailed country-specific annexes were still under negotiation when DR-CAFTA discussions started.
29. In government procurement, Central American countries applied much stronger commitments to each other than they allowed with the United States; they eliminated minimum thresholds or exemptions to any government agency in purchases of goods or services (González 2005).

CHAPTER 4

Economic Effects of DR-CAFTA

More Art Than Science

Like many Latin American countries, the economies of Central America that recently signed DR-CAFTA underwent a period of dramatic trade reforms in the early 1990s. These reforms were implemented in an era when academicians, political leaders, and various civil society organizations from around the globe were questioning the merits of trade liberalization. For example, Rodríguez and Rodrik (2000) criticized influential academic reports on the relationship between trade and economic growth on the grounds that the literature had not adequately addressed the key issue of measuring trade policy, as opposed to other factors that might affect the incidence of international commerce on national economies. In fact, a recent World Bank report on the impact of NAFTA concluded that this controversial agreement had been moderately positive for the Mexican economy, but that it was certainly not enough to spur fast, long-term economic development in Mexico (Lederman, Maloney, and Servén 2005).

This chapter highlights various analytical arguments and their limitations in favor of trade reforms and contrasts them with the findings of various analyses undertaken to assess the potential effects of DR-CAFTA on the developing countries of Central America, namely Costa Rica, El Salvador, Guatemala, Honduras, and Nicaragua.

Assessing the impact of any public policy before it is actually implemented is admittedly difficult. Indeed, Kehoe (2003) pointed out that popular ex ante general equilibrium analyses of NAFTA written in the early 1990s turned out to be quite off the mark in their predictions about NAFTA's structural effects (in terms of industry-level growth) on the Mexican economy, mainly because such models are generally incapable of predicting dynamic effects of trade reforms and free trade agreements. The problem, however, is not necessarily particular to the general equilibrium simulation approach because all methodologies have advantages and disadvantages, and most provide some useful elements for policy discussions. Ex ante analyses, either partial or general equilibrium simulations, have the advantage of focusing on the effects of the FTA on the beneficiary countries. But inasmuch as the agreement has not been implemented, these analyses are limited by a broad set of assumptions required to make such predictions. In contrast, statistical analyses of the effects of international trade and FTAs already in operation have the advantage of using real-world experiences, but the disadvantage of not being related strictly to the DR-CAFTA countries. Hence these econometric exercises need to control for an array of variables in an attempt to identify the average effects of FTAs, independent of other country characteristics. In the end, predicting the effects of DR-CAFTA prior to its implementation remains more art than science, but the technical aspects of the various approaches to some extent determine the results obtained from each one. For this reason the chapter provides a wealth of technical discussions of methodologies.[1]

This chapter applies two broad approaches for estimating the potential economic effects of trade agreements, namely static and dynamic approaches. The static approach includes efforts to simulate the impact of DR-CAFTA on each country's trade structure, returns to factors of production, and the structure of production itself. This approach includes both partial and general equilibrium modeling attempts. These simulations are also complemented with statistical evidence from global data that highlight how country-specific characteristics might affect the outcomes of DR-CAFTA. Two such characteristics are transport infrastructure and the regulatory environment that affect the ease with which workers and firms can take advantage of new opportunities.

The dynamic approach includes statistical analyses of the impact of trade in general and FTAs in particular on factors such as investment and institutions. The underlying idea is that for trade to have dynamic effects, the effects should operate through factors that affect long-term economic growth.

Consequently, the final section of this chapter reviews new estimates of the effects of free trade agreements anywhere in the world on the rate of per capita GDP growth.

The evidence reviewed here supports three key conclusions. First, DR-CAFTA is likely to have positive effects on economic growth in Central America by increasing foreign and domestic investment and increasing both exports and imports, which might help speed up the transfer of technology from abroad. Preliminary evidence, drawn from econometric estimates controlling for the possibility that economic conditions themselves determine the probability of signing an FTA (Gould and Gruben 2005), suggests that economies that sign free trade agreements tend to increase their annual growth rates by about 0.6 percent in the five years following agreement implementation. Moreover, there is evidence that FTAs offer better market access opportunities to the United States than do existing U.S. unilateral preferential programs, such as the Caribbean Basin Initiative (in spite of its recent modifications). The evidence based on data from 2001 and presented by Lederman and Ozden (2005) suggests that, after controlling for various country and industry characteristics, FTAs with the United States are associated with higher exports that can be several multiples of the exports of otherwise similar countries that do not benefit from any commercial preferences. Likewise, exports from FTA members are higher than those from CBI beneficiaries, after controlling for industry and country characteristics. Also, the econometric evidence from Cuevas, Messmacher, and Werner (2002), which was also reported in Lederman, Maloney, and Servén (2005), suggests that FTA members temporarily attract more FDI than nonmembers by increasing the responsiveness of FDI to a country's economic performance.

Second, the magnitude of these positive effects and how they are distributed within the national economies of Central America will depend crucially on each country's ability to take advantage of the opportunities offered by the agreement, particularly because the gains from trade depend on each economy's ability to change its production and employment patterns and to adopt foreign technologies. More specifically, the evidence suggests that institutional reforms and public investments in innovation and infrastructure will affect the magnitude of the impacts on FDI, technology transfer, and international commerce.

Third, the agreement will undoubtedly have differential effects within countries. Perhaps more important, the overall benefits of DR-CAFTA for these countries will depend on their ability to help the sectors, especially workers who will be negatively affected by the expected changes in relative prices. In other words, implementing efficient adjustment programs not only will help the workers who will face important adjustment challenges, but also will affect the magnitude of the overall gains from DR-CAFTA.

The rest of this chapter provides an analytical overview of both the intuition and the empirical evidence that suggests why DR-CAFTA and other trade reforms might not be enough to help Central America enhance its prospects for rapid economic development. The following section reviews the theory and corresponding literature concerning the so-called static gains from trade. The third section examines the theory and evidence concerning the "dynamic" gains from trade. The final section summarizes the main findings and highlights broad policy implications, most of which are discussed in more detail in other chapters.

Trade Liberalization and the Static Gains from Trade

The standard textbook theories that predict gains from international commerce usually do so by comparing the welfare of consumers in a country without trade to welfare of consumers in that same country after full trade liberalization. At the center of these arguments lies the idea of "comparative advantage," whereby certain countries can produce some products at lower *relative* costs than other goods. The gains from trade for small economies come in two parts[2]: those related to the increase in the level of consumption for a given level and structure of production, and those derived from the reallocation of labor and other factors of production toward the sectors with the lowest relative costs of production (or higher relative prices) for the relevant goods. The technical annex at the end of this chapter reviews some of the basics and shows why the gains from trade have never been thought to be automatic.

A finding of particular relevance for Central America is that the gains from trade are unambiguously positive *only* if the structure of production changes as a consequence of the trade reform. This requires that labor move to those sectors where labor productivity is relatively higher. That is, the gains from trade are feasible as long as economies are able to adjust efficiently to the new set of relative prices after trade liberalization by maintaining a constant level of employment. The static gains from trade will make all citizens better off only if workers who will bear the costs of adjustment by having to change their economic activities are compensated for their efforts.

More generally, the potential gains from trade exist in most contexts. When comparative advantage is caused by differences in factor endowments (the Heckscher-Ohlin framework), technologies (the Ricardian model), tastes, the size of domestic markets (in the presence of increasing returns to scale), and even in the presence of trade costs, such as transport and transaction costs, there are welfare gains to be obtained from liberalizing international trade. It is interesting that there are gains from trade for small countries even when the sectors of comparative advantage are unknown in the sense that a country's comparative advantage depends on how (at what price) one measures comparative advantage (Deardorff 2003). But in all these settings, the static gains from trade might not be realized if the adjustment process produces significant and persistent unemployment or if the structure of production does not change.

Some observers have argued that even this conclusion is tenuous in the presence of international capital flows. The argument seems to be that capital will go to countries where, for example, labor standards and wages are lower. Free trade in turn makes these multinational production decisions more profitable, but leaves workers in some countries worse off. Although theoretically plausible, substantial independent reviews of the empirical literature suggest that there is no systematic evidence of increased trade leading to the deterioration of wages. Moreover, figure 4.1 shows that there is actually no statistical relationship between the incidence of international trade and unemployment rates across countries, thus suggesting that there is no *long-term* relationship between international commerce and unemployment. As will be discussed in detail below, there might be short-term effects as economies adjust to changes in trade policies and thus the public sector has a role to play to facilitate a socially and economically efficient adjustment process. Indeed, there is also no evidence that trade or multinational production is associated with the worsening of labor or environmental outcomes (see Stern [2003] and Brown, Deardorff, and Stern [2004] on labor; see Dean [2002], Copeland and Taylor [2003], and Frankel and Rose [2005] on the environment).

However robust is the international evidence about trade, wages, and unemployment, critics of trade agreements often focus on the so-called core labor standards. These have to do with the legal rights of workers to unionize or restrictions imposed on child labor or female worker discrimination rather than with economic outcomes such as wages and unemployment. Busse (2004) found that overall exposure to international trade (measured

Figure 4.1. Unemployment and the Incidence of International Trade in the Long Run

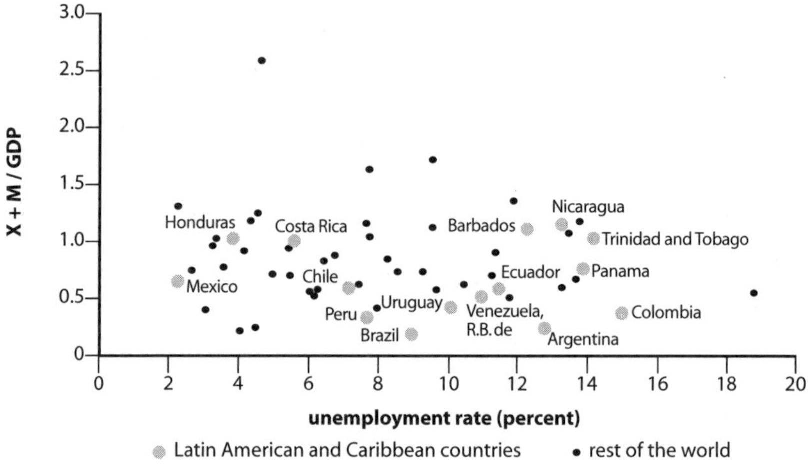

Source: De Ferranti, Perry, Lederman, and Maloney 2002, Figure 5.2.

by the ratio of trade flows to GDP) actually is negatively correlated with female labor discrimination and child labor, thus suggesting that international trade does not promote discrimination against female workers or child labor. But Busse did find that trade is negatively correlated with an indicator of civil liberties (which in turn appears correlated with OECD indicators of union rights). In another article, Busse (2002) presented partial correlations among female labor participation rates, child labor participation, and an index of collective bargaining rights and allegedly labor-intensive exports as a share of total exports. Greater female labor participation actually increases the share of labor-intensive exports, as does the participation of children (ages 10–14), whereas the OECD's index of unions rights tends to reduce comparative advantage in labor-intensive manufactures. This latter study can be amply criticized on various technical grounds, including, as Busse noted, that the econometric estimates suffer from endogeneity biases, and that the data did not permit the inclusion of all relevant labor market variables. More important, Busee (2002) was silent with respect to the impact of trade reforms and FDI on domestic labor market outcomes.

Jones (2000) provided perhaps the most comprehensive treatment of issues related to international commerce in the presence of international capital flows. His main theoretical conclusion with respect to the potential gains from trade is that the presence of international capital flows, or even international migration of labor, does not change the basic finding that trade reforms are potentially beneficial for all countries involved in trade. This is the case even under various assumptions regarding the sector-specific use of such international capital or labor. This result is due to international flows of factors of production that reinforce the incentives to specialize in the production of goods and services where a given country has a relative productivity advantage. International capital or labor flows do make it more difficult to predict in which sectors an economy will specialize, but this ambiguity does not mean that there are no gains from trade.

The Mexican experience with NAFTA highlights how an economy adjusts and changes its pattern of trade and employment, which in turn allows it to benefit from the agreement. Figure 4.2 shows the evolution of Mexico's pattern of net exports, covering 10 broad commodity groups. The implementation of NAFTA in 1994 was associated with the rise of Mexico's share of net exports of machinery (for example, vehicles and parts, telecommunications equipment, and computers). De Ferranti et al. (2002) showed that this change in Mexico's pattern of trade with respect to the United States became apparent by 1993, just prior to the implementation of the trade agreement. Thus, NAFTA had structural effects even before its formal implementation, possibly related to changes in the pattern of FDI. Figure 4.3 shows the evolution of formal employment in agriculture and manufacturing *maquilas* (and does not include other manufacturing establishments), many of which produce the aforementioned machinery products. This evidence is representative of the structural change experienced by the Mexican economy—a healthy structural shift, given that overall unemployment was not higher after NAFTA (except for 1995 during the so-called Tequila crisis).

In fact, the international evidence suggests that long-term development around the world is characterized by structural economic changes whereby the share of agricultural employment and production declines as economies grow (see, for example, Bravo-Ortega and Lederman 2005). Although this does not necessarily mean that the absolute number of jobs in agriculture declines with development, the absolute number tends to decline in the most developed economies.

The structural change experienced by Mexico under NAFTA is thus consistent with gains from trade, but it is likely that public policies can help Central American economies ensure that DR-CAFTA will deliver on its promises of economic development. The following subsections review some

Figure 4.2. Mexico: Structure of Net Exports, 1981–99

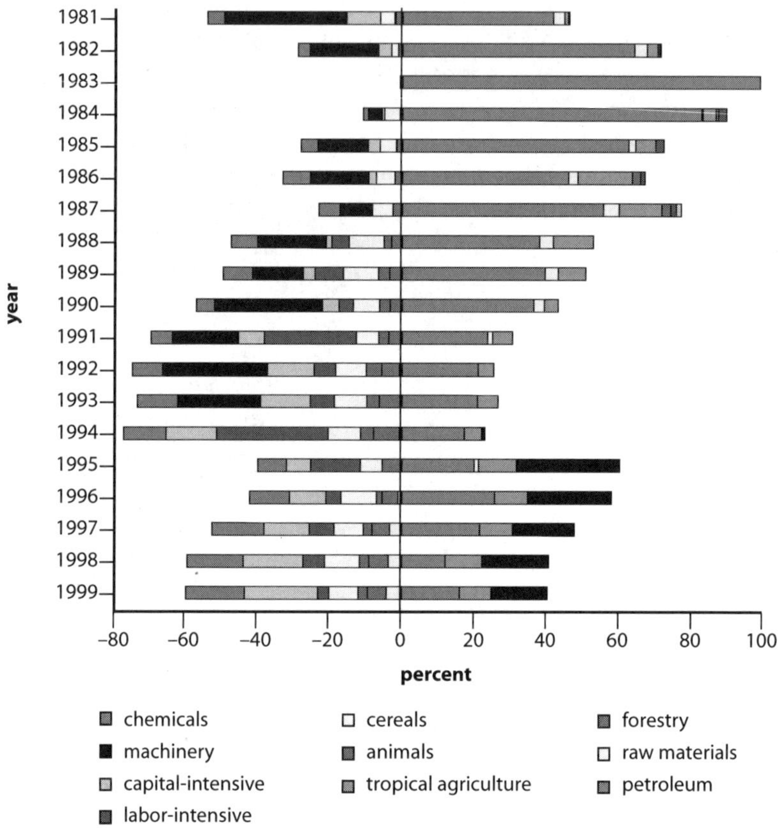

Source: De Ferranti, Perry, Lederman, and Maloney 2002, Figure A.7.

of the policy-sensitive areas that might affect the capacity of Central American economies to adjust to the new trade regime and thus affect the magnitude of the potential static gains offered by DR-CAFTA.

Static Gains from Trade under Various Conditions: The Role of Infrastructure and the Labor Adjustment Process

Theory dictates that international trade can provide significant opportunities for development, but these opportunities depend on the ability of an economy to prevent unnecessary declines in overall employment as the

Figure 4.3. Registered *Maquila* and Agricultural Workers, Mexico, 1983–2003

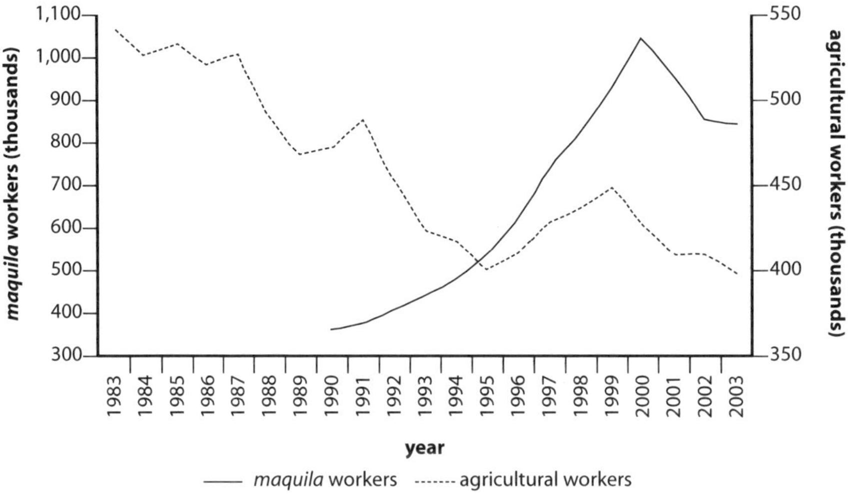

Source: Lederman, Maloney, and Servén 2005, Chapter 4, Figure 9.

economy adjusts to a new set of relative prices. Here we cover three related issues—infrastructure, trade facilitation, and labor adjustment—that seem to be important determinants of an economy's capacity to successfully adjust to a new, more open trade regime.

Infrastructure and Trade Facilitation

As mentioned above, the restructuring of an economy is crucial for taking advantage of the economic opportunities offered by trade agreements. A successful adjustment entails avoiding substantial job losses, and thus might require that workers literally move to regions that have attracted new investment and that exports of activities with the highest labor productivity can overcome transport and transaction costs. In both instances, an economy's infrastructure is critical for helping this process. If national infrastructure covering the movement of both people and goods is not adequate, then exports will not rise as much and labor might thus be stuck in the low-productivity areas, thereby reducing the gains from trade. Indeed, empirical evidence suggests, for example, that for a given economy (in terms of size and geographical location) the international costs of international freight, insurance, and customs procedures affect the value of exports to the United

States. Table 4.1 reports various econometric estimates by Lederman and Ozden (2005) concerning the impact of each additional dollar in transport and transaction costs on the value of exports to this market. Regardless of econometric technique, the impact of these costs seems to be quite high. Although the empirical analyses by Lederman and Ozden do not cover all types of infrastructure, logic dictates that telecommunications or the provision of basic services to emerging sectors can also help the economic transformation promised by DR-CAFTA. Chapter 7 of this volume provides some guidance regarding the types of infrastructure needs that should be prioritized in the complementary agenda of the DR-CAFTA beneficiaries.

Other relevant results from the estimations by Lederman and Ozden (2005) concern the effect of FTAs on exports to the U.S. market, especially when contrasted with the effects of unilaterally provided preferences such as the Generalized System of Preferences (GSP) and the CBI (or the Carib-

Table 4.1. Exports to the United States: Potential Effects of Transport Costs and DR-CAFTA, 2000

Explanatory variables	*TOBIT model[a] (1)*	*TOBIT model[b] (2)*	*Treatment model[c] (3)*	*Heckman selection model[d] (4)*
GSP	–0.14	–1.46**	–0.10	–0.52
FTA	1.60**	1.05**	1.59**	1.75**
CBI	1.55**	1.35**	1.12**	0.53**
Transport Costs	–5.97**	–5.98**	–5.60**	–5.83**

Source: Lederman and Ozden 2005.

Note: Table provides various estimations of the "gravity" model of exports to the United States. All models were estimated with a data set that covers more than 150 countries and 98 product categories, and all included the following (unreported) control explanatory variables: product dummy variables; log GDP and log GDP per capita for each country; log distance in kilometers to the United States; log area in square kilometers of each country; dummy variable for membership in the WTO; dummy variable for English-speaking countries; dummy variable for islands; and variables for the AGOA and Andean trade preferences. In specifications (1) and (3), each preferential trade scheme is represented by a dummy variable so that each product from a beneficiary country takes a value of one for each program. In specifications (2) and (4), the use of preferences by each exporting country is captured by the percent of each sector's exports that entered the U.S. market by using the preferential program. Results for specification (2) were unaffected when country dummy variables were included instead of the country characteristics listed above. In models (3) and (4), the variables that determine the probability of being a beneficiary of U.S. preferential treatment were log distance to the United States, dummy variable for political alliance with the United States, U.S. aid inflows per capita, and a dummy for sharing a border with the United States (Canada and Mexico). All levels of significance were derived from robust standard errors. CBI = Caribbean Basin Initiative; FTA = free trade agreement; GSP = Generalized System of Preferences.

a. Preferences represented by dummy variables.

b. Preferences represented by utilization rates.

c. Preferences as dummies.

d. Preferences as utilization rates.

**Significant at 5 percent.

bean Basin Economic Recovery Act [CBERA]). In the authors' preferred estimations listed under columns (3) and (4) of table 4.1, the effects of FTAs are larger than the estimates for the unilateral preferences. Only in model 2 is the CBI effect larger. Because the average product-country utilization rate of FTAs (58 percent) is significantly higher than that of CBI (36 percent) in the year of analysis (2001), however, even this estimate suggests that the average effect (compared with the marginal effect) had been much higher for FTA beneficiaries than for CBI beneficiaries, while holding a plethora of control variables constant in the regressions (see the note to table 4.1). The data and the coefficients in regression 2, therefore, suggest that DR-CAFTA could raise the value of exports to the United States by almost 11 percent relative to the benefits offered by the CBI.[3] If we take the more generous results under column 4, these benefits in terms of exports increase to more than two times CBI benefits. In any case, the exact magnitude of the contribution of moving to an FTA from unilateral preferences offered through the CBI (and GSP) is less important than the general finding that there are additional gains in terms of access to the U.S. market. These gains probably result from a combination of factors, including the facts that the use of the FTA preferences might be easier because of less restrictive rules of origin (see chapter 3 on the contents of DR-CAFTA) and that FTAs provide more secured market access rules that entrepreneurs can rely on to make long-term business investments, which would then be reflected in rising exports to the United States.

Labor and the Adjustment Process

Another regulatory area concerns labor markets and the ability of firms to enter new markets and the ease with which noncompetitive firms exit other markets. The restructuring of an economy, whereby factors of production migrate from one economic activity to another, requires the disappearance of some firms and the emergence of others. Likewise, it requires workers to find new employment opportunities. Cox-Edwards and Edwards (1994) had previously reviewed various theoretical settings in which lack of labor mobility could reduce the gains from trade and even turn them negative. Consequently, the regulatory environment in these areas could be a crucial element in enabling the economies of Central America to take advantage of the opportunities offered by DR-CAFTA.

One way of examining the role of regulations in determining the gains from trade is to look at how regulations affect the magnitude and sign of the correlation between the incidence of international trade on the domestic economy and the level of development, measured by the value of GDP per capita. Bolaky and Freund (2003) provided figure 4.4a–c, which shows the aforementioned correlations for a large sample of countries, for the subsample of countries exhibiting the lowest regulatory burdens, and those with the highest regulatory burdens. The index of regulatory burden combines ratings on labor regulations and on the bureaucratic procedures that are required to start a new business. The data come from the World Bank database on *Doing Business* (see World Bank 2003a). Figure 4.4a shows that trade openness is positively correlated with the level of development in a sample of 75 countries. However, the correlation is flatter and statistically not significant for the 25 countries with the worst regulatory environments, thus suggesting the gains from trade might not materialize in perverse regulatory environments. Bolaky and Freund (2003) provided further discussion of these important issues, but it is worth noting here that a plethora of econometric estimations support the basic finding reflected in these graphs—that a heavy regulatory burden can seriously reduce the gains from trade.

Upon comparing the regulatory environments in Central American countries with those in other Latin American and other developing countries it becomes evident that regulatory reform should be a key priority in the complementary agenda.[4] The major areas for improvement involve reducing the number of days for entry procedures and reforming employment laws or any other regulations that impede the intersector labor mobility.

Even the best and most flexible regulatory framework cannot ensure that people will automatically change jobs or that capital will instantaneously reallocate to the most productive activities. Moreover, some workers could experience income losses greater than the gains in terms of lower prices of consumption goods. Since the marginal utility loss for poor workers from a given loss of real income is greater than for richer workers, a countries' overall national welfare will also depend on the ability of the economy to provide greater adjustment assistance to the poor rather than the middle and upper echelons of the labor market.

Thus there is a role to be played by the public sector in terms of aiding the adjustment process. In the case of the DR-CAFTA countries, which have already undergone a substantial process of economic adjustment over the past decade and a half, this intervention by the public sector does not need to be characterized by excessively large adjustment assistance programs. Rather, it is likely that any pro-adjustment program can be contained by tar-

Figure 4.4a–c. Trade and Levels of Development: The Regulatory Environment Does Matter

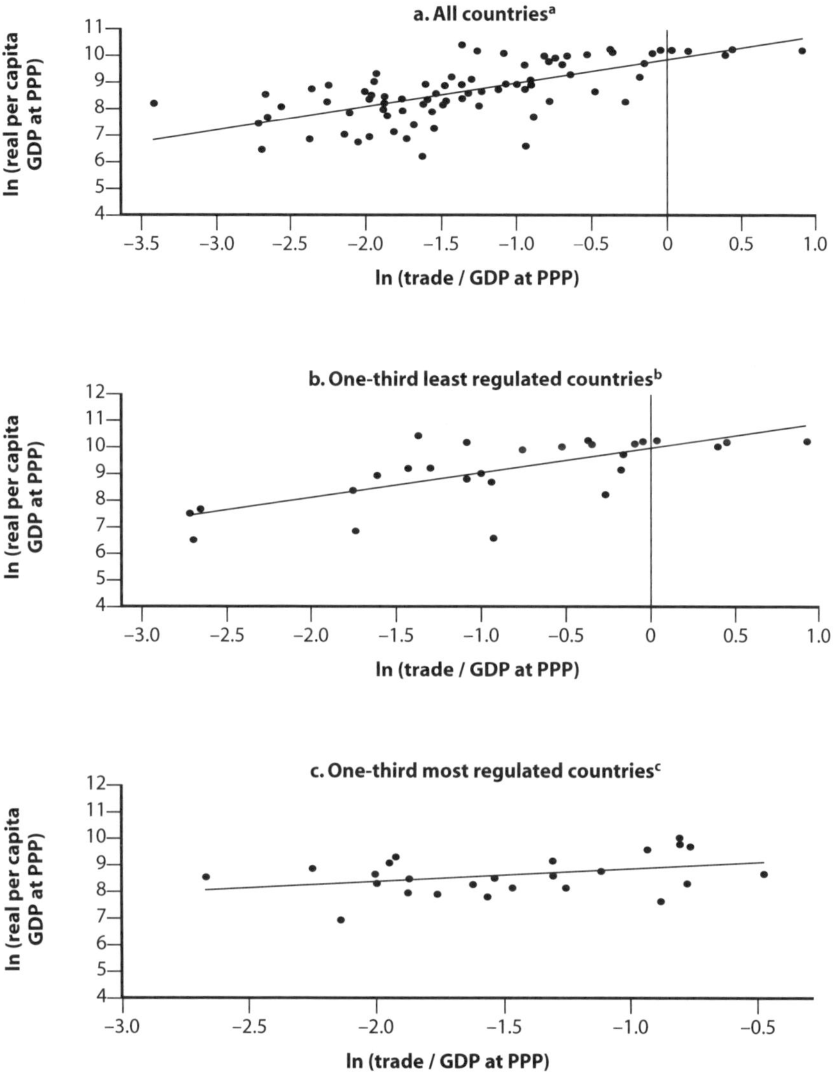

Source: Bolaky and Freund 2003, Figure 1A-1C.

PPP = purchasing power parity.

a. ln (real percapita GDP at PPP) = 9.80 + 0.88 ln (trade / GDP). *T*-statistic 8.26.

b. ln (real percapita GDP) = 9.90 + 0.92 ln (trade / GDP). *T*-statistic 5.22.

c. ln (real percapita GDP) = 9.31 + 0.49 ln (trade / GDP). *T*-statistic 2.11.

geting the workers and small farmers who are most vulnerable to the relative price changes expected from DR-CAFTA. Monge and González-Vega (2003) have identified some key sectors in agriculture that would fall into this category. Moreover, the distinction between net producers and net consumers of the sensitive commodities is an important ingredient for designing efficient adjustment programs, as argued in chapter 5.

Simulations from Partial Equilibrium Models

To quantify the potential short-term effect of eliminating U.S. tariffs on Central American exports, results of partial equilibrium simulations based on market-specific elasticities are reported in summary table 4.2 (see the specifics in annex tables 4A.1 to 4A.5).[5] The simulations suggest that trade gains from DR-CAFTA would amount to a short-term increase in exports ranging from 21 percent (El Salvador) to 47 percent (Guatemala). As expected, most of the estimated gains for Central American economies would be concentrated in the textiles and apparel sector. Smaller absolute gains would also be expected for other textile articles, footwear, and articles of leather and cotton. Nicaragua could see gains in some processed foods (vegetable oils, processed beef) and Guatemala and Honduras may see significant increases in tobacco products.

The partial equilibrium results reported above need to be interpreted with caution. Although employing utilization rates of trade preferences is an improvement over traditional analysis of potential apparel gains, simulations cannot easily deal with the complicated structure of export restrictions associated with rules of origin requirements that are likely to be in place in DR-CAFTA.

For most countries in the region, the greatest potential for expanded Central American apparel exports resides in the loosening up of the rules of origin that govern current tariff preference rules. As explained in chapter 3, DR-CAFTA will facilitate apparel goods to qualify for duty-free treatment by allowing unlimited use of regional inputs, accumulation of origin with regional partners, exceptions for specific types of apparel, and temporary quotas for goods that do not need to meet strict rules of origin for Costa Rica and Nicaragua. Some of these gains should attract investment in yard spinning, fabric making, and other textile processes into Central America, and that could greatly increase local value added in this sector. Similarly, Central American countries are also likely to benefit from the more flexible "short-supply" provisions included in DR-CAFTA, which allow for duty-free exports with inputs from third countries that are not widely available in the United States.

Hopes for expanded apparel exports from the Central America region depend on how the U.S. market responds to the end of the global textile quotas in January 2005. While there has been a noticeable spike in imports into the U.S. market from China in the first few months of 2005, strong import

Table 4.2. Changes in Exports as a Result of U.S. Tariff Elimination, Central America
percent

Item	*Costa Rica*	*El Salvador*	*Guatemala*	*Honduras*	*Nicaragua*
HS.02 Beef	9.3	–	–	9.3	9.3
HS.04 Dairy products, eggs	–	–	–	–	1.9
HS.12 Oilseeds					55.0
HS.16 Beef preparations, seafood	18.6	–	–	–	4.0
HS.17 Sugar and sugar products	3.9	3.9	3.7	3.6	–
HS.18 Cocoa and cocoa products	2.3	3.3	3.2	–	–
HS.19 Cereal preparations	1.6	1.6	1.6	1.6	–
HS.21 Miscellaneous food preparations	3.5	3.5	3.5	3.5	3.5
HS.24 Tobacco	–	–	57.1	51.1	56.1
HS.39 Plastics	–	–	2.8	–	–
HS.42 Leather goods	36.1	42.4	32.7	34.8	22.9
HS.46 Straw manufactures	–	4.9	4.9	4.9	4.9
HS.51 Wool	35.2	–	21.1	–	–
HS.52 Cotton	12.5	17.4	21.9	29.2	–
HS.53 Other vegetable fibers	–	20.5	–	–	–
HS.54 Synthetic filaments	24.4	28.7	34.4	26.8	–
HS.55 Synthetic fibers	13.5	36.8	31.4	31.6	–
HS.56 Yarns	9.2	7.4	7.3	9.9	8.4
HS.57 Rugs	17.2	–	5.2	–	–
HS.58 Special woven fabrics	9.6	8.8	18.5	7.9	6.5
HS.59 Special fabrics	9.7	7.8	10.3	–	–
HS.61 Knitted apparel	35.3	23.8	58.4	24.5	59.2
HS.62 Woven apparel	17.8	39.7	34.3	26.4	36.3
HS.63 Other textile articles	19.8	25.7	25.3	21.0	21.8
HS.64 Footwear	40.9	38.8	42.0	95.7	63.0
HS.65 Hats and their parts	11.9	11.8	11.8	11.8	–
HS.94 Cereal preparations	8.1	7.9	8.0	–	–

Source: See Annex tables A4.1 to A4.5.
– = Not available; HS = Harmonized System.

growth from Central American countries in the same period suggests that other traditional exporters are bearing the brunt of Chinese shipments. In part this may be explained by Central American countries continuing to enjoy a significant tariff advantage over Asian competitors (that is, zero tariffs vs. 10–30 percent most-favored-nation tariffs in apparel categories), an edge that is likely to continue once DR-CAFTA enters into force. In addition, gains achieved by making rules of origin more flexible may be retroactive in the sense that imports that qualify for zero tariff under DR-CAFTA rules (but not under the current tariff preferences) could be allowed to claim refunds for tariff payments. Also, Central American countries benefit from a distance advantage that provides them with a competitive edge in markets where fashion trends change quickly and just-in-time deliveries and rapid supply response are important. These factors together with the know-how capabilities developed and the specialization on "full-package" services by Central American apparel-exporting firms, should create significant opportunities for development of local links for this cluster, beyond the pure assembly model associated with *maquila*.

Partial equilibrium results do not reveal significant short-term export gains aside from *maquila* products because this technique traditionally underestimates the supply response to FTAs. Available estimation methods cannot anticipate new exports aside from those for which positive export levels exist prior to the implementation of the free trade agreement. Simulations made for Mexico before NAFTA also underestimated the expansion of new export categories for the same reason. Before NAFTA, Mexican exports to the United States were concentrated in primary products, including oil. After NAFTA, Mexico's export base broadened substantially, with manufactures largely surpassing traditional primary products, as mentioned above.

Regarding the possible impact on Central American economies of eliminating tariffs on U.S. imported products, Tables 4A.6 to 4A.10 show that there will be trade increments in a wide range of manufactures, following the same partial equilibrium model methodology. The higher absolute increases will be concentrated for most of the countries in vehicles, mineral oils, furniture, electrical machinery, and textiles. The import aggregated increase will vary from 10 percent to 12 percent in El Salvador, Guatemala, and Nicaragua, and up to 26 percent in Honduras.

Simulation from a General Equilibrium Model for Nicaragua

This section[6] describes the main features of the computable general equilibrium model and household survey microsimulation module that were applied by Bussolo and Niimi (2005) to study the sectoral and national effects of further unilateral trade liberalization and DR-CAFTA on Nicaragua. Unlike the previous partial equilibrium models, these CGE simulations consider the interactions across industries and factors of production (labor and capital). Because Nicaragua is a relatively poor country by Latin American standards and even relative to the other DR-CAFTA beneficiaries, it is worthwhile to look at this case in detail from a poverty perspective. Nevertheless, at this point it is worth highlighting that other studies using similar CGE simulations suggest that the overall static gains for DR-CAFTA countries are, on average, well above 1 percent of the region's GDP (or its gross net product, depending on the study) as a whole (see, for example, Hilaire and Yang 2003; Hinojosa-Ojeda 2002 as cited in Paunovic 2004; and Brown, Deardorff, and Stern 2004). Here our focus is on understanding the distributional effects of DR-CAFTA and comparing them with what could be obtained (under the same restrictive assumptions) with further unilateral trade reforms.

The Nicaragua General Equilibrium Model and Its Data

A 2000 Social Accounting Matrix (SAM) has been used as the initial benchmark equilibrium for the CGE model. The SAM, which includes 39 sectors, 39 commodities, 3 factors (skilled and unskilled labor and one composite capital), an aggregate household account, and other accounts (government, savings and investment, and rest of the world), has been assembled from various sources incorporating data from the 2000 Input-Output Table and the 2001 Living Standards Measurement Study households survey. Because the quality of the initial data set represented by this SAM directly influences the quality of the model results, particular attention has been devoted in estimating the value added, the trade, and tariff components of the matrix. The CGE model we use is based on a standard neoclassical general equilibrium model, which is virtually identical to other CGE simulations, including Hilaire and Yang (2003) in terms of the underlying economics concerning constant elasticities of substitution on the production side. The Nicaragua analysis is unique, however, in its treatment of issues related to income distribution, international trade, and factor markets.

Income Distribution and Absorption

Labor income and capital revenues are allocated to households according to a fixed coefficient distribution matrix derived from the original SAM. Notice that one of the main advantages of using the microsimulation module is to enrich this rather crude macro distribution mechanism. Private consumption demand is obtained through maximizing household-specific utility function following the Linear Expenditure System. Household utility is a function of consumption of different goods. When their total value is determined, government and investment demands[7] are disaggregated in sectoral demands according to fixed coefficient functions.

International Trade

In the model we assume imperfect substitution among goods originating in different geographical areas.[8] Imports demand results from a Constant Elasticity of Substitution (CES) aggregation function of domestic and imported goods. Export supply is symmetrically modeled as a Constant Elasticity of Transformation function. Producers decide to allocate their output to domestic or foreign markets responding to relative prices. Because Nicaragua is unable to influence world prices, the small-country assumption holds, and its imports and exports prices are treated as exogenous. The assumptions of imperfect substitution and imperfect transformability grant a certain degree of autonomy of domestic prices with respect to foreign prices and prevent the model from generating corner solutions. The balance of payments equilibrium is determined by the equality of foreign savings (which are exogenous) to the value for the current account. With fixed world prices and capital inflows, all adjustments are accommodated by changes in the real exchange rate: increased import demand arising from trade liberalization must be financed by increased exports, and these can expand owing to the improved resource allocation. Price decreases in importables drive resources toward export sectors and contribute to falling domestic resource costs (or real exchange rate depreciation). Thus, this modeling exercise is subject to at least a few caveats. First, it assumes that tariff reductions at the border are directly transmitted to domestic relative prices as viewed by producers. This is a strong assumption, given that reported tariffs are not always effective because many products, including agricultural commodities, enter Nicaragua (and other Central American markets) through informal channels and often through formal channels as in the cases of zero-duty imports allowed to stem rising prices or for specific uses (such as feed grains for poultry in Nicaragua). Moreover, changes in border policies do not necessarily mean that producer prices in the interior of Nicaragua will change because of the natural protection offered by distance to markets. Thus, all results from this simulation exercise need to be treated with great caution.

Factor Markets

Labor is separated into two categories: skilled and unskilled. These categories are considered imperfectly substitutable inputs in the production process. Moreover, some degree of market segmentation is assumed: composite capital is sector specific, and labor markets are segmented between agriculture and nonagriculture, with labor fully mobile within each of the two broad sectors but fully immobile across them. These restrictive conditions are imposed on the modeling framework so that it mimics in the best possible and least contentious way what would be the short-term impact of trade reforms on the Nicaraguan economy. One could certainly introduce dynamic features, market imperfections, and other complications, but the debate would then move toward assessing the links between trade policy and growth and, although important, that is a much more contentious issue. Finally, the segmented version of the model also facilitates linking the macro results of the CGE model to the household survey micro-model, where households are not allowed to respond to price changes by migrating, increasing their human capital endowments, or even changing their consumption choices.

The labor market specification is a key element of our model and an important driver of poverty and distributional results. Therefore, its specification calls for some clarification and justification. The labor market skill segmentation has become a standard assumption in CGE modeling and it is easily justifiable for the case of Nicaragua, where inequalities in terms of educational endowments and access to education support this assumption. However, the assumption that the market for labor is further segmented into agricultural and nonagricultural activities is more controversial. To test its validity, Bussolo and Niimi (2005) conducted an econometric exercise of wage functions to assess whether Nicaragua exhibits wage gaps across these two sectors after controlling for the individual characteristics of workers. They concluded that the possibility that agricultural workers have different wages from similar workers in other industries cannot be rejected. Although this finding is not conclusive, because the estimated wage gap might have various interpretations and be caused by other factors that were not included in the analysis, it might be sufficient to justify the assumption of segmented labor markets in the CGE simulation exercise.

The Microsimulation Module: Linking Household Surveys to the CGE Model

Poverty effects of trade reforms are estimated using a top-down approach. Initially the CGE model calculates the new equilibrium (that is, new relative prices and quantities for factors and commodities) following a trade shock. Then prices are transferred to the micro module to estimate a new income distribution, and finally poverty effects are calculated. No feedback from the micro module to the macro model is explicitly accounted for in this version.

The following equation[9] represents the core of the micro module:

$$\frac{\partial Wh}{Y_h} = \underbrace{\sum_g -\theta^c_{h,g}\dot{p}g}_{\textit{consumption}} + \underbrace{\theta^l_h\dot{w}}_{\substack{\textit{labor}\\ \text{income}}} + \underbrace{\theta^R_h\dot{w}}_{\textit{remittances}} + \underbrace{\theta^{kap}_h\dot{\pi}}_{\textit{profits}} + \underbrace{\sum_g \theta^T_{h,g}(\dot{t}_g + \dot{m}_g)}_{\textit{tariff}\text{ revenue}} \qquad \text{(Eq. 4.1)}$$

The relative gains or losses (W represents welfare) for each household (h) depend on (1) changes in prices for purchased goods (p_g, where a dot represents percentage change) and the initial share of expenditure on each good ($\theta^c_{h,g}$); (2) changes in factor returns (w stands for returns to skilled and unskilled labor, and π is returns to capital) and the shares of total initial income by source (θ^l_h and θ^{kap}_h); and (3) remittances and other transfers that depend on the wage rate and the government revenues. Income by source is calculated for each member of the household, and to keep notation simple, equation (4.1) shows results after aggregating incomes for each person in the same household. When the changes in welfare are calculated, a new distribution of income is generated and this counterfactual distribution is then compared to the initial distribution.

The main advantage of this approach is that it takes into account important sources of heterogeneity across households, given that the structure of income by type and the composition of consumption by commodity, the various θs in the above equation, are household specific. A large body of literature on trade and poverty has shown that changes in the distribution of income (or consumption) might differ considerably across different groups of households and that predetermined groupings may not capture the whole spectrum of possible outcomes.[10] Poor households themselves are poor for different reasons and designing compensatory policies that are targeted to the right recipients can be greatly facilitated by having at disposal a whole new counterfactual distribution. In the new distribution, households, as well as individuals, can be identified according to the full set of socioeconomic characteristics recorded in the survey. It is thus easier to identify a specific characteristic—such as region of residence, employment status, gender, education, age, and so forth—that may strongly correlate with larger-than-average losses from the trade policy reform and then use this information in targeting compensatory measures.

Clearly, how this new counterfactual distribution is generated is rather important. Equation (4.1) only considers first-order effects and excludes important second-order mechanisms that may account for large income changes. Specifically, movements in and out of employment or across sectors of production are excluded as is substitution in consumption, although not accounting for the latter does not normally result in large errors. This approach is better suited to estimate short-run effects and it may overestimate the effects of a trade shock, given that quantity adjustments and substitutions are ruled out. Knowing these limitations, however, its main advantage is its transparency and low implementation costs in terms of data and time.

Equation (4.1) implies that, for each household, individual incomes can be readily imputed to the relevant factors of production, namely the two labor types and the composite capital. This is fairly straightforward for urban wage-workers; however, for a large group of the Nicaraguan population this imputation is not obvious. As explained in the next subsection, disaggregating income for self-employed workers in the farm sector can be a laborious and error-prone procedure: the labor and capital components are often not easily separable. For households whose heads belong to this group of workers, an approach that bypasses this imputation has been used. This is represented by the following equation:

$$\frac{\partial W}{Y} = \left[\sum_j \theta_j^o \dot{p}_j^o - \sum_k \theta_k^I \dot{p}_k^I\right] + \sum_f \theta_f^w \dot{w}_f - \sum_g \theta_g^c \dot{p}_g^c - \qquad \text{(Eq. 4.2)}$$

As before, the relative change in welfare is represented by a change in consumption (the last term in the left-hand side of the equation), by a change in explicit wage earnings, and by the profit generated by the activity run by the household (the term in square brackets). This is estimated as the difference between sales (holding constant the quantity shares of the different goods sold θ_j^O) and input costs (again without changing the structure of input quantities θ_j^I).

Finally, it should be noted that autoconsumption has been explicitly excluded from the computations in both equations (4.1) and (4.2), given that price changes—in the short run, and those of the order of magnitude considered here—do not affect it. In terms of equation (4.2), this means that not only final consumption needs to exclude autoconsumption but also that input costs have to be netted of those costs that relate to production for autoconsumption.

Poverty Effects of Trade Policy Reforms

This section first presents the results of the general equilibrium model and then the poverty estimations obtained by linking the changes in the macro variables to the household surveys.

Policy Scenarios. The DR-CAFTA agreement has recently been at the center of attention of trade ministers in the Central American region. This agreement should provide almost full free access to one of their major markets; it should assist the implementation of additional domestic market reforms; and, by requiring reciprocal opening, it should produce significant efficiency gains because of resource reallocations toward more competitive sectors. However, as brilliantly illustrated by the Chilean multipronged strategy of trade liberalization, DR-CAFTA is just one of the many trade options that the Central American countries can pursue, and probably the best way to evaluate the opportunities offered by such a regional agreement is to compare it with a benchmark case of full liberalization. Two main scenarios are considered: DR-CAFTA, and a unilateral nondiscriminatory liberalization. The potential advantages and disadvantages of the *reciprocal* liberalization produced by the regional scenario are illustrated by further decomposing the DR-CAFTA scenario into two separate unilateral liberalizations: first, Nicaragua liberalizes in relation to the United States, which does not reciprocate; and then the United States unilaterally liberalizes in relation to Nicaragua. Although not a realistic policy choice, the full unilateral liberalization provides a useful yardstick against which DR-CAFTA can be evaluated.

In all the simulations only tariffs are modified and eliminated in a single sweep. Likewise, each of the simulations is based on a comparative static framework with no capital accumulation, no changes in labor supply or skill levels, and factor market segmentation. Consequently, as happened with the early-1990s CGE modeling attempts of the Mexican experience under

NAFTA, the results from the simulations might be quite off the mark because dynamic effects could overwhelm the static effects predicted by the simulations even if the assumptions regarding the key parameters (that is, elasticities of substitution on the demand and supply sides for each of the 28 industries) were realistic (see Kehoe [2003] for an ex post review of the accuracy of NAFTA CGE models).

Trade Reforms: Macro Results. In a general equilibrium model, all relative prices and quantities are determined simultaneously. To disentangle the trade policy reform effects on the economy, however, it is helpful to describe the adjustment process as if it were sequential. First, tariffs are reduced. That reduction, in turn, has an effect on import flows, which, in turn, displace domestic production and generate resource reallocations. These shifts interact with factors' supply and demand, and determine factor prices. These prices, together with prices for new goods, finally affect households' real income levels. Changed household incomes then feed back into the system through changes in consumption choices, and the process continues until a new equilibrium is reached. Three main elements determine the *position* (that is, the values of the endogenous variables) of the new equilibrium: (1) the starting levels of some key variables in the initial equilibrium—the prices and quantities implicit in the initial SAM; (2) the functional forms of the model's behavioral equations; and (3) some key parameters, namely substitution elasticities among factors in the production process and, for a trade reform analysis, the elasticities of substitution in demand between domestic and imported commodities and the elasticity of transformation in supply between domestic and foreign markets. The values for the different elasticities have been borrowed from the available econometric literature. Depending on the estimation methods as well as on the period or country being examined, however, these values show considerable variation, and this has caused heated controversies between supporters and skeptics of this type of model. Systematic sensitivity analysis, wherein all elasticities are randomly changed and results are presented with accompanying confidence intervals, has been proposed as a solution to these controversies, but even this rather computationally intensive proposal has its problems and we do not attempt it here.

The bottom line is then that results presented here are indicative of a likely response to the analyzed shocks. In most cases, the sign and relative, if not absolute, magnitude of the model's results—for example, a finding that gains for unskilled labor are larger than those for skilled labor—should be reliable.

Major advantages of this type of model are that it represents the whole economy in a consistent and theoretically sound framework, and that the structural features of the country investigated strongly influence the final results. Table 4.3 shows these features for Nicaragua in terms of sectoral shares of gross production, imports, exports, and private demand; the middle panel details, for each sector, the U.S. weight in total trade; the right panel shows Nicaraguan tariffs against the United States and other partners and the U.S. tariffs against Nicaraguan products. For convenience, the bottom panel of the table reports measurements for aggregate sectors, although the model's actual 28 sectors are shown in the top panel. In commenting on the results of the policy simulations, we will be referring repeatedly to data in table 4.3.

The initial import protection, both in its level and sectoral variability, is among the key elements determining the simulation outcomes. Three key features are highlighted by the tariff data: (1) the overall trade-weighted protection rate is rather low, (2) its dispersion is high with a clear bias against agricultural imports, and (3) tariffs against the United States are generally above the trade-weighted average of tariffs against the rest of the world.

Table 4.3 also shows that domestic Nicaraguan agricultural producers may be facing strong competition relative to imports from the United States, which, notwithstanding significant levels of protection, enjoys a large share of total imports of agricultural commodities (41 percent). Anticipating the results shown below, it is likely that a liberalization of U.S. imports, which basically consists of reducing an anti-agricultural imports bias, may lead to an increase of competition in the agricultural sectors, with a potential initial negative shock for households strongly dependent on farming incomes. Clearly, this potentially negative outcome may be exacerbated by the level of sector aggregation used in the model. It may be that, at finer sectoral levels, one finds imports and domestic products to be complements rather than substitutes. Agricultural products, however, are normally fairly homogeneous and thus substitutable, and the risk of negative impacts should not be completely ruled out.

Unilateral Liberalization against All Trading Partners. As outlined above, the adjustment process caused by this reform is initially described in terms of sectoral demand and supply changes, as shown in table 4.4. Consider first the demand/imports side. Initial tariff rates (TM)[11] are highest in the agriculture and food-processing sectors—in particular in *basic grain, meat and fish products, sugar products,* and *dairy;* accordingly these sectors could experience the

Table 4.3. Nicaragua's Economic Structure, 2000

	Sectoral share				*U.S. weight*		*Tariff*		
Sector	*Xp*	*M*	*Ex*	*Xc*	*M US*	*Ex US*	*Nic-US*	*Nic-ROW*	*US-Nic*
Agriculture									
Coffee	2	0	20	0	14	26	8	6	0
Sugar cane	1	0	0	0	0	0	0	0	0
Basic grain	3	1	1	4	72	0	29	17	0
Other agricultural products	3	2	7	5	18	3	8	4	11
Livestock	5	1	3	3	35	0	4	2	0
Forestry	1	0	0	1	93	0	1	1	0
Fishery	1	0	1	0	34	5	10	5	0
Mining and Energy									
Mining	1	10	4	0	1	4	2	0	0
Electricity, gas, water	2	0	0	1	0	0	10	6	0
Water distribution	1	0	0	1	0	0	0	0	0
Food Processing									
Meat and fish products	5	0	23	5	19	27	18	8	3
Sugar products	2	0	5	2	6	11	8	7	0
Dairy	2	1	3	3	32	0	12	8	0
Other food	4	8	2	11	19	0	7	4	1
Beverages	2	1	1	6	9	0	12	6	0
Tobacco	0	1	1	1	2	9	4	0	7
Other Manufacturing									
Textiles, clothing, and leather	3	4	12	5	39	5	4	4	4
Wood products	2	2	2	1	28	0	8	3	0
Paper and print products	1	3	0	1	21	0	3	2	0

continued

Table 4.3, *continued*

	Sectoral share				*U.S. weight*		*Tariff*		
Sector	*Xp*	*M*	*Ex*	*Xc*	*M US*	*Ex US*	*Nic-US*	*Nic-ROW*	*US-Nic*
Other Manufacturing, continued									
Refined oil	3	5	2	2	9	0	7	7	0
Chemicals	1	17	2	6	21	0	3	2	0
Glass no-metal products	1	3	1	0	9	2	4	2	0
Metal products	0	7	1	0	15	0	3	2	0
Machinery and equipment	0	26	1	2	40	0	2	3	0
Services									
Construction	9	0	0	0	0	0	0	0	0
Commerce	10	0	0	1	0	0	0	0	0
Other services	29	5	4	28	24	1	0	0	0
Transport services	5	1	4	8	24	3	0	0	0
Total	100	100	100	100	24	36	4	3	–
Aggregate sectors averages									
Agriculture	17	4	32	13	41	28	20	6	–
Mining and Energy	4	10	4	3	1	64	2	0	–
Food Processing	15	12	36	29	18	54	8	4	–
Other Manufacturing	12	68	20	19	28	14	3	3	–
Services	53	6	8	37	24	40	0	0	–

Source: Nicaragua Social Accounting Matrix estimated by the author.
Note: Under Sectoral Share, Xp represents the sectoral output as a percentage of total output, M represents the sectoral total imports, Ex represents the exports shares, and Xc represents the private consumption shares. Under U.S. Weight, M US represents the initial share of imports coming from the United States over total imports, and Ex US represents the initial share of exports going to the United States. Under Tariff, Nic-US and Nic-ROW are Nicaraguan tariffs against U.S. and other partner imports, respectively, and US-Nic are U.S. tariffs against Nicaraguan exports.

Table 4.4. Sectoral Effects of Full Unilateral Trade Liberalization

	Imports and local sales					*Exports and production*			
Sector	*Tm*	Δ*M*	*M/D*	Δ*S*	Δ*Pd*	Δ*Ex*	*Ex/Xp*	Δ*Xp*	Δ*Px*
Agriculture									
Coffee	6	13	8	−1	−1.4	5	101	4	−0.2
Sugar cane	0	0	0	1	−2.2	0	0	1	−2.2
Basic grain	26	55	11	−4	−6.8	27	3	−3	−6.6
Other agricultural products	5	6	14	0	−2.7	12	26	3	−2.1
Livestock	2	2	4	1	−2.1	10	8	2	−2.0
Forestry	1	−8	1	1	−4.1	19	2	1	−4.0
Fishery	6	24	4	1	0.7	−2	6	1	0.7
Mining and Energy									
Mining	0	−5	85	−2	−1.1	3	55	1	−0.5
Electricity, gas, water	6	12	2	−1	−2.1	8	0	−1	−2.1
Water distribution	0	0	0	−1	−0.8	0	0	−1	−0.8
Food Processing									
Meat and fish products	10	25	4	−1	−1.8	6	53	2	−0.9
Sugar products	7	18	1	−1	−1.2	4	33	1	−0.9
Dairy	9	18	18	−3	−2.3	6	22	−1	−1.8
Other food	5	3	35	1	−3.9	18	7	2	−3.6
Beverages	6	12	8	−1	−1.8	6	3	−1	−1.7
Tobacco	0	−2	85	−1	−0.5	1	96	0	−0.1
Other Manufacturing									
Textiles, clothing, and leather	4	4	38	−2	−1.8	5	55	1	−0.9
Wood products	5	7	23	−1	−2.0	7	12	−1	−1.7
Paper and print products	3	1	55	−3	−1.3	2	3	−3	−1.2

continued

Table 4.4, *continued*

	Imports and local sales					Exports and production			
Sector	*Tm*	*ΔM*	*M/D*	*ΔS*	*ΔPd*	*ΔEx*	*Ex/Xp*	*ΔXp*	*ΔPx*
Other Manufacturing, continued									
Refined oil	7	13	26	−6	−0.7	−3	8	−6	−0.7
Chemicals	2	0	71	−1	−1.7	6	18	0	−1.4
Glass no-metal products	2	2	35	−1	−0.7	2	7	−1	−0.7
Metal products	2	1	72	0	−1.6	7	16	1	−1.4
Machinery and equipment	3	1	83	2	−2.9	15	73	10	−1.0
Services									
Construction	0	0	0	1	−0.5	0	0	1	−0.5
Commerce	0	0	0	−1	−0.4	0	0	−1	−0.4
Other services	0	−3	5	0	−0.9	3	2	0	−0.9
Transport services	0	−5	6	0	−1.6	6	9	0	−1.5
Total	3	2	23	−1	−1.5	6	12	0	−1.3
Aggregate sectors averages									
Agriculture	12	23	7	−0.4	−2.9	7	23	1.1	−2.5
Mining and Energy	0	−4	−48	−0.8	−1.6	3	12	−0.4	−1.5
Food Processing	5	6	21	−0.7	−2.9	7	23	1.1	−2.5
Other Manufacturing	3	2	57	−2.9	−1.3	5	21	−1.6	−1.0
Services	0	−4	3	−0.2	−0.8	5	2	−0.1	−0.8

Source: Authors' calculations.

Tm = initial tariff rates; ΔM = the percent variation in total import volumes with respect to the initial levels; M/D = the ratio of imports to domestic demand (the sectoral import dependency, calculated using preliberalization levels); ΔS = the percent variation in the volumes of domestic sales of domestic output; ΔPd = the percent variation in domestic prices for local sales; ΔEx = the percent variation in the volumes of exports; Ex/Xp = the ratio of exports to domestic output (the sectoral export orientation); ΔXp = the percent change of domestic output; ΔPx = the percent change of output prices.

largest inflows of import volumes when protection is removed, assuming, of course, that the border-price changes are fully transmitted to domestic consumers throughout the Nicaraguan economy and that the model parameters concerning the responsiveness of domestic demand to such price changes are accurate. The model predicts an increase in import volumes (ΔM) of 23 percent with respect to their initial levels for agriculture and 6 percent to their preliberalization levels for food processing. Nevertheless, imports do not represent a large share of local demand (M/D) in agriculture or food processing. Thus, even with a high (presumed) elasticity of substitution between local production and imports (= 3), the impact of increased imports on sales of domestic goods (ΔS) is low in these sectors. In fact, the model predicts that other manufacturing sectors suffer slightly bigger domestic sales contractions as a result of their larger initial share of import dependency despite their lower initial level of protection. Reflecting Nicaragua's dependency on foreign production of capital goods, intermediates, and energy, imports are well above 50 percent of total local demand for other manufacturing and just below that threshold for energy and mining. For the other manufacturing sectors, cheaper imports displace up to approximately 3 percent of domestic production.

For the economy as a whole, these low or moderate domestic market share losses are reflected in small declines of producers' prices for local sales (ΔPd). Some of these effects are larger when disaggregated sectors are examined, and complementary analyses considering much-disaggregated sectors of production may be needed to identify specific sensitive commodities.[12]

These demand/imports side effects are linked to the supply response to which we now turn. For producers of exportable goods, the reduction of prices in local markets (ΔPd) combined with unchanged export prices create incentives to increase the share of sales destined for foreign markets. This export response (ΔEx) varies across sectors and is linked to the pattern of Nicaragua's comparative advantage, which, according to the exports sectoral distribution (column Ex in table 4.3) and the export orientation (Ex/Xp in table 4.4), is within three main sectors: *coffee, meat and fish products,* and *textiles and clothing.* For these sectors, rising export sales more than offset the reduction of domestic sales and lead to an overall increase in sectoral production (ΔXp). In other sectors,[13] with lower export orientation, the change in sectoral production is roughly equal to the change in local sales (ΔS). Sectors enjoying export-led growth also record output price reductions (ΔPx) that are smaller than those of domestic sales prices (ΔPd). This is because output prices are a combination (CES prices) of fixed export prices and domestic prices.

In summary, trade liberalization, even if it consists of the elimination of a relatively low economy-wide protection (3 percent), entails considerable sectoral adjustment.[14] Within agriculture, *basic grain* is the only sector registering a contraction because of its high tariffs and low export orientation; whereas *coffee* and *other agricultural products,* among others, enjoy significant export-led growth. Similarly in the nonfarm portion of the economy, import-competing sectors contract and release resources that move toward sectors that were less protected or that produce for foreign markets. Considering the aggregate averages, the macrosector *Food Processing* is recording positive output changes, whereas the other nonfarm macrosectors' outputs experience moderate contractions.

Changes in factors' remuneration, shown in table 4.5, are another important aspect of the structural adjustment caused by trade reform. Changes in wages and capital return are linked to changes of goods prices through the production technology and the functioning of the factor markets. Different production technologies are approximated by different factors' and intermediate inputs' intensities across sectors, as shown in table 4.6, and factor markets function to mimic short-term adjustment possibilities: capital is sector

Table 4.5. Factor Price Changes Resulting from Full Trade Liberalization

Factor	*ΔP*	*(ΔP/CPI)*
Nonfarm segment		
Skilled labor	–0.3	2.1
Unskilled labor	0.6	2.9
Capital	–0.6	1.8
Skilled/unskilled wage gap		–0.9
Farm segment		
Skilled labor	–4.0	–1.6
Unskilled labor	–6.3	–3.9
Capital	2.7	5.1
Skilled/unskilled wage gap		2.5
Price indexes		
Food Price Index	–3.6	
Nonfood Price Index	–1.5	
Consumer Price Index	–2.4	

Source: Author calculations from model results.
ΔP = the percent variation of the price of each factor with respect to the initial levels; (ΔP/CPI) = the percent variation of the price deflated by the Consumer Price Index.

Table 4.6. Value Added and Employment by Sector and Factor, and Sectoral Intermediate Uses
percent

	Value added							Employment (number of workers)				
	Sectoral Intensity				Sectoral share			Sectoral intensity		Sectoral share		
Sector	Sk	Usk	KandL	Xint	Sk	Usk	KandL	Sk	Usk	Sk	Usk	ΔXp
Agriculture												
Coffee	3	66	31	29	7	21	10	1	99	4	10	4.4
Sugar cane	2	27	71	40	2	3	7	2	98	4	5	0.8
Basic grain	6	77	17	29	17	31	7	2	98	41	55	–3.4
Other agricultural products	17	40	43	35	53	16	18	7	93	9	4	2.5
Livestock	4	32	63	36	20	19	40	4	96	39	23	1.6
Forestry	0	75	25	47	0	8	3	0	100	0	1	1.1
Fishery	1	10	89	37	1	2	15	4	96	3	2	0.5
Mining and Energy												
Mining	9	73	18	48	0	2	1	5	95	0	1	0.5
Electricity, gas, water	34	6	59	42	3	0	6	63	37	1	0	–0.6
Water distribution	20	55	25	37	1	2	1	28	72	1	1	–1.1
Food Processing												
Meat and fish products	25	46	29	82	2	3	2	21	79	1	1	2.3
Sugar products	12	33	55	70	0	1	3	11	89	0	1	0.7
Dairy	35	30	35	71	1	1	2	21	79	0	0	–1.0
Other food	31	42	27	70	3	3	3	13	87	0	0	–1.0
Beverages	48	15	37	60	3	1	3	51	49	1	0	–1.2
Tobacco	4	43	53	47	0	0	0	13	87	0	0	0.5
Other Manufacturing												
Textiles, clothing, and leather	20	72	7	50	2	6	1	22	78	5	6	1.0
Wood products	16	75	9	58	1	4	1	9	91	0	1	–0.5

continued

Table 4.6, *continued*
percent

	Value added							Employment (number of workers)				
	Sectoral Intensity				Sectoral share			Sectoral intensity		Sectoral share		
Sector	*Sk*	*Usk*	*KandL*	*Xint*	*Sk*	*Usk*	*KandL*	*Sk*	*Usk*	*Sk*	*Usk*	*ΔXp*
Other Manufacturing, continued												
Paper and print products	28	66	6	61	0	1	0	25	75	0	0	−2.9
Refined oil	69	0	31	97	0	0	0	100	0	0	0	−5.8
Chemicals	36	35	29	65	1	1	1	27	73	0	0	0.0
Glass no-metal products	29	62	9	72	1	1	0	12	88	1	1	−0.6
Metal products	24	71	5	76	0	1	0	17	83	1	1	1.1
Machinery and equipment	31	63	6	76	0	0	0	20	80	1	2	10.2
Services												
Construction	16	64	20	54	5	17	8	11	89	4	10	1.4
Commerce	33	56	11	29	18	26	7	19	81	23	31	−0.6
Other services	40	21	39	36	55	24	61	35	65	55	32	−0.4
Transport services	27	70	3	71	3	6	0	14	86	3	5	0.2
Total	27	41	32	48	200	200	200	16	84	200	200	0.1
Aggregate sectors averages												
Agriculture	6	48	46	35	100	100	100	3	97	100	100	1.1
Mining and Energy	26	31	43	42	4	4	8	24	76	2	2	−0.4
Food Processing	31	34	35	72	10	9	13	15	85	4	8	1.1
Other Manufacturing	24	66	11	71	6	14	3	20	80	9	11	−1.6
Services	35	37	28	41	80	73	76	25	75	85	79	−0.1

Source: Authors' calculations.
Note: All the values in the table, except those in the last column, are calculated from values in the initial equilibrium; highlighted (shaded) rows are those corresponding to expanding sectors. Sectoral intensity sums to 100 percent in each sector. Sk = skilled labor; Usk = unskilled labor; KandL = capital and land; Xint = the share of intermediate inputs in total output; ΔXp = the percent change of domestic output resulting from full trade liberalization.

specific, and the farm and nonfarm sectors constitute two segmented markets for skilled and unskilled labor.

In the farm segment (which corresponds to the macrosector *Agriculture* in the previous tables), capital (including land) records a positive real price change and skilled and unskilled labor experience reductions. The agricultural expanding sectors—shaded in table 4.6—are those that use capital relatively more intensively than does *basic grains*, the contracting sector. Indeed, *coffee, other agricultural products*, and *livestock*—the largest output gainers—combined use almost 70 percent of the total farm capital value added. On the other hand, because of the contraction of the unskilled labor-intensive sector, *basic grains*, unskilled labor records a greater reduction than skilled labor.

Turning to the nonfarm segment and considering the bottom panel of table 4.6, it is easy to see that *Food Processing*, the sector with the largest output expansion, is relatively intensive in the use of capital and, in terms of number of workers (rather than value added, which includes wage differential biases), is the sector that most intensively uses unskilled workers. *Other Manufacturing*, the sector experiencing the largest contraction, uses unskilled labor to a large extent but not as intensively as does *Food Processing*. These relative intensities in the use of labor combined with initial levels of protection and output changes explain the observed wage movements.

The combination of the trade shock with this production structure explains why unskilled labor is the largest gainer in the nonfarm segment, followed by skilled labor and capital as shown in table 4.5. These results are consistent with the comparative advantage of Nicaragua, a country with abundant unskilled labor, which specializes in the production of agriculture-derived products, and is import dependent for capital goods and intermediates, which are normally produced by sectors using skilled workers intensively.

Even with segmented labor markets, the farm and nonfarm sectors of the economy have strong interconnections that determine the final results. These intersegment links are illustrated in table 4.7 for the *Agriculture* and the *Food Processing* aggregate sectors.[15] Both sectors face the largest average drops in tariff protection and large inflows of imports, but they are also enjoying the largest aggregate output gains. This is achieved by significant structural shifts that are qualitatively different for these two sectors.

For *Agriculture*, the main adjustment consists of a reduction of a single subsector and a specialization toward export-oriented sectors. Prices for imported intermediate goods are reduced by the removal of tariffs, but because of the moderate use of intermediates (35 percent of total input value), cost

Table 4.7. Intersectoral Links between Agriculture and Food Processing

	Agriculture	*Food processing*
Initial tariffs (%)	12	5
Intermediates as percentage of output	35	72
Share of total inputs from sector (%)		
Agriculture	22	63
Mining and Energy	1	3
Food Processing	13	14
Other Manufacturing	52	14
Services	12	6

Source: Authors' calculations.

savings needed to compete with cheaper imports in domestic markets and to increase competitive advantage in export markets have to be realized by factor price reductions. This also explains why labor wages are reduced in *Agriculture.*

For *Food Processing,* the inflow of imports does not entail large sectoral contractions because producers can still compete in domestic markets by enjoying reduced production costs because they use cheaper intermediates, which represent on average almost three-quarters of the total input value. In fact, most of these intermediate inputs come from agriculture whose prices are reduced following the trade shock.

Factor price changes as well as the previously mentioned intersectoral intermediates cost savings also help explain why certain sectors record a reduction or almost no increase of imports following tariff abatement. For instance, the absence of imports surge for *livestock* after the market opening is explained by the increased domestic sales of local producers who can produce at lower costs and are able to gain market share. A partial equilibrium framework in which tariff reduction can only lead to increased imports and lower prices could never account for these types of intersectoral links.

DR-CAFTA Bilateral Trade Liberalization. The full unilateral trade liberalization serves as a benchmark against which the DR-CAFTA regional agreement can be compared. Table 4.8 reports sectoral results for the simulation of this regional free trade area. By discriminating among import origins, this policy has trade-diverting effects that may or may not be compensated by trade creation. As shown below, however, this geographic discrimination is

Table 4.8. Effects of the DR-CAFTA Agreement on Nicaragua's Economic Sectors

	Imports and local sales					*Exports and production*			
Sector	*Tm U.S.*	*ΔM*	*M/D*	*ΔS*	*ΔPd*	*ΔEx*	*Ex/Xp*	*ΔXp*	*ΔPx*
Agriculture									
Coffee	8	3	8	1	−0.6	3	101	3	−0.1
Sugar cane	55	0	0	0	−1.3	0	0	0	−1.3
Basic grain	29	54	11	−4	−4.8	17	3	−3	−4.6
Other agricultural products	8	2	14	1	−0.5	10	26	3	0.1
Livestock	4	5	4	1	−0.2	2	8	2	−0.2
Forestry	1	−3	1	1	−2.2	10	2	1	−2.2
Fishery	10	29	4	2	4.4	−15	6	1	4.2
Mining and Energy									
Mining	2	0	85	−1	0.2	−2	55	−1	0.1
Electricity, gas, water	10	1	2	0	0.3	−1	0	0	0.3
Water distribution	0	0	0	0	0.5	0	0	0	0.5
Other Manufacturing									
Meat and fish products	18	13	4	0	0.4	8	53	4	1.4
Sugar products	8	2	1	0	−0.1	1	33	0	0.0
Dairy	12	11	18	−1	−0.3	0	22	−1	−0.3
Other food	7	1	35	2	−1.9	11	7	3	0
Beverages	12	4	8	0	0.0	0	3	0	0.0
Tobacco	4	0	85	−4	1.5	3	96	2	3.2
Other Manufacturing									
Textiles, clothing, and leather	4	4	38	−1	−0.1	2	55	0	0.2
Wood products	8	4	23	−1	−0.6	1	12	−1	−0.5
Paper and print products	3	1	55	−1	0.1	−2	3	−1	0.1
Refined oil	7	2	26	−1	0.0	0	8	−1	0.0

continued

Table 4.8, *continued*

Sector	Imports and local sales					Exports and production			
	Tm U.S.	*ΔM*	*M/D*	*ΔS*	*ΔPd*	*ΔEx*	*Ex/Xp*	*ΔXp*	*ΔPx*
Other Manufacturing, continued									
Chemicals	3	1	71	–1	–0.2	0	8	–1	0.0
Glass no-metal products	4	1	35	–1	0.2	–1	7	–1	0.2
Metal products	3	0	72	–1	–0.1	0	16	–1	–0.1
Machinery and equipment	2	0	83	–2	–0.2	–1	73	–1	–0.1
Services									
Construction	0	0	0	0	0.3	0	0	0	0.3
Commerce	0	0	0	0	0.7	0	0	0	0.7
Other services	0	1	5	0	0.4	–2	2	0	0.4
Transport services	0	0	6	0	0.2	–1	9	0	0.1
Total	4	2	23	0	0.0	4	12	0	0.1
Aggregate sectors averages									
Agriculture	21	22	7	0.1	–0.9	5	23	1.0	–0.7
Mining and energy	2	0	48	–0.2	0.3	–2	12	–0.4	0.3
Food processing	8	3	21	0.5	–0.4	6	28	1.9	0.0
Other manufacturing	3	1	57	–0.8	–0.1	1	21	–0.5	0.0
Services	0	1	3	–0.1	0.4	–1	2	–0.1	0.4

Source: Authors' calculations.

Tm = initial tariff rates,; ΔM = the percent variation in total import volumes with respect to the initial levels; M/D = the ratio of imports to domestic demand (the sectoral import dependency, calculated using preliberalization levels); ΔS = the percent variation in the volumes of domestic sales of domestic output; ΔPd = the percent variation in domestic prices for local sales; ΔEx = the percent variation in the volumes of exports; Ex/Xp = the ratio of exports to domestic output (the sectoral export orientation); ΔXp = the percent change of domestic output; ΔPx = the percent change of output prices.

not the most relevant aspect to be considered in an evaluation of this policy option.

Nicaragua's liberalization of U.S. imports affects just one-quarter of total imports (as shown in table 4.3) and thus has a smaller aggregate impact. The overall structural adjustment and intersectoral resource reallocation, however, is quite significant. This results from the large U.S. weight in some crucial sectors—such as the 72 percent of *basic grain* imports and the 26 percent of exports for both of the top two exporting sectors in Nicaragua, *coffee* and *meat and fish products.* DR-CAFTA obviously includes increased market access for Nicaraguan products in the U.S. market, but, as will be shown more clearly in the next section, this reciprocal liberalization amounts to a positive but rather small shock. In the model, the implied increased market access is accounted for by increasing border prices for goods exported to the United States, implicitly assuming that Nicaraguan exporters do not influence domestic prices in the United States and that they can enjoy the full rents provided by the initial U.S. tariffs.[16] Given the initial low level of U.S. tariffs, these rents are not very significant.

A preferential bilateral agreement with the United States shows some relevant divergences from a full liberalization, especially with respect to factor price changes (see table 4.9). First, the overall price deflation resulting from partial trade reform is roughly equal to one quarter of the deflation induced by complete tariff abatement. Second, DR-CAFTA entails a liberalization that is geographically and sectorally concentrated. Consider again the shares of imports originating from the United States (table 4.3): the economy-wide average share is 24 percent, but imports of U.S. *Agriculture* goods represent more than 40 percent of total imports in that macrosector, with peaks of 72 percent for *basic grain,* which is also the most protected sector. Additionally, tariffs against U.S. imports are slightly higher than those against other partners (in the data used for these simulations, which correspond to the year 2000). Thus, the DR-CAFTA-induced imports surge of agricultural goods is equal to 94 percent of that induced by a full unilateral liberalization, whereas the economy-wide average stands at 76 percent. These sectoral distortions explain why factor returns in the farm segment undergo changes that are very close to those experienced in a full liberalization scenario; actually the unskilled labor real-wage contraction is the same in the two cases, whereas factor returns in the nonfarm sector record a smaller percentage of the full liberalization shock.

Table 4.9. Factor Price Changes Resulting from DR-CAFTA

Factor	*ΔP*	*(ΔP/CPI)*	*Percentage of full liberalization*
Nonfarm segment			
Skilled labor	0.7	1.2	60
Unskilled labor	1.0	1.6	55
Capital	0.9	1.5	85
Skilled/unskilled wage gap		2.6	
Farm segment			
Skilled labor	−2.0	−1.4	87
Unskilled Labor	−4.5	−3.9	100
Capital	4.1	4.7	92
Skilled/unskilled wage gap		2.6	
Price indexes			
Food Price Index	−1.4		39
Nonfood Price Index	0.0		−1
Consumer Price Index	−0.6		24

Source: Authors' calculations from model results.
Note: In the first column, ΔP represents the percent variation of the price of each factor with respect to the initial levels. In the second column, (ΔP/CPI) is the percent variation of the price deflated by the Consumer Price Index. The third column shows the percent ratio of the real price changes in the DR-CAFTA scenario with respect to the unilateral nondiscriminatory full liberalization case.

In summary, the impact on factor remuneration of the examined trade reforms, full liberalization, and DR-CAFTA arrangements should be positive for urban workers, both wage-employed and self-employed with physical capital, but it may, at least temporarily, be negative for rural wage-earners (although not necessarily negative for subsistence farmers). For agricultural households receiving part of their income from capital and land, or even from nonfarm activities, the unfavorable farm wage changes should have smaller effect. Notice also that the wage gap between skilled and unskilled workers does not significantly change with this kind of trade reform.[17]

Decomposing the DR-CAFTA Scenario. To distinguish the effects of market access from those of own-tariff liberalization, the simulated reciprocal Dominican Republic and Central American trade agreement has been decomposed into two separate reforms. In the first reform, Nicaragua unilaterally eliminates all tariffs against U.S. imports; in the second reform, the United

States unilaterally responds by preferentially liberalizing imports from Nicaragua.[18]

As already anticipated, the opening of the Nicaraguan market corresponds to almost the full DR-CAFTA shock: the unilateral liberalization achieves roughly three-quarters or more of the variation in imports, exports, and domestic output recorded by the reciprocal case. As shown in table 4.10, in the case of unilateral U.S. liberalization, effects on imports and local sales are more or less muted, and the most visible effects consist of some additional specialization in exports of food-processing products.

The two unilateral liberalizations are consistent in their sectoral output effects. Both induce additional growth of agriculture and food processing sectors and, in this sense, help Nicaragua exploit its comparative advantage. Although the United States granted preferential access to Nicaraguan exports in the past, the remaining current U.S. tariffs seem to inhibit potential growth in some key sectors in Nicaragua, and obtaining full access to the U.S. markets may bring some advantages.

As far as factor market effects are concerned, table 4.11 suggests that the nonreciprocal removal of Nicaragua's tariffs causes factor prices in the nonfarm segment to vary almost as much as with the DR-CAFTA scenario, leaving a small contribution to the full price change to the U.S. unilateral response. It is interesting to note that the two unilateral liberalizations have contrasting price effects for factors in the farm segment. In the case of the United States liberalizing its tariffs, factor prices go up because of the increased export demand and this inflationary effect is not counterbalanced by inflows of cheaper imports. However, these inflows explain why factor prices tend to contract with the unilateral liberalization of Nicaragua, thus showing that access to the U.S. market mitigates the potentially negative shocks to farm incomes associated with the liberalization of Nicaraguan agricultural markets. Finally, inasmuch as these simulations predict small effects on factor returns, the corresponding effects on Nicaragua's poverty indicators (the headcount poverty rate and the poverty gap) decline under both scenarios by rather small amounts, as reported by Bussolo and Niimi (2005). But those authors' reported poverty-reduction effect of DR-CAFTA alone is slightly lower than the predicted poverty effect of a full unilateral reform by Nicaragua. That is, Bussolo and Niimi predict that Nicaragua's percentage of poor families would fall by 0.3 percent under DR-CAFTA but by 1.6 percent under the full-liberalization scenario.[19]

Table 4.10. Decomposing the Sectoral Effects of DR-CAFTA

	Nicaragua unilateral liberalization						*U.S. unilateral liberalization*					
	Imports and local sales			*Exports and production*			*Imports and local sales*			*Exports and production*		
Sector	*ΔM*	*ΔS*	*ΔM*	*ΔS*	*ΔPd*	*ΔEx*	*ΔXp*	*ΔPx*	*ΔPd*	*ΔEx*	*ΔXp*	*ΔPx*
Agriculture	19	−0.1	−1.9	5	1.0	−1.7	33	0.2	1.0	0	0.1	1.0
Mining and energy	0	−0.2	−0.2	0	−0.2	−0.2	0	0.0	0.5	−2	−0.2	0.5
Food processing	1	0.5	−1.1	3	13	−0.9	1	−0.1	0.7	3	0.6	0.9
Other manufacturing	1	−0.7	−0.4	1	−0.3	−0.3	0	−0.2	0.3	0	−0.2	0.3
Services	−1	−0.1	−0.1	0	−0.1	−0.1	2	0.1	0.5	−2	0.0	0.5
Total	1	−0.1	−0.6	3	0.3	−0.5	1	0.0	0.6	1	0.1	0.6

Source: Authors' calculations.

ΔM = the percent variation in total import volumes with respect to the initial levels; ΔS = the percent variation in the volumes of domestic sales of domestic output; ΔPd = the percent variation in domestic prices for local sales; ΔEx = the percent variation in the volumes of exports; ΔXp = the percent change of domestic output; ΔPx = the percent change of output prices.

Table 4.11. Decomposing Factor Price Changes Resulting from DR-CAFTA

	Nicaragua unilateral liberalization			U.S. unilateral liberalization		
Factor	ΔP	(ΔP/CPI)	Percentage of DR-CAFTA	ΔP	(ΔP/CPI)	Percentage of DR-CAFTA
Nonfarm segment						
Skilled labor	0.0	1.1	86	0.6	0.2	14
Unskilled labor	0.5	1.5	94	0.6	0.1	6
Capital	0.2	1.2	81	0.8	0.3	19
Skilled/unskilled wage gap		–0.4			0.1	
Farm segment						
Skilled labor	–3.2	–2.2	160	1.3	0.8	–60
Unskilled labor	–5.2	–4.1	106	0.7	0.3	–6
Capital	2.1	3.1	67	2.0	1.5	33
Skilled/unskilled wage gap		2.1			0.6	
Price indexes						
Food Price Index	–2.0			0.6		
Nonfood Price Index	–0.4			0.4		
Consumer Price Index	–1.0			0.5		

Source: Authors' calculations from model results.
Note: In the first column, ΔP represents the percent variation of the price of each factor with respect to the initial levels. In the second column, (ΔC/CPI) is the percent variation of the price deflated by the Consumer Price Index. The third column shows the percent ratio of the real price changes in the unilateral liberalizations with respect to the bilateral DR-CAFTA case.

Complementary Policies and the Dynamic Gains from Trade

The scientific literature on trade and economic growth provides various reasons why trade reforms and trade agreements might have dynamic effects, as opposed to the previously discussed static gains. The term "dynamic effects" is used to refer to the impact of trade policies on factors that can affect the long-term growth rate of developing economies, namely aggregate investment, technological progress, and the quality of public institutions. The following sections review relevant literature and empirical evidence concerning these channels of influence.

Foreign Direct Investment

A specific aspect of DR-CAFTA relevant for investment location decisions was the adoption of rules of origin for the determination of the goods that could benefit from preferences established by the treaty.[20] These rules, which vary across goods (see chapter 3), provided new incentives for the location of investments in the NAFTA region in general and Mexico in particular in those industries where existing levels of regional integration were below the threshold levels determined by the rules.

But the effect of FTAs on the perceived riskiness of investment—the so-called credibility effect—can be even greater than the profitability effect. Although the term *credibility* is somewhat vague, in the present context it encompasses three different things:

1. the FTA's locking-in effect of trade policies
2. the locking-in effect of broader reforms (ranging from regulation and competition policies to property rights, contract enforcement, and macroeconomic stability)
3. the guarantee of access to partners' markets.[21]

Different preferential trade arrangements entail different combinations of the three. For example, European Union (EU) accession is viewed by a majority of observers as having significant effects in all three dimensions, and particularly in the broader area (item 2), because the single market entails a common regulatory framework for all members (leaving aside even broader issues of political unification). In the case of a regional integration arrangement (RIA) such as NAFTA, the main effects in principle should accrue through the secured access channel and the locking in of Mexico's commitment to trade opening initiated in the late 1980s, because the treaty entails fewer automatic repercussions than the EU in the broader policy environment. Many analysts have expressed the view that NAFTA's risk-reducing effect could also be very large, but it is virtually impossible to know with certainty, given that Mexico suffered a major financial crisis during the first years of NAFTA and relatively little time has transpired since then.[22]

To gauge the effect of NAFTA on FDI flows, and disentangle it from that of other factors affecting FDI, we turn to an econometric analysis of the influence of FTA membership on direct investment flows. We then use the empirical estimates to quantify the relative contribution of regional integration, globalization, and other factors to the evolution of FDI in Mexico. This analysis should shed light on what can be expected in DR-CAFTA countries.

The approach is described in detail in Cuevas, Messmacher, and Werner (2002), so here we provide only a summary. The analysis focuses on aggregate FDI flows to 45 countries over the period 1980–2000.[23] This sample includes the same FTAs studied by Frenkel and Wei (1998).[24] The framework assumes implicitly that North–North, North–South, and South–South FTAs are all the same in terms of FDI effects. This is worth noting because NAFTA is the only North–South FTA in the period studied by Cuevas and his coauthors. The empirical model relates FDI to various explanatory variables. The most relevant ones for this report are FTA-related variables, which comprise a dummy indicating FTA membership of the host country (FTAMEM) and another capturing the anticipation of future membership (EXFTAMEM).[25] In addition, we include a measure of the extended market size of the FTAs to which the host country belongs, given by members' total GDP (FTAGDP). These variables should be expected to carry positive signs if FTAs encourage FDI to member countries. Finally, to explore FTAs' potential investment diversion effects, a measure of the degree of other countries' trade integration (INTEGRATION) is used; this is basically a weighted sum of the GDP of all the sample countries participating in FTAs, with the weight of each country's GDP given by the fraction of worldwide GDP covered by its FTA arrangements.[26]

Table 4.12 reports empirical estimates of the determinants of FDI obtained from this specification.[27] Four variants are reported, with different combinations of the FTA-related variables and the institutional variables. On the whole, the explanatory power of the empirical equations is quite satisfactory, given the samples employed. The results concerning the variables capturing FTA membership support the notion that joining a trade block leads to higher FDI inflows. The expectation of joining a free trade area (EXFTAMEM) has a positive effect on foreign investment. The coefficient consistently exceeds one-third, indicating that announcement of an imminent entry into a larger regional market raises FDI in that proportion. The fact that the free trade area dummy has a statistically insignificant coefficient reflects the inclusion in the equations of a more direct measure of integration, extended market size (FTAGDP), which is always significant. The elasticity of FDI with respect to this variable is between one-tenth and one-seventh, implying that if a country joins a free trade area five times as large as the country itself, it should expect FDI inflows to rise by 50 percent or more. In contrast, we find no significant effects of the variable capturing investment diversion (INTEGRATION), perhaps because of the rudimentary nature of this measure.

Table 4.12. Fixed-Effects Regressions of the Log of FDI Against Membership in a Free Trade Area and Other Variables

Variable	*Model (1)*	*Model (2)*	*Model (5)*	*Model (6)*
FTAMEMBR	−0.211		−0.149	
	0.219		*0.249*	
EXPFTA	0.377*	0.437**	0.341*	0.389**
	0.199	*0.188*	*0.202*	*0.185*
LNGLOINT	0.158	0.162	0.256	0.253
	0.141	*0.141*	*0.166*	*0.166*
LNGDPFTA	0.158**	0.110**	0.146*	0.114*
	0.072	*0.053*	*0.079*	*0.059*
WRLDGRWT	−0.072*	−0.070*	−0.100	−0.099
	0.041	*0.041*	*0.062*	*0.062*
US1TBILL	0.006	0.007	0.045	0.045
	0.020	*0.020*	*0.039*	*0.039*
LNFDIWRL	0.747**	0.744**	0.617**	0.614**
	0.116	*0.116*	*0.139*	*0.139*
GDPGRWTH	0.034**	0.033**	0.0617**	0.614**
	0.012	*0.011*	*0.139*	*0.139*
INFLATIO	−1.31E−04	−1.47E−04	−3.45E−05	−4.31E−05
	1.22E−04	*1.21E−04*	*1.22E−04*	*1.21E−04*
CURRACCT	−0.040**	−0.041**	−0.033**	−0.033**
	0.011	*0.011*	*0.013*	*0.013*
RELGNIPH	−2.491**	−2.297**	−5.493**	−5.397**
	1.179	*1.061*	*0.394*	*1.384*
LNEXPORT	0.748**	0.719**	0.638**	0.620**
	0.219	*0.217*	*0.270*	*0.268*
LNGDP	0.170	0.204	−0.036	−0.006
	0.240	*0.237*	*0.300*	*0.296*
GOVSTAB			0.137**	0.139**
			0.048	*0.048*
LAWORDER			0.293**	0.298**
			0.066	*0.065*
BUREAU			0.064	0.061
			0.080	*0.079*
Constant	−14.806**	−14.498**	−11.724**	−11.518**
	1.796	*1.767*	*2.142*	*2.113*
R^2: within total	0.4703	0.4696	0.4937	0.4934
	0.8071	*0.8068*	*0.8250*	*0.8249*
Number of observations	787	787	645	645
Number of countries	45	45	45	45

Source: Cuevas, Messmacher, and Werner 2002; see also Lederman, Maloney, and Servén 2005.
Note: Standard errors appear in italics under the corresponding coefficients.
* Significant at 10 percent.
** Significant at 5 percent.

As for the global variables, world growth carries in all cases a negative coefficient, close to 10 percent significance. This is in agreement with the findings reported by Albuquerque, Loayza, and Servén (2005) on the role of global factors in FDI flows: other things being equal, faster growth in the rest of the world reduces a country's appeal for international investors. In turn, the international interest rate is generally insignificant. Finally, world FDI flows are strongly significant and positive, as should be expected.[28]

Among the local factors, the elasticity of FDI inflows with respect to exports is about 0.7 percent and significant in all models, suggesting that openness is a major attractor of FDI.[29] Host-country growth is also consistently positive and significant, likely reflecting the positive effect of profitability on FDI, and again consistent with Albuquerque. Loayza, and Servén (2005). Inflation has a generally negative effect on FDI, as expected, but the effect is not statistically significant. Likewise, local market size, as measured by GDP, carries a consistently positive but insignificant coefficient. In turn, the negative coefficient on the current account balance in all regressions seems to reflect financing need (likely driven by domestic investment) rather than an unstable macroeconomic environment. Finally, the measure of relative per capita income (RELGNIPH) always carries a significant negative coefficient. If, as already argued, per capita income differentials are proxies for relative wages, the result implies that, all things being equal, countries with lower labor costs attract larger FDI inflows.[30]

The last two columns in table 4.3 add the institutional quality variables. They carry significantly positive signs, as one should expect, with the exception of the quality of the bureaucracy indicator, which fails to be significant. On the whole, the coefficients on the other regressors show only modest changes relative to the previous specifications.

The key result from this analysis is the positive effect of FTAs on FDI inflows to member countries. This agrees with earlier empirical studies of the impact of FTAs based on a variety of methodological frameworks ranging from structural model simulations (for example, Baldwin, François, and Portes 1997) to gravity-based studies of bilateral FDI (Levy-Yeyati, Stein, and Daude 2002). However, it is notable that the estimated impact of FTAs is much less than what proponents of NAFTA, for example, have argued (see the United States Trade Representative's Web site) because FDI to Mexico increased by much more than 40 percent (the effect of NAFTA implied by the aforementioned results). Moreover, the results suggest that it is the interaction of FTA membership with other economic outcomes that really has an impact, rather than an FTA by itself. Finally, the variables representing the quality of public-sector institutions have strong and independent effects on FDI, thus again suggesting that high-quality institutions are key in attracting FDI, not just for improving the allocation of factors of production (labor and capital) for productive uses, as discussed in the previous section on the static gains from trade.

There can be little doubt that FDI increases the host country's capital stock and contributes the technology embodied in that capital. But the evidence on technological spillovers is sparse and pessimistic. López-Córdova (2003) found a *negative* direct impact of FDI on the same industry's total factor productivity (TFP), but positive effects on the productivity of firms that do business with foreign companies. This is consistent with numerous other studies.[31]

The macroeconomic evidence regarding the role of FDI in spurring TFP growth is also pessimistic. First, most studies of the causality between investment and growth indicate that investment follows growth (see, for example, Loayza, Fajnzylber, and Calderón 2005). Carkovic and Levine (2005, abstract) concluded that "the exogenous component of FDI does not exert a robust, independent influence on growth." Thus there seems to be a need to consider the potential role of national innovation and education policies because we cannot assume that fast-paced growth will automatically result from FDI inflows.

Innovation and Education

The most talked-about channel through which international trade can raise long-term productivity growth is through the importation of foreign technologies in the form of capital goods (Keller [2002] and Eaton and Kortum [2002], among others). For the case of Mexico under NAFTA, Schiff and Wang (2003) presented empirical evidence suggesting that capital goods imports from the United States had huge impacts on industrial productivity in Mexico. It is interesting to note that these authors' econometric estimates imply that a marginal increase in the imports of research and development (R&D)–weighted capital goods from the United States are associated with a 5.5–7.5 percent increase in the level of Mexican industrial TFP, whereas capital imports from Europe or other industrial countries had negligible effects. These results are consistent with estimates provided by Keller (2002), who found that the productivity gains resulting from the importation of foreign capital goods declines with geographic distance of the trading partners. This result alone should shed some doubt on the channel of influence because geographic distance should affect the quantity of trade but not necessarily the marginal effects of capital imports. Thus it is likely that the dramatic effects captured by Schiff and Wang for Mexico under NAFTA are due to greater business interactions and learning via contacts rather than through the magic of capital imports.

Recent work in innovation stresses that adopting existing technology is not without cost. Firms and countries need to develop an "absorptive" or "national learning" capacity that, in turn, is hypothesized to be a function of spending on R&D.[32] Though learning is often considered relevant only for basic science dedicated to expanding the knowledge frontier, Cohen and Levinthal (1989), among others, stress learning—knowing where the frontier is and figuring out what adaptations are necessary—as the "second face" of R&D. In fact, Pavitt (2001) argued that investment in pure research is also important for developing countries. First, those most familiar with the frontiers of basic science will best train the applied problem solvers in the private sector. Second, even basic research does not flow easily or without cost across borders, so developing countries cannot simply rely on what is being generated in the advanced countries. Finally, Lederman and Saenz (2005) presented econometric evidence suggesting that innovation outcomes, namely patents per capita, are an important explanation of the levels of development observed around the world.

Low rates of investment in R&D can be the result of low private and social returns to R&D in developing countries, although Lederman and Maloney (2003a) estimated that the economic returns to R&D and to licensing for countries of Costa Rica's level of income are high, at approximately 65 percent. Further statistical analysis by Lederman and Maloney suggested that financial depth, protection of intellectual property rights, ability to mobilize government resources, and quality of research institutions are key determinants of R&D effort across countries. Notably absent as a robust predictor of national R&D effort in the preliminary analyses presented by these authors was the incidence of international trade. That is, after controlling for the aforementioned variables, international trade does not seem to be a crucial factor in determining how much each country invests in R&D.

Low levels of innovation outcomes may also arise from inefficiencies in the way in which existing innovation-related resources are used through the National Innovation System (NIS). One way of estimating the efficiency of an NIS is by examining how R&D investments translate into commercial patents and how the "elasticity" of patents with respect to R&D investment compares to the world average.[33] Chapter 7 includes a review of the efficiency of R&D expenditures in Costa Rica, El Salvador, and numerous other countries. For the case of Latin America and the Caribbean as a whole, econometric exercises described in Bosch, Lederman, and Maloney (2005) showed that the main explanation for the region's inefficiency stems from the lack of collaboration between the private sector and research organizations such as universities.[34] Additional statistical exercises showed that Costa Rica's privileged position compared with the rest of the Latin American and Caribbean countries is the result of higher-quality research institutions and greater collaboration with private firms. El Salvador's negative value can be interpreted as an indication of the extent to which the country underperforms in patenting efficiency relative to the OECD average.

El Salvador seems to be more inefficient than the average of Latin American and Caribbean countries. Additional statistical exercises showed that El Salvador's inefficiency is only partially explained by variables characterizing the NIS, such as quality of research organizations and their collaboration with the private sector. Understanding the shortcomings of El Salvador's NIS remains a topic for future analysis.

A related topic concerns Central America's performance with respect to economic discoveries, namely the introduction of new export products. Hausmann and Rodrik (2003b) provided a theoretical framework suggesting that without public-sector intervention the market will not provide incentives for entrepreneurs to invest in discovering new and potentially profitable businesses. In fact, these authors have argued that countries such as El Salvador can revitalize their economic growth through public-sector subsidies for the introduction of new products (Hausmann and Rodrik 2003a). Furthermore, Klinger and Lederman (2004) did find evidence suggesting the market failures might impede economic discovery, although those authors also found that general export growth is associated with subsequent increases in the probability of experiencing export discoveries (defined as an episode in which a country begins to export products that were not exported at all at the beginning of a 10-year period). Furthermore, Khan (2004) found that the introduction of new products does affect economic growth by stimulating productive investment. For Central America, however, the question is whether policies to stimulate economic discoveries have to be a priority over other policy needs. These issues, including some related to the potential gaps in R&D effort observed in Central America, are addressed in chapter 7 of this volume.

Institutions

Although the role of institutional quality in promoting economic development remains a fertile area for academic research, there is substantial evidence suggesting that law and order and corruption are key factors in the development process (see, among others, Acemoglu et al. 2001, Easterly and Levine 2003, and Rodrik and Subramanian 2003). The economics profession highlighted some time ago the fact that when economic resources are used for rent seeking or directly unproductive activities, the overall level of economic output falls because of the distraction of these potential productive factors. Krueger (1974) was one of the first people to focus on the effects of public policies, including trade policies, through this resource-distraction effect. Others have drawn broader implications for competition policy more generally (Bliss and Di Tella 1997). And there is some evidence that trade policy distortions are positively correlated with empirical (but subjective) measures of corruption (Dutt 2005). This line of reasoning thus suggests that DR-CAFTA itself might have a salutary effect on overall production and potentially national welfare by reducing rent seeking, which would in turn increase potential output. In turn, rent-seeking activities by private agents can themselves breed public corruption and vice-versa.

But does trade really help improve indicators of corruption? Or are there other factors that explain both the incidence of international trade on the domestic economy as well as the incidence of corruption? Table 4.13 presents results from Lederman, Loayza, and Soares (2005) concerning the determinants (of perceptions) of national corruption around the globe during the period 1984–2000. Contrary to previous literature, this evidence suggests that political institutions such as the prevalence and years of experience under democratic governments are stronger and more robust predictors of international measures of corruption than exposure to international trade. Details concerning the two econometric techniques used to derive the two sets of consistent estimates in table 4.13 are present at the bottom of the table. In any case, these results suggest important policy implications, namely that we should not expect international trade to make significant inroads by themselves in the fight against corruption in Central America, at least not in the near future. Rather, governments should encourage proactive policies to improve formal mechanisms of accountability, such as transparency initiatives (publishing budgets, providing time for public comment on regulatory changes, and, of course, protecting the freedom of the press). In the long run, it is likely that democratic governance itself, through the for-

Table 4.13. Determinants of International Corruption: Does Trade Really Matter?

	Ordered probit				*Ordinary least squares*			
Estimation technique	*(1)*	*(2)*	*(3)*	*(4)*	*(5)*	*(6)*	*(7)*	*(8)*
democ	−0.1580	−0.5238	−1.8054	−0.7097	−0.2078	−0.4598	−1.2111	−0.6140
	0.1302	*0.1547*	*0.3149*	*0.2368*	*0.1195*	*0.1227*	*0.2009*	*0.1870*
	0.2250	*0.0010*	*0.0000*	*0.0030*	*0.0820*	*0.0000*	*0.0000*	*0.0010*
presid	1.0367	0.4324	1.2732	1.1194	0.9261	0.3591	0.7589	0.8403
	0.1030	*0.2028*	*0.3340*	*0.2710*	*0.0907*	*0.1679*	*0.2237*	*0.2150*
	0.0000	*0.0330*	*0.0000*	*0.0000*	*0.0000*	*0.0330*	*0.0010*	*0.0000*
reelect	−0.2244	0.0429	−0.3354	−0.3062	−0.2329	0.0385	−0.1668	−0.2676
	0.1375	*0.1810*	*0.2929*	*0.2609*	*0.1254*	*0.1477*	*0.2153*	*0.2149*
	0.1030	*0.8130*	*0.2520*	*0.2410*	*0.0630*	*0.7940*	*0.4390*	*0.2140*
dstab	−0.0340	−0.0423	−0.0410	−0.0453	−0.0272	−0.0307	−0.0234	−0.0284
	0.0024	*0.0032*	*0.0055*	*0.0049*	*0.0019*	*0.0022*	*0.0033*	*0.0035*
	0.0000	*0.0000*	*0.0000*	*0.0000*	*0.0000*	*0.0000*	*0.0000*	*0.0000*
state	−0.0968	0.1525	0.4359	0.1625	−0.1039	0.0828	0.1693	0.0759
	0.0425	*0.0543*	*0.1015*	*0.0768*	*0.0370*	*0.0407*	*0.0618*	*0.0557*
	0.0230	*0.0050*	*0.0000*	*0.0340*	*0.0050*	*0.0420*	*0.0060*	*0.1730*
list	−0.1654	0.0426	−0.0817	0.3171	−0.1553	−0.0018	−0.0501	0.1937
	0.0860	*0.1035*	*0.1733*	*0.1472*	*0.0683*	*0.0689*	*0.0904*	*0.0909*
	0.0550	*0.6810*	*0.6370*	*0.0310*	*0.0230*	*0.9790*	*0.5800*	*0.0330*
control	0.1628	−0.0574	−0.4270	−0.1001	0.1419	−0.0413	−0.3092	−0.0667
	0.0955	*0.1068*	*0.1864*	*0.1429*	*0.0825*	*0.0808*	*0.1112*	*0.1028*
	0.0880	*0.5910*	*0.0220*	*0.4830*	*0.0860*	*0.6090*	*0.0060*	*0.5170*
press	−0.0113	−0.0056	−0.0210	−0.0014	−0.0099	−0.0043	−0.0152	−0.0006
	0.0022	*0.0031*	*0.0061*	*0.0043*	*0.0020*	*0.0024*	*0.0042*	*0.0033*
	0.0000	*0.0690*	*0.0010*	*0.7500*	*0.0000*	*0.0740*	*0.0000*	*0.8500*
govrev			0.0389				0.0239	
			0.0098				*0.0065*	

	(1)	(2)	(3)	(4)	(5)	(6)	(7)	(8)
			0.0000				*0.0000*	
transf			−0.0632				−0.0184	
			0.0221				*0.0110*	
			0.0040				*0.0950*	
open			0.0000				−0.0015	
			0.0030				*0.0019*	
			0.9930				*0.4510*	
lngdp				−0.1826				−0.1940
				0.1412				*0.1056*
				0.1960				*0.0670*
tyr15				−0.1090				−0.0469
				0.0443				0.0304
				0.0140				0.1230
leg_brit		0.2598	0.3293	0.6279		0.1518	0.1735	0.3470
		0.1122	*0.2510*	*0.1672*		*0.0844*	*0.1485*	*0.1216*
		0.0210	*0.1900*	*0.0000*		*0.0730*	*0.2430*	*0.0040*
elf		0.0123	0.0210	0.0109		0.0100	0.0132	0.0103
		0.0021	*0.0040*	*0.0029*		*0.0016*	*0.0024*	*0.0020*
		0.0000	*0.0000*	*0.0000*		*0.0000*	*0.0000*	*0.0000*
Period dummies	Yes	Yes	Yes	Yes	Yes	Yes	Yes	Yes
reg/nature variables	No	Yes	Yes	Yes	No	Yes	Yes	Yes
Number of Observations	1158	1010	490	605	1158	1010	490	605
Pseudo R^2/R^2	0.24	0.33	0.45	0.38	0.57	0.70	0.79	0.74

Source: Lederman, Loayza, and Soares 2005, table 7.

Note: Standard errors followed by *p*-values appear in italics below the coefficients. Dependent variable is ICRG corruption index (0–6, higher values indicate more corruption). Independent variables are (*d* for dummy): democracy *d*, presidential *d*, possibility of reelection *d*, time of democratic stability, indicator of local elections for state governments, government control of legislative *d*, freedom of press index, government revenues (percentage of GDP), transfers from central government to other levels percentage of GDP), openness to trade (imports as percentage of GDP), In of per capita GDP, average schooling in the population above 15 years of age, British legal tradition *d*, index of ethnolinguistic fractionalization, period *d*s, region *d*s (East Asia and Pacific, Eastern Europe and Central Asia, Middle East and North Africa, Southeast Asia, Sub-Saharan Africa, and Latin America and the Caribbean), and nature variables (landlock *d*, area, tropical *d*, longitude, and latitude). Lagged are *govrev, transf, open, lngdp,* and *tyr15.* Regressions include all observations available between 1984 and 1997. Robust standard errors used. Intercept terms for each level of corruption (1–6) are not reported.

mal mechanisms of checks and balances, will become the underpinning of clean governments and more vigorous economies. Nevertheless, certain elements of DR-CAFTA call for public transparency in government procurement and regulatory changes, thus reducing the scope for discretionary normative changes that can breed corruption among the public sectors of Central America. Moreover, DR-CAFTA also mandates that governments implement their own labor and environmental regulations, which also reduces the scope for selective enforcement of laws. Consequently, modern trade agreements such as DR-CAFTA, whose scope goes beyond traditional trade matters, do hold some promise for tackling institutional deficiencies.

Growth Effects of Free Trade Agreements

The previous paragraphs examined literature that provides insights into the potential dynamic effects of trade through intermediate outcomes, such as FDI, innovation, and the quality of public institutions. This section turns our attention to evidence concerning the overall effects of FTAs on the rate of growth of GDP per capita across countries.[35]

In this section we examine whether DR-CAFTA is likely to have an impact on economic growth. Although our empirical results will be indicative, they are not expected to produce precise point estimates of the impact of the FTA on economic growth. Rather the results should provide the average growth impact of FTAs after controlling for a wide variety of country-specific factors. Because countries and institutions differ in myriad ways, both measurable and immeasurable, one would ideally like to have country-specific empirical results that capture the idiosyncratic circumstances of each country. Because of obvious data limitations, and the fact that most countries in the region typically have only one (or no) prior regional free trade agreement, statistical analysis of past experience on a country-by-country basis is not feasible. Consequently, the empirical analysis undertaken is a cross-sectional time-series panel data analysis that uses the experience of 132 countries over a 30-year period. The 30 years of data are divided into six 5-year growth periods and the countries included encompass both industrial and developing countries with 151 country episodes of regional trade agreements. A full description of the data can be found in table 4A.11 in the annex to this chapter.

As a starting point for the empirical analysis, we estimate a fixed-effects panel growth model that includes the number of regional free trade agreements to determine whether they have any power in explaining economic growth. We also add a variety of important economic and political variables to control for external and internal factors that may also influence economic growth to confirm the robustness of the results. Following this, we account for possible selectivity bias (that is, the choice of signing a free trade agreement may be endogenously determined by the state of the economy) by explicitly taking into consideration a country's choice to enter into an FTA.

Fixed-effects Ordinary Least Squares Regressions

We begin with standard panel data analysis using a fixed-effects regression model and five-year growth periods. Our benchmark model is the Solow growth model with measures for both physical and human capital investment. The benchmark estimation model takes the following form:

$$\hat{Y}_t = \sum_{i=1}^{n} a_i CountryDUM_i = \lambda_1 \ln(Y_{t\text{-}1}) + \lambda_3 \ln(K) + \lambda_4 \ln(H) + \mu \qquad \text{(Eq. 4.3)}$$

where $\hat{Y}_t$ is real GDP per capita growth during period t, $CountryDUM_t$ is a country-specific dummy variable, $Y_{t\text{-}1}$ is initial level of real GDP per capita, K is physical capital investment, H is human capital investment, and μ is the error term.

As table 4.14, column 1, indicates, the standard benchmark Solow model generally behaves as expected—conditional convergence in growth rates is found as indicated by the negative and statistically significant coefficient on the initial value of log real GDP per capita, and physical capital investment is found to have a positive and statistically significant impact on growth. Our proxy for human capital investment (log of secondary school enrollment as a percentage of total population of that age group that corresponds to secondary school age), however, is negative and not statistically significant. Despite using alternative measures of human capital investment, such as primary and tertiary school enrollment rates as proxies for human capital investment, measures of human capital investment did not become significant. The results would indicate that investment in education, as least for the five-year growth periods, does not appear to have a significant impact on growth. However, these results may be caused by the relatively short period of growth (five-year periods) or the lack of a good proxy for human capital investment.

Table 4.14. Fixed-Effects Panel Regressions, 1970–2000, Five-Year Averages

	(1)	*(2)*	*(3)*	*(4)*	*(5)*	*(6)*	*(7)*
Log initial real GDP per capita ($)	–0.017	–0.021	–0.024	–0.035	–0.032	–0.033	–0.034
	(–3.27)	(–3.89)	(–4.37)	(–6.28)	(–5.02)	(–5.10)	(–5.14)
Log secondary school enrollment (%)	–0.004	–0.009	–0.006	–0.003	–0.007	–0.007	–0.007
	(–1.26)	(–2.52)	(–1.64)	(–0.76)	(–1.61)	(–1.48)	(–1.51)
Log investment share of GDP (%)	0.016	0.017	0.015	0.014	0.013	0.013	0.013
	(3.90)	(4.15)	(3.68)	(3.24)	(2.58)	(2.63)	(2.68)
Number of regional FTAs		0.008	0.007	0.008	0.007	0.007	0.007
		(3.59)	(3.23)	(3.51)	(3.15)	(2.90)	(2.83)
World GDP growth (%)			0.011	0.010	0.007	0.007	0.007
			(5.37)	(5.36)	(3.69)	(3.45)	(3.47)
Trade share of GDP (%)			0.0004	0.0003	0.0002	0.0002	0.0002
			(5.13)	(3.19)	(2.20)	(2.08)	(2.07)
Black market premium (%)				–0.000006	–0.000004	–0.000004	–0.000004
				(–2.22)	(–1.70)	(–1.67)	(–1.66)
Government share of consumption (%)				–0.0002	–0.0001	–0.0001	–0.0001
				(–0.81)	(–0.43)	(–0.50)	(–0.52)
Fiscal balance as share of GDP (%)					0.001	0.001	0.001
					(3.46)	(3.57)	(3.59)
Choice to liberalize						0.008	0.008
						(1.09)	(1.11)
Freedom							0.002
							(0.66)
Constant	0.134	0.171	0.145	0.241	0.255	0.260	0.258
	(3.06)	(3.83)	(3.16)	(5.04)	(4.61)	(4.70)	(4.66)
Observations	743	743	743	655	557	557	556
R^2 within	0.058	0.076	0.144	0.202	0.206	0.208	0.209
R^2 between	0.002	0.002	0.049	0.008	0.015	0.016	0.019
F-statistic	13.13	13.25	17.99	16.01	12.22	11.12	10.14

Source: Authors' calculations.

Note: The *t*-statistics are in parentheses. Dependent variable: current per capita real GDP growth.

Regional Trade Agreements

Regression 2 in table 4.14 (column 2) includes a measure for the number of regional free trade agreements in force. To account for the possibility that regional FTAs may be signed in the middle of a five-year growth period, the value of the variable is the portion of the period during which it is in force. For example, if a country signs its first regional FTA in 1971, then the value of the variable is zero prior to 1970, is equal to 0.8 during the five-year growth period between 1970 and 1975, and is equal to 1 thereafter (or until another regional FTA is signed). As regression 2 indicates, regional FTAs appear to have a positive and significant effect on growth. The coefficient on the variable is 0.008, which suggests that a regional free trade agreement would add about 0.8 percentage points to annual growth, all else held constant.[36]

Regressions 3 to 7 add assorted control variables to the benchmark growth model with regional FTA effects. After including these control variables stepwise into the benchmark model with the regional trade agreements variable, we find that the regional trade agreement variable maintains its statistical significance but the size of its impact on growth falls marginally (from 0.8 percentage point impact on annual growth to 0.7 percentage point). As far as the other variables are concerned, world real GDP growth has significant and positive spillover effects on country growth (in the range of 0.7 percent to 1.1 percent); trade as a share of country GDP also has a positive and significant impact in country growth, but is much smaller than the spillover impact of world income growth (in the range of 0.04 to 0.02 percent); as expected, the black market premium has a negative and significant impact on growth, although the impact is rather small (only a –0.0004 to –0.0006 percent impact) and the significance level is lower (95–85 percent range); government consumption as a share of total consumption is negative as expected, but is not statistically significant; the fiscal balance as a share of GDP is positive, as expected, and is highly significant, suggesting that higher fiscal balances (either resulting from greater revenues that occur during an economic expansion, or fiscal restraint from greater tax collections or expenditure cuts) are associated with greater economic growth. A 1 percent increase in the fiscal balance as a share of GDP is associated with about a 0.1 percent increase in annual growth. Finally, the political and civic freedom index is positively related to economic growth, but is not statistically significant.

The choice to liberalize or, in other words, the period in which a regional FTA is implemented is associated with additional higher real GDP growth—

about the same effect as that of the number liberalizations (0.8 percent of annual growth)—but is not statistically significant partly because of multicollinearity (by definition, an increase in the number of liberalizations is always associated with the choice to liberalize). Taken together, the longer-term effect of the number of regional trade agreements variable and the shorter-term initial impact indicate that the near-term effects may be about twice as high as the longer-term impacts on growth.

Additional exercises not reported here used 10-year growth periods in the time-series dimension rather than the 5-year growth periods. This reduces the number of observations in the time-series dimension by nearly one-half, but the effect of the regional trade agreement variable is only slightly smaller (about 0.6 percent compared with 0.7 percent) and is still statistically significant at the 95 percent level or higher when including all the control variables. The signs of the control variables are broadly similar to the five-year regressions, but, in general, the significance of the control variables drops below the 90 percent level when including the fiscal balance as a share of GDP in the regression equation. The fiscal balance as a share of GDP is significant at the 99 percent level and appears to dominate the impact of the other control variables that affect growth in the shorter time horizon shown in table 4.14. Over a longer period of time, a more prudent fiscal policy may be a much stronger proxy for policies that affect economic growth (outside of investment and trade policies) than any of the other control variables by themselves. Finally, it is worth noting that further econometric exercises that rely on the Arellano and Bond (1991) estimator indicate that the results concerning the average growth effect of FTAs were unaffected by the change in methodology, which suggests that results discussed thus far are quite robust.

Selectivity Bias in the Choice to Liberalize

In this section we take into consideration the possibility that regional trade agreements might be chosen during periods of above-normal growth and, as a consequence, may be the result rather than the cause of higher growth. A problem with the empirical analyses above—as well as that used in numerous other studies on trade and economic growth—is that they rest on the implicit assumption that the choice to enter into a free trade agreement is exogenous and does not depend on the state of the economy or other factors that, in turn, may be related to growth. But, this assumption may be too restrictive. Indeed, during periods of economic expansion, import-competing interests may be less apt to lobby *against* freer trade if they see the overall economic pie growing. Labor in the import sectors may find employment and wages rising and may be less likely to actively oppose freer trade—even though their gains may not be as large as other sectors. In the literature on the political economy of protectionism it has been observed that protectionist pressures are the highest during periods of economic contractions; the corollary to this is that protectionist pressures are the lowest during periods of expansion (see, for example, Lederman 2005 and literature cited therein).

In other words, the choice to enter into an FTA may be endogenously determined by the economy and prospects for future growth. It may simply be the case that FTAs are signed during periods of higher-than-average economic growth and are not the cause of that growth. Those countries with prior economic reforms, international financial support, and better prospects for economic growth may be the most likely to pursue free trade negotiations because of the support of exporters and the lack of strong protectionist pressures from import-competing interests. In those countries experiencing weaker economic growth, contraction, and/or diminished prospects, internal political dynamics and protectionism may be much more difficult to overcome.

If the decision to enter into a free trade agreement is endogenous, how will the correction for this potential endogeneity affect the estimated impact of regional FTAs on economic growth? To address this question a simple framework for analyzing growth and policy choice is presented and then the econometric techniques used to estimate such a model are discussed.

Specification of the Selectivity Model

Equations (4.4) through (4.6) describe the benchmark growth model with the endogenous choice of entering into an FTA. The model assesses whether output growth differs significantly between those periods during which an FTA is signed. It departs from the previous analysis in that the choice to liberalize is modeled as endogenous and selectivity bias is explicitly addressed. The model is specified as

$$\hat{Y}_{it} = \alpha Y_{it\text{-}1} + \beta D_{it} + \gamma X_{it} + \delta n_i + \varepsilon_{it} \qquad \text{(Eq. 4.4)}$$

$$d_{is} = aZ_{is} + cn_i + \eta_{is} \qquad \text{(Eq. 4.5)}$$

$$D_i = 1 \text{ if } d_i > 0;\ D_i = 0 \text{ if } d_{is} < 0. \qquad \text{(Eq. 4.6)}$$

In equation (4.4), real GDP growth in each period is a function of initial GDP, a dummy variable indicating whether country i signed an FTA during the period, D_{it}, a vector of internal and external country environmental characteristics, X_{it}, such as world growth, fiscal balance, and black market premium, a vector of country-specific dummy variables n_i (fixed effects) to account for country-unique trend growth differences, and an error term that includes unobservable country-specific growth factors (more discussion on this below) and random disturbances. Equations (4.5) and (4.6) specify the policy choice decision: a country signs a particular regional free trade agreement in period s if the latent variable d_{is} rises above zero. This policy choice equation is based on the notion that the choice to enter into a regional free trade agreement depends on the net benefit a country expects to receive from freer trade and the lobbying efforts of domestic interest groups. The latent variable is a function of a vector of characteristics, Z_{is}, which include lagged variables such as real GDP per capita growth, initial level of GDP per capita, world GDP growth per capita, trade share of GDP, political freedom index, dummy variables to account for unspecified "free trade trends" in the 1980s and 1990s, and a vector of country-specific dummy variables (fixed effects).

Table 4.15 shows the results of the model that explicitly takes into consideration the potential selectivity bias in the choice of trade liberalization. Maximum likelihood and two-step estimation techniques are shown, but the results are broadly similar. In short, selectivity bias does not appear to be a significant problem since the estimated hazard variable (selectivity bias) in both equations ($\hat{H}$) is not statistically significant. Despite prior years of slower-than-normal growth and higher-than-normal world growth being a good predictor of the signing of a regional free trade agreement, in neither estimation procedure (the maximum likelihood or the two-step procedure) are the estimated coefficients, nor the significance of the regional trade agreements variables, diminished substantially. Consequently, the evidence suggests that endogeneity in the choice of liberalization does not appear to be a significant problem and does not change the finding that regional free trade agreements tend to boost economic growth.

Potential Impact on the Poor

Having established that the effect of an FTA on annual per capita growth is an increase in the per capita growth rates of 0.6 percentage points a year, the repercussions on poverty rates can be roughly estimated using elasticities of

Table 4.15. Treatment Effects Model, 1970–2000, Five-Year Averages[a]

	Maximum likelihood estimates	*Two-step estimates*
Current per capita real GDP growth		
Log Initial real GDP per capita ($)	−0.039 (−2.90)	−0.039 (−3.88)
Log secondary school enrollment (%)	−0.0003 (−0.05)	−0.0004 (−0.06)
Log investment share of GDP (%)	0.007 (0.46)	0.007 (1.02)
World GDP growth (%)	0.0063 (2.57)	0.006 (2.60)
Trade share of GDP (%)	0.00003 (0.19)	0.00003 (0.19)
Black market premium (%)	−0.00001 (−0.57)	−0.00001 (−0.94)
Government share of consumption (%)	0.0003 (0.91)	0.0003 (0.84)
Fiscal balance as share of GDP (%)	0.001263 (2.62)	0.001 (2.28)
Choice to liberalize	0.0103 (1.39)	0.011 (1.45)
Number of regional FTAs	0.006 (2.48)	0.006 (2.42)
Choice to liberalize		
Lagged per capita real GDP growth	−9.701 (−1.7)	−9.569 (−2.11)
Two-period lagged per capita real GDP growth	−14.511 −2.11)	−14.322 (−2.77)
Lagged log level of real GDP per capita	2.42493 (2.18)	2.420 (3.01)
Lagged world real GDP growth per capita	0.427 (2.28)	0.434 (2.61)
Lagged trade share of GDP	−0.017 (−1.39)	−0.017 (−1.62)
Lagged freedom index	0.455 (1.46)	0.454 (1.59)
Dummy for 1980	−0.821 (−2.25)	−0.818 (−2.48)
Dummy for 1990	−0.047 (−0.11)	−0.042 (−0.13)
Hazard (*H*)	−0.001 (−0.20)	−0.002 (−0.32)
Number of observations	297	297
Wald chi-square	...	325.59
Log pseudo-likelihood	552.11	...

Source: Authors' calculations.

.. Negligible.

Note: The *z*-statistics are in parentheses.

poverty to changes in economic growth. Such elasticities allow for the calculation of changes in poverty rates that result from economic growth, holding other factors constant (including income distribution), and are available for most Central American countries from recent World Bank studies. Table 4.16 presents the estimated changes in poverty and extreme poverty rates five years after implementation of DR-CAFTA, assuming that the estimated growth effect materializes for all five countries. Results suggest that overall poverty reductions would vary by country, ranging from 0.6 percentage points in Costa Rica to 1.6 points in Guatemala. The corresponding range

Table 4.16. Five-Year Poverty Reduction Effects of DR-CAFTA for Central American Countries

	Headcount poverty rate			*Extreme poverty rate*		
	2005	*2010*	*Difference*	*2005*	*2010*	*Difference*
Costa Rica	20.4	19.8	−0.6	6.0	5.7	−0.3
El Salvador	36.4	35.0	−1.4	14.7	14.1	−0.6
Guatemala	55.9	54.3	−1.6	15.5	14.4	−1.1
Honduras	63.1	61.9	−1.2	45.7	44.4	−1.3
Nicaragua	45.6	44.7	−0.9	14.9	14.2	−0.7

Source: Elasticities for Costa Rica are derived using results from López and Servén (2005).
Note: Poverty rates for 2005 are World Bank estimates based on the most recent official data. The 2010 estimates assume an annual per capita growth rate of 0.6 percent and poverty elasticities taken from the most recent World Bank Poverty Assessment studies.

for extreme poverty rates goes from 0.3 percentage points in Costa Rica to 1.3 points in Honduras. In five years, this translates into an absolute reduction in the total number of poor people of about 530,000 adding the five countries involved, and nearly 380,000 for those people living in extreme poverty.

Summary

This chapter has reviewed various analyses undertaken to assess the potential impacts of DR-CAFTA on the developing countries of Central America. It began by highlighting that standard theoretical treatments of the gains from trade indicate the dependence of such gains on an economy's capacity to change its productive structure. Otherwise, the gains are limited to the gains on the consumption side, which allow domestic agents to consume a bundle of goods that is larger in economic value than the one without trade reforms. The gains from productive transformation can be substantially higher than the gains from enhanced consumption alone. These conclusions refer to static analyses of the gains from trade.

Regarding empirical analyses of the potential static gains from trade, the evidence reviewed in the chapter highlighted two key complementary factors, namely the infrastructure that affects international transport costs and the regulatory environment. There is strong evidence suggesting that exports to the U.S. market will benefit from the shift from unilateral preferences (CBI) to a free trade agreement, but perhaps more important, international transport costs (freight, insurance) have a robust and large effect on the value of exports, regardless of the type of preferential treatment. Also, the evidence reviewed suggested that the gains from trade in terms of increases in GDP per capita are intermediated by the regulatory environment that determines how quickly firms and workers can change their sectors of operation and employment. Thus a complementary agenda to enhance the impact of DR-CAFTA should consider these factors, even when concerned about the static gains from trade.

Partial equilibrium analyses of the potential sectoral effects of DR-CAFTA suggested that the main short-term winners of the agreement would be concentrated in the apparel industries, abstracting from any impact of the elimination of world quotas in this sector. Nevertheless, these analyses suffer from an inability to capture the potential effects on sectors that are relatively small, because the effects predicted by these models are proportional to the initial level of exports. In addition, they have difficulty dealing with technical issues such as the restrictiveness of rules of origin. Furthermore, such partial equilibrium models do not consider the effects of the trade reforms in the economy as a whole because they do not consider intersector interactions through factor and goods markets.

This chapter also presented the simulation results from a so-called computable general equilibrium model for Nicaragua linked to household data. The simulation related the macroeconomic results of the model to changes in the returns to unskilled labor to poverty outcomes. Indeed, under a restrictive set of conditions (for example, segmented labor markets, no dynamic effects, effective transmission of tariff reductions to relative producer prices, and no further unilateral trade reforms). DR-CAFTA could have an overall modest positive effect on Nicaragua's welfare (income per capita) but with a very small (positive) effect on poverty, and with the potential for poor rural households to be negatively affected. Thus, as with the other static analyses, these results further support the contention that DR-CAFTA might not be enough to reduce poverty, although these results need to be interpreted with caution because they are obviously limited by key theoretical and empirical assumptions.

The rest of the chapter was dedicated to understanding the potential dynamic gains from DR-CAFTA. The first part covered evidence concerning the potential effect of free trade agreements —and trade more generally— on foreign investment, corruption, and innovation. Existing evidence suggests that FDI responds to FTAs indirectly by enhancing the effect of exports and GDP on FDI. The evidence also indicates that trade might not have a direct effect on corruption, and thus we should not expect large dynamic gains from DR-CAFTA to come from the impact of international trade on the quality of public institutions. The process of democratic consolidation seems much more important, although certain aspects of DR-CAFTA that put pressure on governments to improve the enforcement of their own laws could also be helpful. The existing literature on innovation and economic discovery suggests a mixed picture. On one hand, innovation efforts might not be related to the incidence of international trade. On the other hand, the probability of observing episodes of "economic discovery" seems to be positively correlated with overall export growth.

This chapter also reviewed the econometric challenges and results by investigating the empirical link between FTAs and subsequent economic growth in a large sample of countries. The main result is that the growth rate of GDP per capita is positively associated with a country's participation in FTAs. This finding is robust to the inclusion of assorted control variables and econometric methods. Unlike the evidence presented in previous work, the new evidence reviewed does not find that the increase in GDP growth of about 0.6 percent a year was sensitive to the type of partner in the FTA. In contrast, a previous empirical study using a different set of control variables and specifications of the empirical models did find that access to larger markets has a larger effect on growth than do FTAs with smaller partners. In any case, there seems to be substantial evidence that FTAs might help accelerate the pace of economic development, at least for the first five years subsequent to implementation. In the long run, the steady-state level of income will be determined by a plethora of other factors and, as economies get richer, their pace of growth will tend to decline. Consequently, there does not seem to be a silver bullet, and DR-CAFTA is unlikely to be the solution to all development challenges faced by Central America.

The evidence reviewed should make clear that ex ante analyses of the potential effects of DR-CAFTA (and trade reforms in general) remain an art rather than a science because the results are highly sensitive to theoretical assumptions and empirical methods. Chapters 5, 6, and 7 of this volume provide more guidance regarding the complementary agenda, which includes policies that can help DR-CAFTA beneficiaries overcome the challenges posed by the adjustment process as well as the long-term challenge of economic development in the context of DR-CAFTA.

Technical Annex: Gains from Trade for Small Economies and the Underlying Assumptions

The purpose of this annex is to summarize a textbook model of the gains from trade by highlighting the role of the gains resulting from consumption and the gains resulting from the productive transformation of a small open economy. The starting point is the standard simplifying assumption, whereby we assume that the economy produces two broad categories of products, 1 and 2. Furthermore, each good is produced with labor and sector-specific technology, which determines the amount of labor required to produce a unit of each good. Thus, equations (4A.1) and (4A.2) below represent the production functions of each good, where a_1 and a_2 represent the output per unit of labor for each sector, and L_1 and L_2 represent the number of workers dedicated to producing each good.

$$Q_1 = a_1 \bullet L_1 \qquad \text{(Eq. 4A.1)}$$

$$Q_2 = a_2 \bullet L_2 \qquad \text{(Eq. 4A.2)}$$

Consequently, the economy's total labor force (L) is simply the sum of workers in sectors 1 and 2, as expressed in equation (4A.3). This assumption also implies that the labor participation rate does not change, or that the economy maintains a constant level of employment equal to L. As argued in this chapter and subsequently in chapter 5, government policies designed to help the process of adjustment can be instrumental in maintaining a given level of total employment as relative prices change because of trade policies (DR-CAFTA).

$$L = L_1 + L_2 \qquad \text{(Eq. 4A.3)}$$

Hence the economy's production frontier, which represents the quantities of both goods that it can produce when all labor (L) is employed in production, can be expressed as the quantity of good 1 (Q1) that can be obtained if all labor is employed in that industry and the quantity of good 2 (Q2) that can be produced if all labor were in this sector. In other words, the production frontier for the economy in this simple model is the line joining both of these maximum production possibilities. This production frontier is formally expressed in equation (4A.4):

$$Q_1 = a_1 \bullet L - \left(\frac{a_1}{a_2}\right) \bullet Q_2 \qquad \text{(Eq. 4A.4)}$$

In this framework, the composition of production depends on available technologies in this economy compared to the technologies of production in the rest of world (or in the economy's trading partners). Here we assume that the economy under consideration can produce good 1 relatively more efficiently than good 2 when compared with its trading partners:

$$\frac{a_1}{a_2} > \frac{a_1^*}{a_2^*}. \qquad \text{(Eq. 4A.5)}$$

Thus, we assume that this economy has a comparative advantage in the production of good 1. Note that it can have lower labor productivities in both sectors, but it would still have a comparative advantage.

Figure 4A.1 illustrates the economy's production frontier as the downward-sloping line that goes from point $a_1 \bullet L$ on the vertical axis to point A in the horizontal axis. As mentioned, point $a_1 \bullet L$ is the maximum quantity of good 1 that can be produced if all labor were employed in that sector, whereas point A is equal to $a_2 \bullet L$. The slope of this line is equal to the negative ratio of a_1 over a_2, as shown in equation (4A.4) above.

Now assume that the initial structure of production is represented by some point along the production frontier. In this case, the value of this pro-

Figure 4A.1. Gains from Trade, from A to C

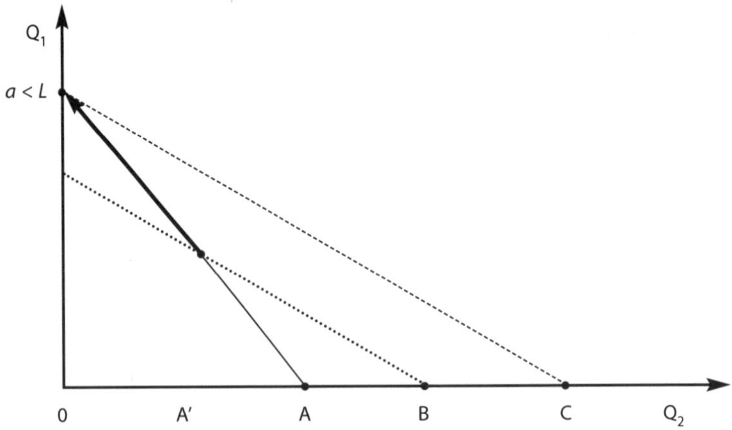

Source: Authors' calculations; see text for explanations.

duction mix based on the economy's trading partners' relative efficiencies is given by the consumption frontier portrayed by the dotted line that goes through the production point and extends down to point B on the horizontal axis. In terms of the quantity of good 2 that the economy can consume, the gains from trade without changes in the structure of production are given by the distance between points A and B in figure 4A.1. That is, with free trade, consumers in this economy can consume larger quantities of good 2 than would be possible without free trade because in autarky consumption must lie on the production frontier.

The gains from trade become larger if the economy is able to change its production structure. In the graph, this entails a movement of the production point from the previous point to the point on the vertical axis where all of the economy's labor is dedicated to production in sector 1. In turn, the consumption frontier shifts outward from point B to point C on the horizontal axis. Consequently, the gains from trade depend on the ability of the economy to change its production structure even if the so-called dynamic gains from trade are not considered. This report argues that the capacity of the economy to be transformed will depend on key public policies and thus the gains from trade are not automatic.

Annex Tables

Tables 4A.1 through 4A.11 are on the following pages.

Table 4A.1. Costa Rica: Estimated Effects of U.S. Tariff Elimination in Partial Equilibrium

HS code and product description		Actual exports 2001 ($000)	DR-CAFTA potential gain ($000)	Change (%)
	Total	731,448	197,550	27
61	Articles of apparel and clothing accessories, knitted or crocheted	396,414	139,893	35
62	Articles of apparel and clothing accessories, not knitted or crocheted	293,864	52,198	18
02	Meat and edible meat offal	26,176	2,446	9
42	Articles of leather; saddlery/harness; travel goods	3,529	1,276	36
64	Footwear, gaiters, and the like; parts of such articles	1,730	708	41
56	Wadding, felt and nonwoven; yarns; twine, cordage	4,045	371	9
58	Special woven fabric; tufted textile fabric; lace; tapestries	1,840	177	10
55	Manmade staple fibers	1,175	159	14
54	Manmade filaments	568	138	24
16	Preparation of meat, fish or crustaceans, mollusks, etc.	379	70	19
59	Impregnated, coated, cover/laminated textile fabric	517	50	10
17	Sugars and sugar confectionery	515	20	4
21	Miscellaneous edible preparations	428	15	4
94	Furniture; bedding, mattress, mattress support, cushion	98	8	8
65	Headgear and parts thereof	56	7	12
63	Other made-up textile articles; sets; worn clothing	32	6	20
52	Cotton	38	5	13
57	Carpets and other textile floor coverings	9	2	17
18	Cocoa and cocoa preparations	29	1	2
51	Wool, fine/coarse animal hair, horsehair yarn	2	1	35
19	Preparation of cereal, flour, starch/milk; pastry	4	0	2

Sources: Estimations using SMART, exports from UNCOMTRADE, tariffs from TRAINS, adjusted by utilization rates of CBI's preferential tariffs.

Note: DR-CAFTA is estimated as a unilateral tariff elimination by the United States to Central American countries. HS = Harmonization System.

Table 4A.2. El Salvador: Estimated Effects of U.S. Tariff Elimination in Partial Equilibrium

HS code and product description		*Actual exports 2001 ($000)*	*DR-CAFTA potential gain ($000)*	*Change (%)*
	Total	1,664,350	355,512	21
61	Articles of apparel and clothing accessories, total	1,209,455	181,827	15
62	Articles of apparel and clothing accessories, total	408,666	160,667	39
63	Other made-up textile articles set total	22,246	5,716	26
64	Footwear, gaiters and the like par total	7,698	2,988	39
42	Articles of leather; saddlery/harness total	4,772	2,023	42
52	Cotton total	7,580	1,319	17
60	Knitted or crocheted fabrics total	1,309	683	52
54	Manmade filaments total	626	180	29
46	Manufactures of straw, esparto/other total	1,037	51	5
65	Headgear and parts thereof total	195	23	12
21	Miscellaneous edible preparations total	469	17	4
55	Manmade staple fibers. total	18	7	38
56	Wadding, felt and nonwoven; yarns; tw total	70	5	7
17	Sugars and sugar confectionery total	88	3	4
19	Preparation of cereal, flour, starch/milk total	89	1	2
94	Furniture; bedding, mattress, mattress support total	13	1	8
18	Cocoa and cocoa preparations total	15	1	4
58	Special woven fabrics; tufted textile fabrics total	4	0	11
59	Impregnated, coated, cover/laminate total	1	0	8
53	Other vegetable textile fibers; pap total	1	0	12

Source: Estimations using SMART with trade data from UNCOMTRADE and tariffs from TRAINS.

Note: DR-CAFTA is estimated as a unilateral tariff elimination by the United States to Central American countries. HS = Harmonization System.

Table 4A.3. Guatemala: Estimated Effects of U.S. Tariff Elimination in Partial Equilibrium

	HS code and product description	*Actual exports 2001 ($000)*	*DR-CAFTA potential gain ($000)*	*Change (%)*
	Total	1,652,343	777,969	47
61	Articles of apparel and clothing accessories, knitted	880,543	514,248	58
62	Articles of apparel and clothing accessories, not knitted	743,844	255,137	34
24	Tobacco, manufactured tobacco substitutes	8,185	4,673	57
63	Other textile articles; sets; worn clothing	5,223	1,322	25
64	Footwear, gaiters and the like	2,954	1,241	42
42	Articles of leather; saddlery/harness	863	282	33
52	Cotton	1,063	232	22
65	Headgear and parts thereof	1,599	188	12
55	Manmade staple fibers	540	170	31
54	Manmade filaments	470	162	34
21	Miscellaneous edible preparations	3,120	110	4
17	Sugars and sugar confectionery	2,387	87	4
56	Wadding, felt and nonwoven; yarns; twine	1,005	74	7
58	Special woven fabrics; ace; tapestry	116	22	19
46	Manufactures of straw, esparto/other plaiting materials	192	9	5
18	Cocoa and cocoa preparations	164	5	3
94	Furniture; bedding, mattress, mattress support	37	3	8
51	Wool, fine/coarse animal hair, horsehair yarn	8	2	21
57	Carpets and other textile floor coverings	13	1	5
59	Impregnated, coated, cover/laminated textile	6	1	10
39	Plastics and articles thereof	6	0	3
19	Preparation of cereal, flour, starch/milk; pastry	5	0	2

Source: Estimations using SMART with trade data from UNCOMTRADE and tariffs from TRAINS.
Note: DR-CAFTA is estimated as a unilateral tariff elimination by the United States to Central American countries. HS = Harmonization System.

Table 4A.4. Honduras: Estimated Effects of U.S. Tariff Elimination in Partial Equilibrium

HS code and product description		*Actual exports 2001 ($000)*	*DR-CAFTA potential gain ($000)*	*Change (%)*
	Total	2,235,949	559,178	25
61	Articles of apparel and clothing accessories, knitted or crocheted	1,757,745	431,312	25
62	Articles of apparel and clothing accessories, not knitted/crocheted	459,781	121,411	26
24	Tobacco and manufactured tobacco substitutes	11,163	5,699	51
63	Other made-up textile articles; sets; worn clothing	1,755	369	21
02	Meat and edible meat offal	1,285	120	9
17	Sugars and sugar confectionery	3,012	108	4
65	Headgear and parts thereof	563	66	12
56	Wadding, felt and nonwoven; yarns; twine, cordage	297	30	10
54	Manmade filaments	84	23	27
55	Manmade staple fibers	58	18	32
64	Footwear, gaiters and the like; parts of such articles	8	8	96
42	Articles of leather; saddlery/harness; travel goods	18	6	35
58	Special woven fab; tufted tex fab; lace tapestry	38	3	8;
52	Cotton	7	2	29
46	Manufactures of straw, esparto/other plaiting materials	35	2	5r
21	Miscellaneous edible preparations.	44	2	4
19	Prep. of cereal, flour, starch/milk; pastry	56	1	2

Source: Estimations using SMART with trade data from UNCOMTRADE and tariffs from TRAINS

Note: DR-CAFTA is estimated as a unilateral tariff elimination by the United States to Central American countries.. HS Harmonization System.

Table 4A.5. Nicaragua: Estimated Effects of U.S. Tariff Elimination in Partial Equilibrium

HS code and product description		*Actual exports 2001 ($000)*	*DR-CAFTA potential gain ($000)*	*Change (%)*
	Total	384,027	153,653	40
62	Articles of apparel and clothing accessories, not knitted/crocheted	248,174	90,035	36
61	Articles of apparel and clothing accessories, knitted or crocheted	96,647	57,182	59
12	Oil seed, oleaginous fruits; miscellaneous grain, seed, fruits	5,515	3,031	55
02	Meat and edible meat offal	31,195	2,913	9
24	Tobacco and manufactured tobacco substitutes	666	373	56
63	Other made-up textile articles; sets; worn clothing	208	45	22
56	Wadding, felt and nonwoven; yarns; twine, cordage	438	37	9
04	Dairy products; birds' eggs; natural honey; edible products	748	14	2
21	Miscellaneous edible preparations	393	14	4
64	Footwear, gaiters and the like; parts of such articles	6	4	63
42	Articles of leather; saddlery/harness; travel goods	16	4	23
17	Sugars and sugar confectionery	16	1	4
46	Manufactures of straw, esparto/other plaiting materials	3	0	5
58	Special woven fabric; tufted textile fabric; lace; tapestries	2	0	7

Source: Estimations using SMART with trade data from UNCOMTRADE and tariffs from TRAINS.
Note: DR-CAFTA is estimated as a unilateral tariff elimination by the United States to Central American countries. HS = Harmonization System.

Table 4A.6. Costa Rica: Estimated Effects of Tariff Elimination on U.S. Imports in Partial Equilibrium

HS code and product description		*Imports 2004 ($000)*	*Change in imports ($000)*	*Change (%)*
	Total	1,124,249	248,154	22
61	Articles of apparel and clothing accessories, knitted	78,565	39,624	50
39	Plastics and articles thereof	99,039	23,536	24
87	Vehicles	50,392	19,980	40
85	Electrical machinery and parts	82,093	15,800	19
27	Mineral fuels, oils	118,157	13,634	12
94	Furniture, bedding, mattress, mat support	19,947	12,658	63
62	Art. of apparel and clothing accessories, not knitted	17,758	10,629	60
41	Raw hides and skins and leather	21,615	8,119	38
84	Boilers machinery and mechanical appliance	45,733	7,311	16
40	Rubber and articles thereof	19,012	6,779	36
48	Paper and paperboard, articles of paper pulp	40,549	6,537	16
10	Cereals	89,877	6,321	7
95	Toys, game and sports parts	10,046	5,610	56
38	Miscellaneous chemical products	41,466	5,005	12
33	Essential oils, resins, cosmetics and toiletries	18,882	4,501	24
64	Footwear, gaiters and the like	5,580	3,916	70
21	Miscellaneous edible preparations	14,902	3,260	22
58	Special women fabric, ace, tapestry	25,715	3,180	12
73	Articles of iron or steel	18,605	3,147	17
71	Pearls, precious stones, and metals	25,080	2,977	12
20	Preparations of vegetables, fruit, nuts, or other	13,119	2,588	20
52	Cotton	20,875	2,587	12
19	Preparation of cereal, flour, milk, or pastry	9,842	2,246	23
54	Manmade filaments	17,267	2,148	12
83	Miscellaneous articles of base metal	11,030	2,081	19
96	Miscellaneous manufactures articles	5,250	1,887	36
30	Pharmaceutical products	25,150	1,813	7
60	Knitted or crocheted fabrics	5,573	1,724	31
34	Soap, organic surface agents, washing	6,314	1,667	26
42	Articles of leather, saddlery/harness	2,421	1,535	63
08	Edible fruit and nuts: peel of citrus fruit	7,673	1,485	19
35	Albuminoidal substances, modified starches, glues	9,620	1,443	15
	Other exports	147,103	22,425	15

Source: Estimations using SMART, exports from UNCOMTRADE, tariffs from TRAINS.
Note: DR-CAFTA effect estimated as a unilateral tariff elimination (immediate drop to zero of all tariffs) by Costa Rica to U.S. imports. HS = Harmonization System.

Table 4A.7. El Salvador: Estimated Effects of Tariff Elimination on U.S. Imports in Partial Equilibrium

HS code and product description		*Imports 2004 ($000)*	*Change in imports ($000)*	*Change (%)*
	Total	1,485,314	177,416	12
87	Vehicles	1414,227	36,141	26
27	Mineral fuels, oils	178,037	14,140	8
94	Furniture, bedding, mattress, mat support	16,630	12,054	72
85	Electrical machinery and parts	147,014	10,048	7
39	Plastics and articles thereof	80,458	7,338	9
40	Rubber and articles thereof	14,818	7,071	48
10	Cereals	108,427	5,556	5
21	Miscellaneous edible preparations	27,482	5,520	20
48	Paper and paperboard, articles of paper pulp	68,064	5,304	8
52	Cotton	57,693	5,221	9
33	Essential oils, resins, cosmetics, toiletries	16,099	5,190	32
62	Art. of apparel and clothing accessories not knitted	5,173	5,143	99
61	Art. of apparel and clothing accessories knitted	5,918	5,078	86
84	Boilers machinery and mechanical appliances	233,803	4,924	2
95	Toys, games and sports parts	8,704	4,837	56
64	Footwear, gaiters and the like	5,017	4,171	83
63	Made up textile articles, sets, worn clothing	9,561	2,498	26
04	Dairy products, eggs, honey	6,015	2,487	41
30	Pharmaceutical products	21,431	2,209	10
73	Articles of iron or steel	15,232	2,081	14
96	Miscellaneous manufactures articles	5,848	1,741	30
23	Residues and waste from the food industry	39,631	1,622	4
08	Edible fruits and nuts: peel of citrus fruit	8,739	1,619	19
42	Articles of leather, saddlers/harness	2,353	1,532	65
16	Preparations of meat, fish or crustaceans	3,060	1,488	49
54	Manmade filaments	5,859	1,444	25
19	Preparations of cereal, flour, milk, or pastry	6,548	1,349	21
38	Miscellaneous chemical products	20,126	1,308	7
06	Meat and edible meat offal	2,712	1,229	45
20	Preparations of vegetable, fruit, nuts, or other	4,674	1,119	24
83	Miscellaneous articles of base metal	7,052	1,009	14
71	Pearls, precious stones, and metals	2,202	985	45
	Other exports	209,708	13,959	7

Source: Estimations using SMART, exports from UNCOMTRADE, tariffs from TRAINS.

Note: DR-CAFTA effect estimated as a unilateral tariff elimination (immediate drop to zero of all tariffs) by El Salvador to U.S. imports. HS = Harmonization System.

Table 4A.8. Guatemala: Estimated Effects of Tariff Elimination on U.S. Imports in Partial Equilibrium

HS code and product description		*Imports 2004 ($000)*	*Change in imports ($000)*	*Change (%)*
	Total	2,944,125	346,750	12
87	Vehicles	368,319	101,750	28
27	Mineral fuels, oils	507,906	33,499	7
85	Electrical machinery and parts	305,766	23,197	8
40	Rubber and articles thereof	33,583	17,139	51
94	Furniture, bedding, mattress, mat support	19,926	13,487	68
52	Cotton	129,662	13,469	10
39	Plastics and articles thereof	146,240	12,180	8
95	Toys, games and sports parts	20,692	10,982	53
48	Paper and paperboard; art. of paper pulp	121,478	8,456	7
62	Articles of apparel and clothing accessories, not knitted	14,499	8,391	58
33	Essential oils, resins, cosmetics, and toiletries	33,007	7,811	24
10	Cereals	153,683	7,789	5
64	Footwear, gaiters and the like	10,663	6,862	64
84	Boilers machinery and mechanical appliances	287,924	6,583	2
63	Made up textile articles, sets, worn clothing	26,080	4,682	18
38	Miscellaneous chemical products	39,439	4,134	10
21	Miscellaneous edible preparations	21,257	4,030	19
23	Residues and waste from the food industry	61,474	3,835	6
61	Articles of apparel and clothing accessories, knitted	6,434	3,751	58
72	Iron and steel	59,569	3,542	6
02	Meat and edible meat offal	24,550	3,492	14
96	Miscellaneous manufactures articles	9,825	2,835	29
30	Pharmaceutical products	23,914	2,717	11
73	Articles of iron or steel	24,305	2,466	10
19	Preparation of cereal, flour, milk, or pastry	9,122	2,175	24
04	Dairy products	8,648	2,166	25
08	Edible fruit and nuts, peel of citrus fruit	11,342	2,093	18
42	Articles of leather, saddlers/harness	3,026	1,956	65
20	Preparation of vegetable, fruit, nuts, or other	9,781	1,855	19
16	Preparations of meat, fish or crustaceans	8,215	1,747	21
83	Miscellaneous articles of base metal	12,436	1,661	13
69	Ceramic products	3,313	1,637	49
	Other exports	428,046	24,675	6

Source: Estimations using SMART, exports from UNCOMTRADE, tariffs from TRAINS.

Note: DR-CAFTA effect estimated as a unilateral tariff elimination (immediate drop to zero of all tariffs) by Guatemala to U.S. imports. HS = Harmonization System.

Table 4A.9. Honduras: Estimated Effects of Tariff Elimination on U.S. Imports in Partial Equilibrium

	HS code and product description	*Imports 2004 ($000)*	*Change in imports ($000)*	*Change (%)*
	Total	2,671,912	700,776	26
61	Art. of apparel and clothing accessories, knitted	422,583	210,392	50
60	Knitted or crocheted fabrics	339,708	175,135	52
62	Art. of apparel and clothing accessories, not knitted	253,998	132,120	52
27	Mineral fuels, oils	232,524	33,855	15
52	Cotton	307,130	31,226	10
87	Vehicles	47,042	14,217	30
39	Plastics and articles thereof	81,088	13,800	17
55	Manmade staple fibers	85,389	9,355	11
48	Paper and paperboard; articles of paper pulp	83,920	7,514	9
58	Special women fabric, ace, tapestry	53,079	7,324	14
94	Furniture, bedding, mattress, mat support	11,730	7,177	61
85	Electrical machinery and parts	83,510	6,778	8
40	Rubber and articles thereof	7,890	4,318	55
21	Miscellaneous edible preparations	19,053	4,042	21
54	Manmade filaments	23,986	3,156	13
64	Footwear, gaiters and the like	5,029	3,041	60
84	Boilers machinery and mechanical appliances	223,749	2,510	1
83	Miscellaneous articles of base metal	13,066	2,470	19
10	Cereals	77,244	2,369	3
95	Toys, games and sports parts	4,870	2,108	43
33	Essential oils, resins, cosmetics, and toiletries	5,610	1,810	32
02	Meat and edible meat offal	10,028	1,808	18
63	Made up textile articles, sets, worn clothing	9,063	1,700	19
23	Residues and waste from the food industry	31,616	1,531	5
22	Beverages, spirits and vinegar	5,769	1,288	22
96	Miscellaneous manufactures articles	8,632	1,269	15
56	Wadding, felt and non woven, yarns, twine	18,260	1,256	7
73	Articles of iron or steel	11,294	1,253	11
38	Miscellaneous chemical products	16,142	1,219	8
20	Preparation of vegetable, fruit, nuts, or other	5,401	1,135	21
44	Wood and articles of wood; wood charcoal	5,179	930	18
19	Preparation of cereal, flour, milk, or pastry	3,193	845	26
	Other exports	165,137	11,825	7

Source: Estimations using SMART, exports from UNCOMTRADE, tariffs from TRAINS.

Note: DR-CAFTA effect estimated as a unilateral tariff elimination (immediate drop to zero of all tariffs) by Honduras to U.S. imports. HS = Harmonization System.

Table 4A.10. Nicaragua: Estimated Effects of Tariff Elimination on U.S. Imports in Partial Equilibrium

HS code and product description		*Imports 2004 ($000)*	*Change in imports ($000)*	*Change (%)*
	Total	440,592	45,971	10
27	Mineral fuels, oils	33,375	5,617	17
94	Furniture, bedding, mattress, mat support	6,809	4,510	66
87	Vehicles	16,495	3,997	24
85	Electrical machinery and parts	44,301	2,371	5
39	Plastics and articles thereof	16,517	2,209	13
40	Rubber and articles thereof	9,174	2,196	30
21	Miscellaneous edible preparations	5,365	1,922	21
33	Essential oils, resins, cosmetics, and toiletries	54,359	1,831	34
84	Boilers machinery and mechanical appliances	54,359	1,785	3
15	Animal or vegetable fats, and oils	26,643	1,780	7
63	Made up textile articles, sets, worn clothing	7,681	1,749	23
61	Articles of apparel and clothing accessories, knitted	2,827	1,505	53
04	Dairy products, eggs, honey	7,225	1,479	20
10	Cereals	28,104	1,244	4
48	Paper and paperboard; articles of paper pulp	14,107	1,055	7
38	Miscellaneous chemical products	8,383	995	12
95	Toys, games and sports parts	2,225	922	41
73	Articles of iron or steel	7,575	857	11
64	Footwear, gaiters and the like	1,123	808	72
19	Preparation of cereal, flour, milk, or pastry	33,548	578	16
34	Soap, organic surface agents, washing preparations	2,124	518	24
62	Art. of apparel and clothing accessories, not knitted	794	501	63
20	Preparation of vegetable, fruit, nuts, or other	2,408	483	20
83	Miscellaneous articles of base metal	1,621	367	23
96	Miscellaneous manufactures articles	1,865	328	18
16	Preparations of meat, fish or crustaceans	1,089	288	26
32	Tanning/dyeing extract, tannins and derivatives	4,027	278	7
42	Articles of leather, saddler/ harness	410	265	65
11	Prod. mill industry, malt, starches, wheat	2,344	259	11
02	Meat and edible meat offal	1,521	255	17
68	Art. of stone, plaster, cement, asbestos	1,802	242	13
07	Edible vegetables and certain roots and tubers	2,201	195	9
	Other exports	115,312	2,584	2

Source: Estimations using SMART, exports from UNCOMTRADE, tariffs from TRAINS.

Note: DR-CAFTA effect estimated as a unilateral tariff elimination (immediate drop to zero of all tariffs) by Nicaragua to U.S. imports. HS = Harmonization System.

Table 4A.11. Summary Statistics of Variables Used by Gould and Gruben in Estimating Growth Effects of Free Trade Agreements, 1960–2002

	Observations	*Mean*	*Standard Deviation*	*Minimum*	*Maximum*
Current per capita real GDP growth	1,122	0.020492	0.035773	–0.2306	0.235846
Log real per capita GDP ($)	1,122	8.115969	1.043246	5.773635	10.41356
Log secondary school enrollment (%)	744	3.592764	0.968234	0.113329	5.079913
Log investment share of GDP (%)	1,124	2.608961	0.689849	0.081122	4.044216
Regional trade agreement index	1,076	0.60855	0.827527	0	5
Regional integration agreements (share of world GDP)	1,009	0.051133	0.107988	0	0.608453
Economic freedom of the world	621	5.726087	1.207982	2.3	9.1
World GDP growth (%)	1,009	1.857951	1.018959	0.568824	3.667349
Trade share of GDP (%)	1,124	62.06638	42.38338	5.244616	393.7483
Black market premium (%)	834	65.47042	458.6325	–9.93	11662.38
Government share of consumption (%)	1,124	18.18883	10.38591	1.430759	70.71793
Fiscal balance as share of GDP (%)	831	–3.02481	4.239407	–43.499	19.19231
Choice to liberalize	1,009	0.126858	0.332979	0	1
Freedom	835	2.103772	0.773869	1	3
Number of observations: 743					

Source: Gould and Gruben 2005.

Notes

1. Nontechnical readers are encouraged to browse the various results and proceed to the other chapters.
2. The term *small* is used here to refer to any economy that cannot affect international prices of goods and services.
3. This, calculation comes from the fact that the model is estimated in log-log form. Thus the effect of FTAs relative to CBI is equal to the ratio of the exponential of the product of the FTA coefficients reported in table 4.1 multiplied by the average utilization rate divided by the CBI coefficients times the average CBI utilization rate.
4. El Salvador is covered in the World Bank regulatory database and thus we leave it to the interested reader to undertake the necessary evaluation of this country's regulatory burden. The data reviewed in chapter 7 of this volume, however, suggest that this country might not suffer from excessive regulations more generally.
5. Simulation results calculated with SMART software, using tariffs that are corrected by the 2001 utilization rates of the Caribbean Basin Trade Partnership Act preferences (that is, the share of U.S. imports from El Salvador that actually enjoy the zero-tariff treatment upon entry for each item). Results reflect a scenario where all CACM countries gain zero-tariff access to the United States simultaneously.
6. This section draws heavily from Bussolo and Niimi (2005).
7. Aggregate investment is set equal to aggregate savings, whereas aggregate government expenditures are exogenously fixed.
8. See Armington (1969) for details.
9. The formal derivation of this equation is presented in the annex of Bussolo and Niimi (2005).
10. See Winters, McCulloch, and McKay (2004) for an excellent survey.
11. Note that column Tm in table 4.4 is the trade weighted average of the Nicaraguan tariffs against United States and the rest of the world (which are separately shown in table 4.3).
12. Usually these analyses consider data at a very fine degree of disaggregation, namely the tariff line. Although trade data at this level may be available, production, consumption, and other important variables are unavailable.
13. Because of the sectoral classification, some sectors in table 4.4, notably *tobacco* and *machinery and equipment*, appear to be both import and export intensive. The apparent export intensity in these sectors results from dividing low levels of exports (probably re-exports) by even lower levels of domestic production. Exports of *tobacco* and *machinery and equipment* jointly account for just 2 percent of total exports.

14. Because of the closure rule of the external account, namely the fixing of foreign savings, and the full employment assumption, the larger expansion of the volumes of exports, with respect to import volumes, is compensated with a real exchange rate depreciation that originates from falling domestic resource costs. In other words, exporting sectors expand by employing resources whose relative prices have declined because of their falling demand from the contracting import-competing sectors.
15. These two sectors account for a third of total production and for almost 40 percent of total employment.
16. A regional multicountry model that includes the whole U.S. economy, rather than the current single-country model, would be better suited to account for all the direct and indirect effects of a liberalization of U.S. tariffs. However, the approach used here, namely to model the United States simply as one of Nicaragua's trading partners, can be considered a reduced form of a more complete multicountry model that, although theoretically more appealing, has much higher data intensity and empirical implementation costs.
17. This outcome may not hold under a different production specification where skilled workers, for example, are modeled as a complement to capital, rather than as substitutes.
18. This decomposition is not exact, given that the sequence in which these reforms are carried out matters for the final results. In this particular case, however, given that the magnitude of the shocks (especially the reduction of U.S. tariffs against Nicaraguan products) is not too large, the order in which the two simulations are carried out is almost indifferent.
19. These numbers were calculated with respect to a national poverty rate of 49.8 percent, which was used as the initial level of poverty in Bussolo and Niimi (2005).
20. This section appears in chapter 4 of Lederman, Maloney, and Servén (2005), and the econometric analysis was undertaken by Cuevas, Messmacher, and Werner (2002).
21. Note that even though FTAs do not necessarily preclude the imposition of antidumping duties, they do offer formal mechanisms for dispute resolution. In this sense, they do provide a guarantee of uninterrupted market access. See Fernández and Portes (1998).
22. Mexico has not suffered a major financial crisis since the 1994–95 Tequila crisis, but it is not clear that the absence of a crisis results from NAFTA.
23. This is in contrast with other recent reports focusing instead on bilateral FDI flows or stocks, which often use empirical models based on gravity variables. For example, see Levy-Yeyati, Stein, and Daude (2001).

24. Specifically, the Association of Southeast Asian Nations, the European Free Trade Association, what today is the EU, NAFTA, the Group of Three, the Andean Group in its recent revival, Mercado Común del Sur, and the Common Market for Eastern and Southern Africa (which in the analysis is included only as an expected FTA).
25. The results below correspond to the case when FTA membership is anticipated two years ahead of its occurrence. Alternative time horizons were used, too, without any substantial changes in results.
26. Thus, an increase in INTEGRATION holding FTAGDP constant would imply a reduced FDI appeal for the host country in question. Note that this variable has only time-series variation.
27. The dependent variable is net FDI inflow. All variables with a monetary dimension are measured in constant dollars and expressed in logs. Country fixed effects were added in al the regressions. Endogeneity is potentially an issue, especially in the case of GDP growth. However, specification tests could not reject its exogeneity. Additional experiments are reported in Cuevas, Messmacher, and Werner (2002).
28. The fact that the coefficient on global FDI is less than unity likely reflects the fact that increasingly important FDI recipients are excluded from the sample because of a lack of complete data. Our measure of total FDI inflows is not the sum of the inflows into the sample countries, which are obtained from a World Bank database, but a worldwide total reported by the U.N. Conference on Trade and Development's World Investment Report.
29. Although this result is consistent with expectations and previous results concerning the role of openness, simultaneity is a potential concern, as FDI may target traded sectors and lead to stronger export performance. However, there is likely a long gestation period between new investment and exports, which reduces the risk of simultaneity.
30. Albuquerque, Loayza, and Servén (2005) reported this result using direct measures of real wages for a reduced country sample.
31. Lipsey (2002), in a comprehensive review of the literature, argued that the evidence is vast that foreign firms tend to be at least as productive as domestic firms and hence their presence pushes up average productivity. The evidence on positive productivity spillovers from foreign firms is ambiguous. The majority of studies that find these effects employ cross-sectional data and thus do not control for unobserved time-invariant country characteristics.
32. At the firm level, see Cohen and Levinthal (1989); Forbes and Wield (2000); Griffith, Redding, and Van Reenen (2003); and Pavitt (2001). At the national level, see Baumol, Nelson, and Wolff (1994).

33. Bosch, Lederman, and Maloney (2005) discussed in detail how these elasticities are estimated and how they vary across regions of the world.

34. This result was derived by estimating a patenting function that includes the interaction between R&D investment and a dummy variable for Latin American and Caribbean countries. In turn, the same function was estimated but included additional explanatory variables. Among these, the variables from the Global Competitiveness Report on the private sector's perception of the quality of research institutions and the extent of collaboration between private firms and universities were the ones that eliminated the statistical significance of the Latin American and Caribbean variable interacted with R&D. See Bosch, Lederman, and Maloney (2005) for details.

35. This section was written by David Gould (World Bank) and William Gruben (Federal Reserve of Dallas).

36. Berthelon (2004) estimated the effects of regional FTAs on growth using a dummy variable for the period a country enters a regional FTA weighted by the size of the share of world GDP represented by the FTA trading partners. He also created another variable that takes the value of this variable but measures it relative to the size of the country's own share of world GDP. Although he found a significant positive value for this variable, we do not find significant results using a similarly weighted variable, nor do we find that the effects of regional FTAs are significantly stronger between countries in the North (developed) and countries in the South (developing) or for any other types of regional FTA partners (South–South or North–North). Although we do find that growth effects are larger for North–South FTAs, they are not significantly different from South–South or North–North FTAs. Our inability to replicate Berthelon's results may be because our data sets are not identical in time periods or countries and that we have different control variables in the regression (including world growth and other variables).

CHAPTER 5

Policy Approaches to Managing the Economic Transition

Ensuring That the Poor Can Benefit from DR-CAFTA

Although the vast majority of people in Central America are expected to benefit from DR-CAFTA in the medium to long term, there are at least some people who risk bearing the costs of trade-related economic adjustment in the short term. For example, although the Central American economies are already relatively open, because of the unilateral trade liberalization efforts undertaken in the 1990s (described in chapter 2), a handful of sensitive agricultural commodities (such as maize, beans, dairy, and poultry) still have significant levels of protection. This protection will be reduced or eliminated as a result of DR-CAFTA (see chapter 3), potentially resulting in short-term employment and income losses to those farmers who currently produce sensitive goods. Especially if the people adversely affected are among the poor or near-poor population, some kind of trade adjustment assistance or social safety net may be warranted to ensure that those negatively affected are able to maintain a minimum level of welfare while they make the transition to new and more remunerative economic opportunities arising from the agreement.

The main objectives of this chapter are to (1) analyze ex ante the potential impacts on household welfare arising from DR-CAFTA, and (2) examine policy approaches that may be useful in enabling trade adjustment and mitigating any negative effects of the agreement. The chapter focuses on the five original parties to DR-CAFTA—Costa Rica, El Salvador, Guatemala, Honduras, and Nicaragua—and explores approaches to ensure that those people who might bear the cost of trade adjustment in the short term are able and equipped to take advantage of opportunities arising from DR-CAFTA in the medium to long term. Because the largest changes in trade protection are expected to affect a handful of so-called sensitive agricultural commodities, this chapter focuses predominantly on the effects of liberalizing trade in these commodities.

The rest of this chapter is organized as follows. Section 2 briefly outlines the state of trade protection for sensitive agricultural goods in Central America, as well as the types of trade reforms negotiated under DR-CAFTA. Section 3 lays out a framework for assessing the welfare impacts of DR-CAFTA ex ante, focusing on how price changes are transmitted to households and how households manage risk in the face of changing economic circumstances. Section 4 presents new evidence of the expected welfare impacts of DR-CAFTA in El Salvador, Guatemala, and Nicaragua, based on analysis of national household survey data. Section 5 examines two broad policy approaches to addressing possible negative impacts of DR-CAFTA, comparing the relative benefits of phasing out trade protection as negotiated under the agreement versus coupling quick trade reform with compensatory measures targeted toward adversely affected groups. Section 6 reviews specific possible policy instruments for mitigating short-term costs of DR-CAFTA under a quick liberalization scenario, as well as approaches to facilitating trade adjustment among those people who might be adversely affected by terms-of-trade changes. This section includes a review of selected transfer programs, as well as interventions to enhance people's economic mobility and public information efforts that can help facilitate adjustment. The chapter concludes with an assessment of the relative strengths and weaknesses of different policy alternatives with respect to enabling a successful economic transition and ensuring that poor people are equipped and prepared to benefit from DR-CAFTA.

Liberalization of Sensitive Agricultural Commodities under DR-CAFTA

Unilateral trade liberalization on the part of the Central American countries during the 1990s left trade protection levels low, with the exception of those for a handful of so-called *bienes sensibles agrícolas*, or sensitive agricultural commodities, including corn (maize), beans (*frijoles*), milk and other dairy items, rice, sugar, beef, pork, and poultry meat.

As can be seen in table 5.1, pre-DR-CAFTA levels of tariff protection on these sensitive commodities were often quite high in the five Central American countries.[1] As of 2001, tariffs on the import of poultry meat were as high as 170 percent in Nicaragua, 150 percent in Costa Rica, 50 percent in Honduras, and 45 percent in Guatemala. Tariff rates were as high as 65 percent on milk (Costa Rica), 62 percent on rice (Nicaragua), and 55 percent on sugar (Nicaragua). Table 5.1 also shows that the dispersion of tariff rates on sensitive agricultural goods was high within individual countries and highly variable across the five countries.

In addition to tariffs, several of the countries imposed various nontariff barriers. For example, there is a system of tariff-rate quotas—sometimes called "within-quota" and "out-of-quota" tariffs—that results in different levels of protection, depending on the quantity of imports. This is illustrated in table 5.1 by the tariff ranges shown for certain commodities. This system enables a limited quantity of sensitive commodity imports to come into a country at relatively low tariff rates. Imports above quota levels are charged a high tariff. In the case of yellow maize, for instance, tariff levels rise from 0 percent to 15 percent in El Salvador, from 5 percent to 35 percent in

Table 5.1. Tariffs on Key Sensitive Commodities in DR-CAFTA Countries[a]
percent

	Crop							
Country	*Milk*	*Maize (yellow)*	*Rice*	*Beans*	*Sugar*	*Bovine meat*	*Pork*	*Poultry*
Costa Rica	65	1	35	30	50	15	48	150
El Salvador	40	0–15[b]	0–40	20	40	15	0–40	20/164[c]
Guatemala	15	5–35	6–36	15	20	0–30	15	15–45
Honduras	15	1–45	0–45	15	40	15	15	35–50[c]
Nicaragua	40	0–30	62	10	55	15	15	170

Sources: Monge, Loría, and González-Vega 2003; Pörtner 2003; Marques 2005; Marques for Honduras, personal correspondence.

a. Data from latest available year, 2001–05.

b. Where tariff ranges are indicated, this signifies tariff levels for imports of products within and outside established quota levels.

c. In the case of poultry imports to El Salvador, tariffs are 20 percent for non–Central American Common Market countries, except for the United States, from which poultry imports carry a tariff level of 164 percent. For both El Salvador and Honduras, the tariff levels also differ depending on the type of poultry meat.

Guatemala, and from 0 to 30 percent in Nicaragua once imports exceed nationally established quota levels. Likewise, tariffs on rice rise from 0 to 40 percent in El Salvador and from 6 percent to 35 percent in Guatemala once imports exceed quota levels (table 5.1).

In addition several commodities face sanitary and phytosanitary restrictions. For example, both milk and poultry meat face trade-related health and safety restrictions within the Central American Common Market, whereas trade in beef faces heath- and safety-related restrictions with countries outside the CACM (for example, related to hoof-and-mouth disease, mad cow disease, and so forth).[2]

Reduction or elimination of tariff and nontariff protections under DR-CAFTA would thus be expected to lead to lower domestic prices for sensitive commodities in each country.[3] Given the high levels of protection on some of these goods, the expected price declines could be considerable in some countries. For this reason, DR-CAFTA includes a wide range of provisions (described in chapter 3) for dealing with the liberalization of trade restrictions on sensitive goods, including grace periods for initiating liberalization, extended phase-out periods for tariffs, interim quotas and/or phase-downs of TRQs, as well as special safeguard measures to protect local farmers from undue harm. The exact provisions were negotiated country by country. Overall, however, the Central American countries were successful in negotiating generous timetables for reducing protection on their *bienes sensibles agrícolas,* as discussed in chapter 3. For some commodities, phase-out periods are as long as 20 years and, at least for a few countries, white maize, an important staple crop produced by poor rural households, was exempted from liberalization (box 5.1).

In sum, although the specifics differ from country to country, DR-CAFTA has built into it a prolonged and predictable period over which these *bienes sensibles agrícolas* can be liberalized, providing for an extended period during which, at least in principle, producers can adapt to expected price declines in these commodities. These provisions themselves represent important protections for producers of sensitive crops, giving them an extended timeframe over which to undertake the necessary adjustments.

Framework for Analyzing Welfare Effects of DR-CAFTA

The literature on trade reform identifies a number of channels through which trade reforms can affect people's welfare, including through (1)

Box 5.1

DR-CAFTA Schedules for Liberalizing Sensitive Agricultural Commodities: The Cases of El Salvador and Honduras

The Central American countries have, overall, negotiated generous timetables for liberalizing sensitive agricultural commodities under DR-CAFTA, including grace periods, extended timetables for tariff reduction or elimination, phasing down of TQRs, and various safeguard provisions. Although the exact reform schedules were negotiated country by country, the broad parameters are similar in many ways, as can be seen in the context of liberalization in El Salvador and Honduras.

In El Salvador,

- tariffs on imports of beans will be phased out in equal installments over a 15-year period, with no grace period
- tariffs on rice for imports exceeding (the currently high) quota levels will be phased out over 7 years, following a 10-year grace period
- tariffs on poultry will be phased out over 7 years, following a 10-year grace period
- the current TRQ on pork will increase by 10 percent a year, and tariffs are to be phased out over an 8-year period starting in year 7
- although prime beef parts already enter duty free, TRQs on all other bovine meat will increase by 5 percent a year; tariffs will be phased out over a 12-year period, following a 2-year grace period
- tariffs on milk and cheese are to be phased out over 10 years, following a 10-year grace period.

In Honduras,

- tariff reductions on rice can be phased over an 18-year period, following a 10-year grace period
- tariff reductions on pork can be phased over a 15-year period, following a 6-year grace period
- whereas the United States will receive immediate market access for high-quality cuts of bovine meat (for example, choice, prime), lower-quality cuts of beef will be liberalized over a 15-year period
- tariff reductions on poultry meat can take place over an 8-year period, starting in 2015

continued

Box 5.1, *continued*

- tariff reductions on dairy products can be phased over a 20-year period
- tariff reductions on yellow maize can be phased over a 15-year period, following a 6-year grace period.

In an important exception in both El Salvador and Honduras, white maize, a key staple produced and consumed by the countries' rural poor populations, will be exempted indefinitely from liberalization. Moreover, for all the sensitive products, special safeguard measures have been agreed on to ensure against unforeseen harm to local producers caused by rapid increases in imports from the United States.

Sources: Government of Honduras 2003; Marques 2005.

changes in the prices and availability of goods; (2) changes in factor prices, employment, and incomes; (3) changes in government tax revenues and transfers, which may be affected by changes in revenues from trade-related taxes; (4) improved incentives for investment and innovation, which strengthen prospects for long-run economic growth; (5) increased exposure to external shocks, particularly through changes in the terms of trade; and (6) the costs of adjusting to changes in the economic environment.[4]

Early concerns about the impacts of DR-CAFTA focused on the short-term price effects of liberalization and, in particular, what they would mean for producers of sensitive agricultural crops in Central America. For this reason, this section focuses largely on the effects of border price changes expected to occur from liberalizing sensitive agricultural commodities in Central America—although other channels of impact (such as those related to growth prospects and the role of transfers) are discussed later in the chapter in the context of public policy responses. Specifically, the section lays out a framework for understanding the pathways through which border price changes are transmitted to households and how households manage relative price changes (or "shocks").

A key message of applying this framework is that the effect of a price change on household welfare (such as the kind resulting from liberalizing the *bienes sensibles agrícolas*) will be smaller than the change in the market price—sometimes significantly smaller. This result occurs because households

- have diverse consumption bundles and often have multiple income sources
- at least in rural areas, are often both consumers and producers of key goods (and the consumption and production effects of price changes work in opposite directions)
- adjust their consumption and production patterns in response to relative price changes
- employ a number of ex ante and ex post strategies to manage price and income risks.

This section examines each of those factors in turn.

Multiple Consumption Goods and Sources of Income

Households, whether rich or poor, consume a diverse bundle of goods. They also often have multiple sources of income. This multiplicity of consumption goods and income sources serves, among other things, to moderate the short-term effects of good-specific price changes on household well-being—both positively and negatively. Analysis of household consumption patterns using Nicaragua's 2001 national household survey, the *Encuesta de Medición del Nivel de Vida* (EMNV) indicates, for example, that commodities such as maize and rice make up between 3 and 6 percent of households' consumption bundles, on average, and between 7 and 8 percent of the consumption bundle of Nicaragua's poorest 20 percent of households (table 5.2). Together, the group of sensitive agricultural commodities makes up about 54 percent of all food consumption, on average, and about 31 percent of total household consumption. Price declines for these goods will thus have a positive impact in households' ability to purchase these goods for consumption, with the largest effects being felt in the bottom half of the welfare distribution. At the same time, increase in purchasing power will be less than if the bundle of sensitive agricultural commodities (whose prices are expected to decline) made up a larger proportion of total household consumption—say, 50, 80, or even 100 percent.

The same data set shows that households also tend to have a diversified set of income sources (or income "portfolios"). As can be seen in figure 5.1, income from self-employed agricultural enterprises such as production of maize, beans, and rice—or chickens and cows in the case of smallholder farm households—makes up about 19 percent of the income, on average, among the poorest rural households in Nicaragua and about 28 percent of incomes among rural households in the fourth quintile.[5] In contrast to the case of

Table 5.2. Consumption Shares of Key Commodity Groups, Nicaragua, 2001

Share of household consumption(national)	*Quintile* 1	2	3	4	5
Food consumption	0.61	0.60	0.57	0.51	0.36
Sensitive commodities (all)	0.32	0.32	0.31	0.23	0.15
Rice	0.08	0.07	0.06	0.04	0.02
Maize	0.07	0.04	0.03	0.01	<0.01
Tortilla	0.01	0.01	0.01	0.01	<0.01
Milk and cheese	0.07	0.13	0.11	0.08	0.05
Sugar	0.05	0.04	0.03	0.03	0.01
Poultry	0.03	0.02	0.03	0.03	0.03
Bovine meat	0.01	0.02	0.03	0.03	0.03
Nonfood consumption	0.39	0.40	0.43	0.49	0.64
Sensitive commodities as a share of household food consumption	0.53	0.54	0.54	0.45	0.42

Source: Based on analysis of Nicaragua's 2001 national household survey, *Encuesta de Medición del Nivel de Vida* (EMNV).

consumption, declines in the prices of the sensitive agricultural commodities will act to reduce the incomes of households producing these goods. Nonetheless, the fact that households generally have multiple income sources means that the negative income effect operates only on a portion of households' total income portfolio, again serving to moderate the impact of the price change.

Households As Both Consumers and Producers of Key Goods

The fact that households, particularly in rural areas, are often both consumers and producers of key goods also serves to soften the impact of a price change on family welfare. This is because the effect of a price change has opposite effects on consumption and production. If, for example, a household were to consume exactly the same amount of a particular good—say, maize—as it produces, then a decline in the border price would have no net impact on household welfare because the purchasing power benefits of consuming less expensive maize would be exactly offset by the loss in income associated with lower producer prices for maize. If a household were to consume more maize than it produced, then a reduction in the maize price would, on net, benefit the welfare of that household. However, the benefits

Figure 5.1. Distribution of Income Sources for Rural Households in Nicaragua, by Quintile, 2001

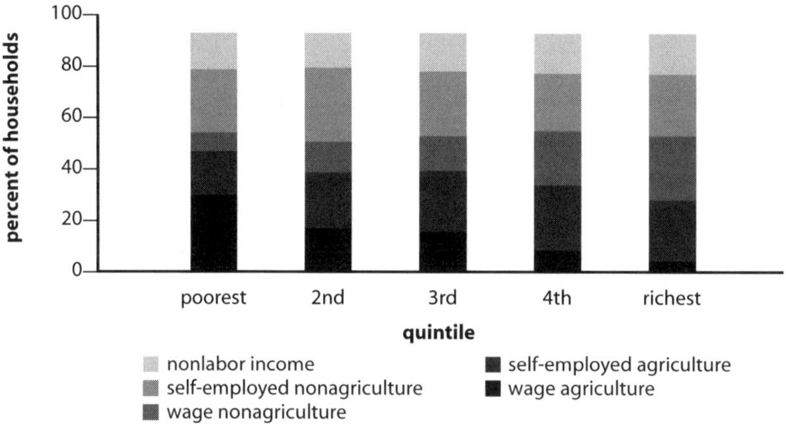

Source: World Bank staff estimates, using the 2001 EMNV.

would only equal the amount of the price decline multiplied by the excess of maize consumption over maize production (that is, the net amount of maize purchased from the market). In contrast, if a household were to produce more maize than it consumed, then it would experience a welfare loss as a result of a decline in the maize price. In this case, the loss would be the amount of the price change multiplied by the excess of maize production over consumption (that is, the net amount of maize sold to the market). Similarly, offsetting price effects would occur with any other sensitive commodities that households both consumed and produced.

The economics literature terms households that consume more than they produce of a good *net consumers* of that good, whereas those households that producer more than they consume of a good are termed *net producers* of that good.[6] Stated simply, net consumers of a good would be expected to benefit from a decrease in the price of that good (at least at the margin), and net producers would be expected to lose from a price decline. Conversely, a price increase for a particular good would be expected to benefit net producers of that good and negatively affect the welfare of net consumers.

Analysis of 2000 household survey data from Guatemala (*Encuesta Nacional de Condiciones de Vida* [ENCOVI]) shows that the vast majority of Guatemalans are net consumers of maize—about 80 percent of households overall. This compares with only about 12 percent of Guatemalan households, in all, that are net producers of maize. The remaining roughly 8 percent of households are neither net consumers nor net producers; they consume and produce equal amounts. It should be noted that the percentage of households that are net consumers (net producers) of maize varies somewhat across the welfare distribution, however (figure 5.2). For example, approximately 71 (17) percent of the poorest households are net consumers (net producers) of maize, whereas about 92 (4) percent of the wealthiest households are net consumers (net producers).[7] The share of households that are net consumers of maize also varies significantly across regions of Guatemala. Roughly 69 (18) percent of rural households are net consumers (net producers) of maize, whereas 91 (5) percent of urban households are net consumers (net producers).[8]

Adjustment to Relative Price Changes

It is important to highlight that households are not simply passive recipients of price changes. Rather, households often adjust their consumption and production practices in response to changes in relative prices to help make the most of their limited resources and mitigate adverse price and income shocks (Deaton 1997). On one hand, households adjust to take the best advantage of favorable changes in prices. For example, if the price of chicken goes down, households tend to increase their consumption of this protein-

Figure 5.2. Net Consumers and Net Producers of Maize in Guatemala, by Quintile, 2000

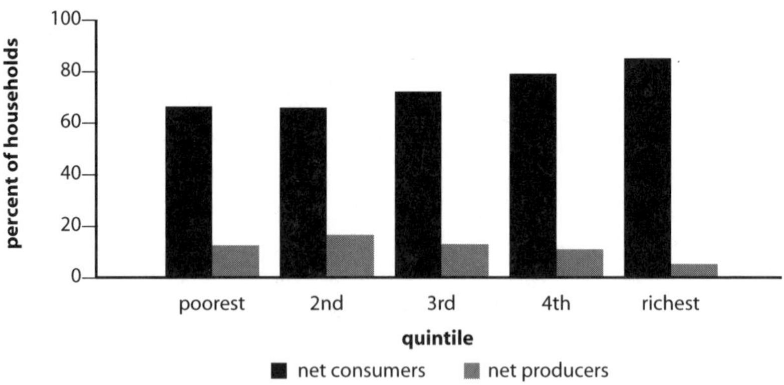

Source: World Bank staff estimates, using the 2000 ENCOVI.

rich food, if all other prices remain constant. On the other hand, households adjust their consumption and production patterns in ways that help mitigate the effects of negative price shocks. For example, when world coffee prices fell dramatically between 1997 and 2001, coffee farmers in El Salvador and Nicaragua reduced their coffee production or abandoned it altogether, shifting their work effort toward more remunerative economic activities within and outside of agriculture (Beneke de Sanfelíu and Shi 2004; Trigueros and Avalos 2004).

It is worth noting that although there is extensive empirical evidence from developed and developing countries showing that households adjust to changing prices, such adaptations may neither be smooth nor instantaneous, especially with respect to production. In general, households' abilities to adjust their consumption will be greater in the short term than their ability to adjust production patterns. The facts that households' consumption bundles tend to be more diverse than their production/income portfolios and that at least some portion of household consumption can be purchased in markets, makes substituting one consumption good for another (at the margin) relatively easy. On the production side, however, households may face a variety of constraints to adjusting their income portfolio, at least in the short term. For example, for poor rural households that are relatively specialized in agricultural production, the agronomic potential of their farmland, seasonal or weather-related constraints on crop production, absence of irrigation or other production technologies, and/or limited availability of credit (or other forms of working capital) may serve to limit households' ability to adjust their income portfolios quickly. Such production-side constraints tend to loosen over the longer term, and can be reduced through strategic investments in education and training and in infrastructure and technology that reduce agronomic constraints, lower transaction costs, and increase the profitability of alternative rural enterprises.[9]

Household Risk Management Strategies

Central American households employ a number of strategies to manage risk in uncertain and changing economic environments. Indeed, empirical evidence from Central America and beyond indicates that having a relatively diversified income portfolio (ex ante) and adjusting to price changes (ex post) are but two strategies that Central American households—and those in neighboring countries—seem to employ. In El Salvador, migration and remittances have also been key elements of household risk management—both ex ante and ex post (Arias 2004; Beneke de Sanfelíu and Shi 2004). In Nicaragua, evidence indicates that households also rely in important ways on informal social networks, including through memberships in community, religious, or neighborhood organizations, that can provide an alternative fount of resources—as loans or gifts—in the event of an adverse shock (Klugman, Kruger, and Withers 2003).

A new empirical study of the effects of the coffee crisis in four Central American countries also illustrates how households in the region have managed recent changes in relative prices (World Bank 2005d). In El Salvador, in response to declines in the coffee price—and related labor demand in the coffee sector—many wage-earning households increased their hours devoted to nonagricultural enterprises. These sectoral shifts in employment, along with remittances, have helped Salvadoran families involved in the coffee economy mitigate considerably the effect on household income of the significant fall in the world coffee price (Trigueros and Avalos 2004; Beneke de Sanfelíu and Shi 2004). In Honduras, evidence also indicates that coffee sector families increased their labor supply in an attempt to offset effects of the coffee price decline (Coady, Olinto, and Caldes 2003).

Some household risk management strategies, such as developing diversified income-earning portfolios (ex ante), increasing adult labor supply, or drawing down financial savings (ex post), may be seen as appropriate responses to price and income risk. Other strategies, however, like engaging in distress sales of productive assets such as land, withdrawing children from school, or deferring use of preventive or curative health services, may create other risks to long-term family welfare. Indeed, there is evidence that, in Nicaragua and Guatemala, some coffee farmers sold off assets, such as land or livestock, as a means of coping with the lower coffee prices (Vakis, Kruger, and Mason 2004). Thus, this risk management mechanism can result in long-term losses in their productivity, both adversely affecting their economic productivity and increasing the likelihood of the intergenerational transmission of poverty.

A number of recent empirical studies within and outside Latin America have tried to measure how effectively households smooth their consumption—or "self-insure"—in the face of adverse income shocks. Although the specific findings differ from country to country, these studies find that households are *partially* effective at mitigating the impacts of shocks to household income. Overall, the evidence suggests that households, on aver-

Table 5.3. Recent Evidence on Household Consumption Smoothing in Developing Countries

Country	*Change in household per capita consumption*[a] *(percent)*	*Source*
Nicaragua (whole country)	2.5	Klugman, Kruger, and Withers 2003
Peru (urban)	3.0–3.6	Glewwe and Hall 1998
China (rural)		Jalan and Ravallion 1999
Poorest	4.0	
Richest	1.0	

a. Change results from a 10 percent change in per capita income.

age, are able to protect between 60 and 90 percent of their consumption per capita in the face of changes in income (table 5.3). That is, a 10 percent shock to household per capita income translates roughly into a 1 to 4 percent change in per capita consumption. Nevertheless, poor households seem to face limitations that inhibit their ability to protect themselves against risk than better-off households. In China, for example, the wealthiest households only experienced a 1 percent decline in per capita consumption in the face of a 10 percent decline in per capita income; in contrast, the poorest households experienced a 4 percent consumption decline in response to the same decline in income (table 5.3).

Together, the evidence suggests that public social protection programs are an important part of a country's ability not only to ensure a minimum level of well-being among its population in the event of shocks, but also to help protect human capital investments and other productive assets of the poor in the event of shocks. Safety nets can play an important role in a country's long-term strategy for economic development and poverty reduction.[10]

Expected Impacts of Liberalizing the Sensitive Agricultural Commodities: New Evidence from El Salvador, Guatemala, and Nicaragua

Given the above information, what might a policymaker expect to be the impacts of liberalizing trade in sensitive agricultural commodities under DR-CAFTA? Three empirical studies—Pörtner (2003), Monge, Castro, and Saavedra (2004), and Marques (2005)—commissioned for this report shed light on the issue. All three studies use nationally representative household survey data and apply a *net consumer–net producer* framework to assess the likely first-order impacts on household welfare of eliminating quotas and reducing to zero the tariffs on several *bienes sensibles agrícolas,* including maize, beans, milk, poultry meat, bovine meat, pork, wheat, and rice.[11]

As discussed above, a decrease in the price of any of these commodities can be expected to benefit net consumers of that good and have a negative impact on the well-being of net producers of that good. One difference between the analysis in the discussion of net consumers and producers above and the analysis presented here is that this section focuses largely on the net welfare impacts of liberalizing the entire basket of sensitive commodities in each country—although the role and importance of several specific commodities on household welfare are discussed below. (For additional information on the methodology used in the country case studies, see box 5.2.[12])

The analyses here present expected impacts *as if* all tariffs and quotas were going to be removed completely and immediately under DR-CAFTA. Although this is obviously not what was ultimately negotiated under the

Box 5.2

Analyzing the Expected Impacts of Liberalizing Sensitive Agricultural Commodities in El Salvador, Guatemala, and Nicaragua: A Net Consumer–Net Producer Approach

The case studies presented in this chapter apply a partial equilibrium approach, sometimes known as a *net consumer–net producer* approach. This approach enables analysts to estimate the first-order effects of a price change on household welfare. The theoretical underpinnings for the approach used here are described in Deaton (1997), McCulloch (2002), and Chen and Ravallion (2003). The approach assumes that each household has a utility function that fulfills certain requirements such as the separability between consumption and production and between leisure and other consumption. Given a set of (small) price changes, the gain or loss to the household can be calculated by the money metric change in the household utility, and is simply equal to the price change multiplied by total sales of the product minus the price change multiplied by the total consumption of the product.

Households can be divided into *net producers* and *net consumers* of a given product. If with the implementation of DR-CAFTA there is a reduction in the import tariff of that product and of its domestic price, then all households that are net producers of that product would experience a loss, while all households that are net consumers of that product would realize a gain. There also may be households that neither produce nor buy the product or that produce only for self-consumption; in these cases, under this framework there would be no change in welfare. Note that the framework ignores transport costs and/or the costs of intermediaries.

The estimation procedure requires calculating the price changes brought about by DR-CAFTA. Here, expected price changes following the elimination of tariffs under the trade agreement are calculated as weighted average (by quantity) of the tariffs applied at the within- and out-of-quota levels. Estimates of expected changes in the prices of sensitive agricultural commodities in El Salvador, Guatemala, and Nicaragua, as a result of DR-CAFTA are presented in the annex to this chapter.

Other approaches—such as computable general equilibrium models—exist for estimating the welfare effects of trade reform. In principle, these models can account for several different channels through which welfare effects are transmitted, although CGE models are considerably more demanding in terms of data and computational costs. Moreover, as Hertel and Reimer (2005) noted in their review of the various approaches to analyzing the poverty impacts of trade, CGE models can be quite complex, making it hard to know whether simulation results are due to the plethora of model assumptions or whether they are robust to alternative specifications and thus driven by the relevant data.

That said, the "comparative static" results presented here should be interpreted with several caveats in mind. First, the approach assumes that, in the short run, households neither adjust their production or consumption patterns in response to price changes nor engage in any other household risk-management strategies. Second, the estimates do not attempt to incorporate any longer-term benefits associated with increased labor demand that might be associated with the increased foreign investment, expansion of exports, or increased economic growth expected.

Third, the analysis assumes implicitly that tariffs are eliminated at once and that the price impact is immediate. Therefore, consumers would realize an immediate gain and the producers would experience an immediate loss. DR-CAFTA, however, has been negotiated to include long phase-out periods, often following an initial

continued

Box 5.2, *continued*

grace period. In this context, the effect of price changes would only be felt over a much longer period of time.

Fourth, even if elimination of tariffs were immediate, there are reasons why the price changes experienced by households might be lower than those suggested by nominal tariff changes. For example, remote and isolated rural communities may only have weak links to commercial markets and thus households in those areas may experience only weak price effects, relative to people living in urban or well-connected rural areas. Indeed, recent empirical analyses of local price changes resulting from border price changes have found that the transmission effect is commonly less than one-to-one (Winters, McCulloch, and McKay 2004). Moreover, the fact that Central American trade is already highly integrated—with zero tariffs on intraregional trade for many sensitive commodities and, probably, some contraband—may also mean that price effects arising from DR-CAFTA may be somewhat muted. For these and related reasons, the types of estimates presented here are generally referred to in the net consumer–net producer literature as "worst-case" impact scenarios (McCulloch 2002).

It is important to note, however, that there also are factors that could work in the opposite direction in terms of actual versus estimated impacts. For example, capital allocation away from adversely affected sectors could reduce the marginal product of labor in those sectors, compounding the static losses faced by net producers of affected goods. Indeed it is possible, at least in principle, to imagine a longer-run worst-case scenario in which the dynamic gains from DR-CAFTA are low and where returns to unskilled labor fall economy-wide as a result of both the direct price effects and the indirect effects of reallocation of capital from adversely affected sectors. A final caveat is that, strictly speaking, partial equilibrium analysis is valid only for small price changes. As can be seen in the annex, the expected price changes are substantial in some cases.

Despite these caveats, the net consumer–net producer approach is useful in helping policymakers identify the expected first-order effects of DR-CAFTA, including which types of households are most likely to gain or lose as a result of liberalizing the trade restrictions on sensitive agricultural commodities, as well as the likely size of the impacts. In doing so, it provides an important analytical base on which to develop policy and programmatic responses to support those likely to be adversely affected by reforms.

agreement, the approach provides useful insights into the first-order impacts of liberalizing the sensitive commodities. As will be discussed further below, this approach is also a useful baseline from which to discuss policy options, as well as some important policy trade-offs associated with the gradual liberalization that was negotiated versus an approach in which liberalization is undertaken quickly and combined with targeted transfers to negatively affected households.

Identifying Prospective Winners and Losers from the Reforms

To assess who is likely to win and who is likely to lose from the liberalization of the sensitive agricultural commodities, the analysis first examines whether households are net consumers or net producers of each sensitive commodity, as in the case of maize in Guatemala highlighted above (figure 5.2). It then estimates the per capita consumption gains to winners and losses to losers associated with liberalizing each good. Finally, it calculates for each household the net welfare impact of removing tariffs and nontariff barriers on the basket of sensitive commodities in each country. As can be seen in figure 5.3, the vast majority of people in Nicaragua, Guatemala, and El Salvador are net consumers of the *basket* of sensitive commodities.

Figure 5.3. Net Consumers and Net Producers of Sensitive Agricultural Commodities in Nicaragua, Guatemala, and El Salvador, by Quintile

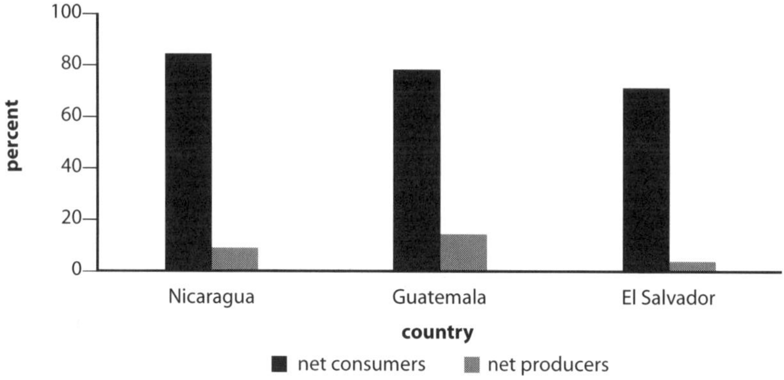

Sources: Pörtner 2003; Monge, Castro, and Saavedra 2004; and Marques 2005.
Note: For data reasons, in the case of El Salvador, the proportion of both net consumers and net producers may be underestimated.

Specifically, the evidence indicates that 90 percent of Nicaraguan households, 84 percent of Guatemalan households, and 68 percent of Salvadoran households are net consumers of the basket of sensitive agricultural commodities and, thus, on net, can be expected to benefit from the sum of the price changes expected to occur when these commodities are liberalized. Conversely, about 9 percent of Nicaraguan households, 16 percent of Guatemalan households, and 5 percent of Salvadoran households are net producers of the basket of sensitive commodities and thus would be expected to experience (static) welfare losses arising from the price changes induced by DR-CAFTA. Some proportion of households, perhaps as high as 19 percent in the case of El Salvador, would neither benefit nor lose as a result of agreement-related price changes either because they do not consume or produce the sensitive commodities or because they consume and produce them in roughly equal amounts.

It is important to note here that in the case of El Salvador it is likely that the proportion of both net consumers and net producers is underestimated. Both the Guatemalan ENCOVI and the Nicaraguan EMNV surveys are designed as consumption, expenditure, and income surveys, which also include detailed data on food prices. As such, they are ideally suited for undertaking the type of net consumer–net producer analysis presented here. In contrast, El Salvador's *Encuesta de Hogares para Propósitos Múltiples* (EHPM) survey is designed primarily as an income and employment survey. The EHPM does contain information on agricultural production, self-consumption, and data on purchase of food items, but in practice these latter data have rarely been used. Review of the EHPM modules suggests that both agricultural production for personal consumption and household consumption expenditures may be underreported, with some households (especially many poor ones) reporting no such production or consumption spending. This is reflected in the fact that the proportion of both net producers and net consumers is lower in the El Salvador analysis than in the cases of Guatemala or Nicaragua.

The El Salvador findings, therefore, must be interpreted with some caution, especially in the case of the disaggregated results reported by region (rural vs. urban) and by welfare quintile, which are analyzed using smaller data cell sizes and where measurement problems among a single or small group of households could significantly influence the results. In this context, it should be noted that Marques (2005) conducted some tests of the robustness of the findings to outliers in the data. He found that the results are robust to outliers, although that is no guarantee that there are missing data reports, especially among poor households, that might have altered the findings somewhat. That said, the overall patterns of net consuming and net producing households for El Salvador are very consistent with those from Guatemala and Nicaragua, giving some level of confidence that they reflect real income and consumption patterns on the ground.[13]

Rural–Urban Differences

Whereas the majority of Guatemalans, Nicaraguans, and Salvadorans are likely to benefit even in the short term from price declines in sensitive agricultural commodities, the distribution of beneficiaries differs somewhat across rural and urban areas (table 5.4). In Guatemala and Nicaragua, for example, the evidence indicates that a higher proportion of households in urban areas will benefit than of households in rural areas. In Nicaragua, 97.6 percent of urban households are expected to benefit compared with 78.8 percent in rural areas. The pattern is similar in Guatemala: 93.6 percent of urban households are likely to benefit from price changes under DR-CAFTA compared to 75.1 percent in rural areas. Note that although the proportion expected to benefit is lower in rural than in urban areas, the percentage is still high—three-quarters or more in those two countries are expected to benefit.

Table 5.4. Net Consumers and Net Producers of the Basket of Sensitive Agricultural Commodities in Nicaragua, Guatemala, and El Salvador, by Rural–Urban Location and Quintile
percent

	Nicaragua		*Guatemala*		*El Salvador*	
Group	*Net consumers*	*Net producers*	*Net consumers*	*Net producers*	*Net consumers*	*Net producers*
All country	90.2	8.8	83.8	15.7	68.2	4.1
Rural	78.8	19.4	75.1	24.5	72.1	4.1
Urban	97.6	1.8	93.6	5.8	65.2	4.1
Poorest quintile	85.7	12.4	78.5	20.8	22.1	7.5
2nd quintile	86.5	11.8	75.4	24.1	76.6	4.1
3rd quintile	91.1	8.5	81.2	18.6	82.1	2.8
4th quintile	92.9	6.5	85.5	14.2	81.4	3.1
Richest quintile	94.8	4.7	92.0	7.5	79.0	2.8

Sources: Pörtner 2003; Monge, Castro, and Saavedra 2004; and Marques 2005.
Note: Net consumers benefit; net producers lose.

Conversely, the proportion of net producers—households expected to experience negative effects of DR-CAFTA-related price changes—is considerably higher in rural areas than in urban areas. In the case of Nicaragua, for example, nearly 20 percent of the rural households are expected to be negatively affected by DR-CAFTA-related price changes, compared with less than 2 percent in urban areas. In Guatemala, nearly a quarter of rural households are likely to be adversely affected by price changes associated with liberalizing sensitive agricultural commodities under DR-CAFTA; this compares with just less than 6 percent in urban areas. It is important to note, moreover, that there is likely to be considerable variation in the impacts of DR-CAFTA *within* rural and urban areas in Central America because of considerable heterogeneity in production and consumption patterns. For example, data from Nicaragua indicate that approximately 34 percent of rural households in the Atlantic region are net producers of the basket of *bienes sensibles agrícolas,* considerably higher than the rural average; for Guatemala, the data suggest that more than 60 percent of households in the Peten region may, in fact, be net producers.[14]

The data from El Salvador tell a slightly different story regarding rural versus urban effects, with a slightly higher proportion of rural than urban households being net consumers: 72.1 versus 65.2 percent, respectively. It is not completely clear why this is the case because rural households generally would be expected to produce a greater share of sensitive agricultural commodities than would urban households. Nor is it clear whether this pattern might be related to the limitations of the data mentioned above. El Salvador is a country in which the economic importance of agriculture has declined dramatically in recent years. One possibility, then, is that Salvadoran households, whether rural or urban, now tend to be net consumers of the basket of sensitive agricultural commodities.

Another possibility could be related to how *rural* and *urban* are defined in the EHPM survey. El Salvador is a geographically compact and densely populated country, which may limit the usefulness of the traditional, administrative definitions of *rural* and *urban* used in the survey. Potentially compounding this problem is El Salvador's not having had a population census since 1992. Combined, the EHPM identification of *rural* versus *urban,* based on administrative definitions and a series of post-1992 assumptions about population dynamics may have led to a blurring of functional rural–urban differences in the data.[15] The main message from the El Salvador data, however, as in the other countries, is that the proportion of households that are net consumers—and thus expected to benefit from price changes induced by DR-CAFTA—still greatly outnumber the proportion of households that are net producers, both in rural and in urban areas.

Differences Across the Welfare Distribution

The country case studies also indicate a common pattern of likely winners and losers across the welfare distribution; specifically, a higher percentage of the nonpoor population are expected to benefit than of the poor population. In Nicaragua, for example, 94.8 percent of households in the wealthiest quintile are net consumers, compared to 85.7 percent of households in the poorest quintile (table 5.4). In Guatemala, 92.0 percent of households in the wealthiest quintile are net consumers, opposed to 78.5 percent in the poorest quintile. The mirror image of these patterns is that a higher proportion of poor households are net producers and thus likely to be adversely affected by DR-CAFTA-related price changes. In Guatemala, for instance, 20.8 percent of households in the poorest quintile are net producers, compared with only 7.5 percent of households in the wealthiest quintile.

In El Salvador, this pattern is less strong on the net consumer side, with the highest proportion of net consumers found in the third and fourth quintiles. Nonetheless, the pattern is still seen clearly among net producers: at 7.5 percent, the percentage of net-producing households in the poorest quintile is roughly 1.5 times higher than the percentage of net-producing households in the wealthiest quintile. Again, it is important to highlight that nonresponses in the production for home consumption as well as the consumption expenditures module appear to be affecting the point estimates of net consumers and net producers in El Salvador—although probably not the overall qualitative findings. This problem appears to be the strongest among households in the poorest quintile where the data seem to suggest that more than 70 percent of all households are neither net consumers nor net producers (that is, neither positively nor negatively affected by price changes in sensitive agricultural commodities).

Prospective Gains to Net Consumers and Losses to Net Producers

Because of differences in household patterns of consumption and production, net consumers (net producers) stand to gain (lose) different amounts across countries and within different subgroups in a particular country. This can be seen clearly in table 5.5, which presents the estimated gains to net consumers

Table 5.5. Estimated Gains by Net Consumers and Estimated Losses by Net Producers of the Basket of Sensitive Agricultural Commodities in Nicaragua, Guatemala, and El Salvador, by Rural–Urban Location and Quintile
percent of per capita consumption

	Nicaragua		*Guatemala*		*El Salvador*	
Group	*Estimated net consumer gains*	*Estimated net producer losses*	*Estimated net consumer gains*	*Estimated net producer losses*	*Estimated net consumer gains*	*Estimated net producer losses*
All country	3.8	−0.8	0.5	−2.3	2.0	−2.2
Rural	3.3	−1.7	0.6	−2.3	2.0	−2.3
Urban	4.2	−0.2	0.4	−2.3	2.0	−2.1
Poorest quintile	n.a.	n.a.	0.8	−2.2	1.4	−3.4
2nd quintile	n.a.	n.a.	0.6	−2.0	2.0	−2.2
3rd quintile	n.a.	n.a.	0.5	−1.8	2.2	−1.9
4th quintile	n.a.	n.a.	0.4	−2.8	2.0	−1.0
Richest quintile	n.a.	n.a.	0.2	−3.2	1.8	−0.7

Sources: Pörtner 2003; Monge, Castro, and Saavedra 2004; and Marques 2005.
n.a. = not reported.

and estimated losses to net producers in Nicaragua, Guatemala, and El Salvador. Expected gains and losses are presented at the national level, for rural and urban areas, and across the welfare distribution.[16] In Nicaragua, it is estimated that if all *bienes sensibles agrícolas* were liberalized instantaneously, the 90.2 percent of households that are net consumers would experience a benefit of 3.8 percent of per capita consumption, on average. This compares with an expected benefit of only 0.5 percent of per capita consumption for net consumers in Guatemala (83.8 percent of households), and an intermediate benefit of 2.0 percent of per capita income predicted among net consumers in El Salvador (no less than 68.2 percent of Salvadoran households).

Expected losses among net producers also differ across countries. In the case of Nicaragua, expected losses are relatively low, on average: only 0.8 percent of per capita consumption (for the 8.8 percent of households that are net consumers). This compares with estimated losses of between 2.2 and 2.3 percent of per capita consumption (or income) among net producers in Guatemala (15.7 percent of households) and El Salvador (4.1 percent of households).

Patterns of gains and losses also differ somewhat across rural and urban areas within a country (table 5.5). The clearest example of this appears to be in

Nicaragua where gains to net consumers are estimated to be as high as 4.2 percent of per capita consumption in urban areas, compared with 3.3 percent in rural areas. At the same time, prospective losses to net producers are expected to be higher among rural than among urban households. Indeed, net producers in rural areas are expected to lose the equivalent of 1.7 percent of per capita consumption, on average, as a result of DR-CAFTA-related price changes, compared with only 0.2 percent of per capita consumption among net producers in urban areas. Differences in gains and losses for rural and urban inhabitants are estimated to be much smaller, and at times nonexistent, in Guatemala and El Salvador. Moreover, in contrast to Nicaragua, the small differences in estimated benefits to net consumers in Guatemala slightly favor rural households. In all three countries, gains to winners and losses to losers vary noticeably across different locations within rural and urban areas—again because of location-specific differences in production and consumption patterns.[17]

Although no data are reported for Nicaragua on the expected size of gains by net consumers and losses by net producers across quintiles, the Guatemala and El Salvador case studies do not show somewhat different patterns of gains and losses as a function of wealth. In Guatemala, the largest expected benefits—albeit still relatively small—are likely to accrue to the poorest net consumers, whereas the data in El Salvador suggest that middle-income net consumers stand to benefit most. In contrast, although the data from El Salvador suggest that the poorest net producers stand to lose the most, the Guatemalan data indicate that net-producing households in the top two quintiles stand to lose the most as a percentage of their per capita consumption. The expected household gains and losses in Nicaragua, Guatemala, and El Salvador are determined by country- and location-specific patterns of production and consumption. In this context, the contrasting distributional effects of liberalizing trade in maize and poultry are shown in box 5.3.

Average Impacts

Adding up and averaging the expected gains among net consumers and expected losses among net producers in each country, it can be seen that these societies will benefit overall as a result of the price changes associated with DR-CAFTA. The size of the average gains differs considerably across countries and sometimes across socioeconomic groups within countries. This reflects both the composition of net consumers and net producers in each society and the sizes of gains and losses among these groups.

Box 5.3

The Distribution of Losses and Gains to Different Sensitive Commodities in Guatemala: The Differential Impacts of Corn Versus Poultry Liberalization

Pörtner (2003) examined the predicted effects of individual commodities by consumption percentile for Guatemala to better understand (1) the distributional effects of liberalizing sensitive agricultural commodities and (2) the role for public intervention to mitigate the poverty and social effects of DR-CAFTA. His analysis pointed to a tremendous heterogeneity of impacts across different commodities. It also pointed to the political economy of reform of different commodities.

Figures 5B.1 and 5B.2 present contrasting patterns of estimated effects on per capita consumption associated with liberalizing two different commodities—maize and poultry meat—in Guatemala.[1] These figures show, by percentile of per capita consumption, (1) the median effect on per capita income (shown by the Xs), (2) the interval between the 5th and 95th percentile of effects (indicated by the solid vertical lines), and (3) the maximum and minimum predicted effects of removing trade protection (indicated by the upper and lower solid lines, respectively).

As can be seen from the Xs in figure 5B.1, the average estimated effect of eliminating trade protection on maize is positive across the consumption distribution, although the size of the net effect is very small (on the order of 0.10 percent of per capita consumption). At the same time, the graph shows that there is considerable heterogeneity of expected outcomes across net consumer and net producer households, even among the poor. For example, among the poorest 30 percent of households in the consumption distribution, there are a substantial number of households that are net consumers of maize that are predicted to experience significant gains relative to their current per capita consumption. Indeed, the expected gains to per capita consumption resulting from maize liberalization, at least in percentage terms, are actually largest among the poorest households. At the same time, however, a considerable number of the poorest households are net producers of maize who seem likely to experience relatively large losses. Indeed, the largest losses (as a percentage of per capita consumption) appear likely to be experienced by the poorest 20 percent of households. These findings frame a central challenge for policymakers—how to help net-producing households deal with declining producer prices, without forfeiting the benefits to be accrued by the majority of net-consuming households.

Figure 5B.1. Estimated Gains and Losses of Liberalizing Maize, by Consumption Percentile

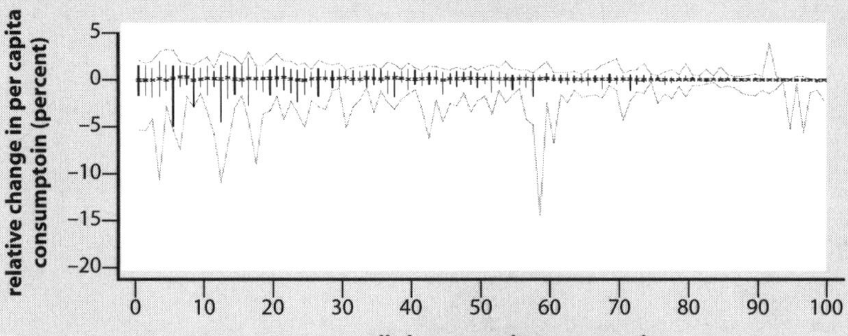

Source: Pörtner 2003.

Figure 5B.2. Estimated Gains and Losses of Liberalizing Poultry Meat, by Consumption Percentile

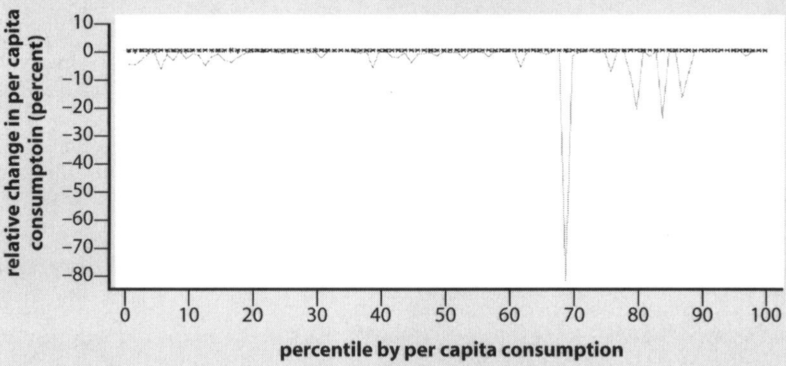

Source: Pörtner 2003.

In contrast to the situation for maize, analysis of eliminating trade protection for poultry meat provides a striking picture of production specialization (figure 5B.2). On average, positive welfare gains to liberalizing trade in poultry are predicted—although, again, the magnitude is very small (on the order of 0.01 percent of per capita consumption). Indeed, the vast majority of households will neither gain nor lose significantly from liberalization of poultry. At the same time, the large downward

continued

Box 5.3, *continued*

spikes pictured at the 70th percentile and above suggest there are a few relativey wealthy producers of poultry who stand to lose significantly. (Similar patterns are also seen in the case of beef.) Although these patterns of large losses among a handful of relatively wealthy households may not call for trade adjustment assistance on poverty or basic welfare grounds, they do suggest that for some commodities there may be small numbers of (potentially politically influential) producers opposed to liberalization who might try to lobby for extending grace or liberalization periods as grace periods end or for other types of special support.

Note

1. It should be noted that because Guatemala data do not differentiate between the production and consumption of yellow and white maize, Pörtner (2003) examined the effects of liberalizing trade in all maize. As such, Pörtner's calculations will overestimate (to an undetermined degree) the impacts of maize price changes resulting from DR-CAFTA among those households that produce and/or consume white maize.

Source: Pörtner 2003.

Benefits related to price changes are expected to be greatest in Nicaragua—equivalent to 3.0 percent of per capita consumption, on average (figure 5.4). Average benefits are estimated to be higher in urban than in rural areas, equivalent to 4.0 and 1.6 percent of per capita consumption, respectively. Static, price-related benefits are estimated to be much smaller in Guatemala, equivalent to an average of only 0.03 percent of per capita consumption. Indeed, households in rural areas are expected to experience small welfare losses—about 0.12 percent of per capita consumption, on average. Estimated average gains in El Salvador are also small, although considerably larger than those estimated for Guatemala. Average gains are expected to be about 1.3 percent of per capita income, with average gains to rural and urban households being nearly identical.[18]

The ways in which DR-CAFTA affects households with different levels of income or consumption also differ across countries—although not necessarily in predictable ways. In Nicaragua, for example, there is no clear pattern of average benefits across the welfare distribution. Average benefits in the

Figure 5.4. Average Estimated Gains (Losses) from DR-CAFTA–related Price Changes in Nicaragua, Guatemala, and El Salvador

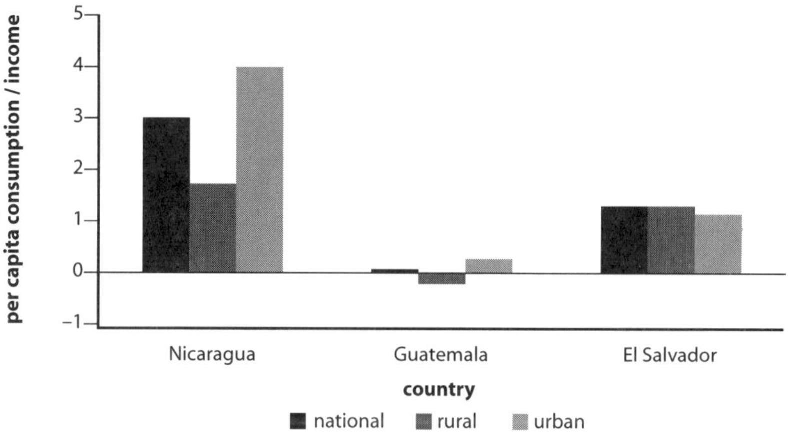

Sources: Pörtner 2003; Monge, Castro, and Saavedra 2004; and Marques 2005.

poorest quintile are slightly above the national level, and essentially equal to those in the 3rd and 4th quintiles (table 5.6). By contrast, benefits expected in Guatemala are largest, on average, among households in the lowest quintile, and they are *slightly negative* among households in the highest two quintiles. (The latter, while quite small as a percentage of per capita consumption, reflects mostly expected losses among relatively wealthy producers of poultry and beef.) In El Salvador, with the exception of the poorest quintile for whom average gains appear to be close to zero, there are no obvious patterns in the size of benefits across the welfare distribution. And, as discussed earlier, it is not clear to what extent the benefit figure for the poorest quintile reflects real benefits rather than underreporting (or nonreporting) problems in the data.

Summary of Effects

New analysis of the first-order welfare impacts of DR-CAFTA in Nicaragua, Guatemala, and El Salvador indicates that the vast majority of households in these countries stand to gain from the price changes associated with liberalizing trade in the so-called sensitive agricultural commodities.

Although most people in these three countries are likely to benefit, the evidence suggests that the number of people who could be adversely affect-

Table 5.6. Average Estimated Gains (Losses) in Nicaragua, Guatemala, and El Salvador, by Rural–Urban Location and Quintile
percent of per capita consumption

Group	*Nicaragua average gain (loss)*	*Guatemala average gain (loss)*	*El Salvador average gain (loss)*
All country	3.0	0.03	1.3
Rural	1.6	(–0.12)	1.3
Urban	4.0	0.19	1.2
Poorest quintile	3.3	0.21	0.1
2nd quintile	2.5	0.01	1.4
3rd quintile	3.3	0.08	1.7
4th quintile	3.3	(–0.06)	1.6
Richest quintile	2.8	(–0.01)	1.4

Sources: Pörtner 2003; Monge, Castro, and Saavedra 2004; and Marques 2005.

ed by DR-CAFTA-related price changes is not trivial—at least in the absence of measures to mitigate those impacts. The proportion of net producers estimated for each country implies, for example, that roughly 1.9 million Guatemalans (out of 12.3 million), 484,000 Nicaraguans (out of 5.5 million), and 260,000 Salvadorans (out of 6.5 million) would be negatively affected by price effects of DR-CAFTA. The analysis also suggests that specific subgroups face higher-than-average risks of experiencing negative impacts of price changes in the absence of complementary policy measures.

Although the average estimated size of losses to net producers is relatively small, such impacts may not be trivial for the poorest Central Americans. As with patterns of net consumers and net producers, the actual size of gains and losses that households experience will be determined in important ways by local patterns of production and consumption. Hence, despite similarities in patterns of impacts across the Central American countries, it will be important to take local circumstances into account in designing policies and programs to ensure that all Central Americans will be able to benefit from DR-CAFTA in the medium to long run. This point will be discussed at greater length in the following section.

Finally, the country case evidence suggests that whereas the average gains associated with liberalizing the sensitive agricultural commodities are positive in all three countries, the static gains associated with the price changes may not be large. The largest static gains appear likely in Nicaragua, where average gains are estimated at 3.0 percent of per capita consumption. At an estimated 1.3 percent of per capita income, the estimated gains in El Salvador are smaller. They are even smaller in Guatemala, where average gains are estimated to be less than one-tenth of 1 percent of average per capita consumption. The general-equilibrium static analysis of Nicaragua discussed in the previous chapter and conducted by Bussolo and Niimi (2005) also predicted rather small effects on both average incomes and poverty rates. These analyses thus suggest that the largest benefits from DR-CAFTA are likely to come from dynamic gains associated with increased foreign direct investment and related improvements in technology and productivity, increased employment, and higher levels of economic growth (see chapter 4). This in turn highlights the prospective importance not only of working to mitigate any negative impacts of DR-CAFTA-related price changes, but also of investing in people and places in Central America so as to maximize all people's ability to participate in emerging opportunities arising from DR-CAFTA.

Alternative Approaches to Mitigating the Adverse Impacts of DR-CAFTA

As discussed in the section above, DR-CAFTA includes a wide range of provisions for dealing with the liberalization of sensitive agricultural commodities, including grace periods for initiating liberalization, extended phase-out periods for tariffs, interim quotas and/or phase-downs of TQRs, and special safeguard measures to protect local farmers from undue harm due to increased agricultural imports under the agreement. While the exact provisions were negotiated country-by-country and, therefore, differ somewhat across the region, collectively the Central American countries were successful in negotiating generous timetables for reducing production on their *bienes sensibles agrícolas*. As shown earlier (box 5.1), phase-out periods are as long as 20 years in some cases. Built into the agreement itself is a type of safety net for those who might be adversely affected by liberalization of sensitive agriculture commodities: a prolonged and predictable timeframe over which producers can undertake the necessary economic adjustments. Let us consider some alternative approaches to mitigating losses resulting from DR-CAFTA.

Quick Liberalization Combined with Compensatory Transfers vs. Phased Reduction of Trade Protection: Can Countries Do Better?

Although the grace periods and extended tariff and quota phase-out periods do provide reasonable protection to producers of sensitive crops, the approach negotiated under DR-CAFTA also has some economic costs. Specifically, although phasing of reforms gives producers an extended period to make the necessary economic adjustments, for that same extended time period it also deprives consumers of the benefits associated with lower prices for key agricultural staples.

One alternative to the negotiated approach would simply be to liberalize trade in the sensitive crops quickly as assumed in the case studies above. This would provide immediate benefits to consumers, but would impose costs on net producers of sensitive goods, many of whom are poor staple crop farmers in rural areas of Central America. Given the painstaking negotiations to provide for phasing of trade reform, specifically to protect these poor groups, it is unlikely that this approach would be taken in practice. So, is there an alternative that would enable consumers to benefit quickly while producers are given a reasonable period for making the economic adjustment? Indeed. Such an approach would involve quick liberalization of trade in the sensitive agricultural commodities, coupled with the provision of compensatory transfers for some finite time period to those people who are expected to be negatively affected by DR-CAFTA in the short term.

In principle, quick liberalization coupled with transfers targeted to households affected negatively would be more economically efficient than the approach actually negotiated under the agreement, because consumers would not have to wait as long as 20 years to reap the full benefits of lower prices. Indeed, real food prices have been declining in Central America in recent years, and these declines in prices have themselves contributed in important ways to poverty reduction in El Salvador and Nicaragua (see, for example, World Bank 2003b, 2004c). Coupling well-designed transfer programs with quick liberalization would thus be a way to enhance households' purchasing power—with important positive welfare effects on the poor—while providing producers with financial support to help them manage the economic transition.

To be effective in practice, however, several conditions have to hold. First, implementing a program of compensatory transfers requires budgetary resources that are not required to implement the approach negotiated under

DR-CAFTA. Ensuring that producers of sensitive commodities are protected and that consumers reap the benefits of lower staple prices would require a commitment of fiscal resources. Second, to be effective and efficient, it would require that the county-level institutions have adequate administrative capacity to implement a transfer programs as well as the ability to target interventions effectively to adversely affected households. And, third, because the objective point of any trade-related compensatory transfer program would be to provide *temporary* assistance, there would have to be transparently and clearly communicated "rules of the game," including a finite time-horizon for assistance, to ensure that the transfers function as support for trade adjustment rather than as a permanent rural entitlement program.

Options for Compensatory Transfers

If DR-CAFTA countries in Central America were to pursue quick liberalization coupled with a system of compensatory transfers, there is a wide range of possible compensation and safety net–type programs among which countries might choose. These include "decoupled" income support payments to farmers, conditional cash transfers, cash-for-work or food-for-work programs (that is, workfare), or single compensation payments, among others (Castañeda 2004). Indeed, several of these programs have been or are currently being implemented with some success in Latin America and beyond:

- Decoupled income payments to farmers, which de-link payments from current production and prices, have been used recently in several countries, including in the European Union, Mexico, Turkey, and the United States. Mexico's decoupled income support program, PROCAMPO, was initiated in 1994 to provide support to farmers who were expected to be affected adversely by price changes occurring under NAFTA.
- Conditional cash transfer programs, which condition cash payments on family investments in children's human capital development, have been introduced recently in a number of Latin American and Caribbean countries, including Brazil, Colombia, Honduras, Jamaica, Mexico, and Nicaragua, as well as in countries outside the region, such as Turkey.
- Workfare programs have been implemented worldwide to address problems of unemployment, including over an extended period of time in Argentina and in response to periodic employment shocks (for example, during the recent coffee crisis in Nicaragua).[19]

Not all possible categories of support provide equal protection or show equal promise in the context of DR-CAFTA, however. Although workfare has been a staple of social assistance in many developing countries, such programs are better suited for employment than income shocks. But given that most of the sensitive agricultural commodities are staple crops produced on family farms, the income effects should significantly dominate employment effects, weakening the likely impact of workfare-type interventions (World Bank 2005b). Similarly, to be effective, support should enhance a household's ability to make the necessary economic transition, which in many cases will take multiple production seasons to complete. In this context, and in the absence of strong rural capital markets in Central America, one-time payments are unlikely to provide sufficient support to implement the necessary transition successfully. Although decoupled income payments to farmers and conditional cash transfers to households respond to somewhat different needs of poor, rural households, each intervention shows some promise to assist households in weathering the economic transition associated with DR-CAFTA.

Decoupled Income Support Payments

Decoupling can be defined broadly as replacing agricultural support programs that are based on current or future production and prices with direct payments that are based on clearly defined and fixed historical measures (Baffes and de Gorter 2003). In principle, decoupling income transfers avoids creating the economic distortions caused by many traditional agricultural support programs through their influence on domestic prices, input use, technology choice, or current or future production decisions. By not distorting production and, in turn, trade, properly designed decoupled transfer programs also fall into the "Green Box" category of income support programs as agreed under WTO rules (box 5.4).

Using decoupled income supports to farmers is, in essence, the approach Mexico adopted under NAFTA. Although Mexico, like DR-CAFTA countries, had negotiated extended grace and phase-out periods for protection of sensitive agricultural commodities, the government has never invoked those provisions, opting rather for a de facto quick liberalization and transfers. Specifically, Mexico introduced in 1994 a decoupled income support program, PROCAMPO, to assist farmers who were likely to experience negative effects from agricultural sector liberalization undertaken under NAFTA.

Box 5.4

Ensuring That Compensation Measures Are Consistent with WTO Agreements

If appropriately designed and implemented, decoupled direct income payments to farmers as well as income safety net programs like conditional cash transfers conform to allowable ("Green Box") interventions under existing multilateral trade agreements. To be allowable under WTO rules, such programs are required to adhere to the following criteria:

- *Decoupled direct income payments:* Under the Uruguay Round of the General Agreement on Tariffs and Trade in 1994 there was an agreement about reduction in and expenditure limits on domestic agricultural subsidies, with some exemptions. The exemptions included domestic support measures that have no, or at most minimal, distorting effects on trade and production. If support is provided via public funding and not via transfers from consumers, and if it does not have the effect of providing price support to producers, then direct payments to producers can then be used if they meet the following conditions:
    - Eligibility for such payments shall be determined by clearly defined criteria such as income, status as a producer or landowner, factor use or production level in a defined and fixed base period;
    - The amount of such payments in any given year shall not be related to, or based on, the type or volume of production (including livestock units) undertaken in any year after the base period;
    - The amount of such payment in any given year shall not be related to, or based on, the prices, domestic or international, applying to any production undertaken in any year after the base period;
    - The amount of such payment in any given year shall not be related to, or based on, the factors of production employed in any year after the base period;
    - No production shall be required to receive such payments.

- *Safety net programs*: According to Annex 2 of GATT rules, another type of direct payment that is permitted is government financial participation in income insurance and income safety net programs. These programs must meet the following criteria:

continued

Box 5.4, *continued*

- Eligibility for such payments shall be determined by an income loss, taking into account only income derived from agriculture, which exceeds 30 percent of average gross income or the equivalent in net income terms (excluding any payments from the same or similar schemes) in the preceding three-year period or a three-year average based on the preceding five-year period, excluding the highest and the lowest entry. Any producer meeting this condition shall be eligible to receive the payments.
- The amount of such payments shall compensate for less than 70 percent of the producer's income loss in the year the producer becomes eligible to receive this assistance.
- The amount of any such payments shall relate solely to income; it shall not relate to the type or volume of production (including livestock units) undertaken by the producer; or to the prices, domestic or international, applying to such production; or to the factors of production employed.
- Where a producer receives in the same year payments under income insurance/safety net provisions and under provisions for relief from natural disasters, the total of such payments shall be less than 100 percent of the producer's total loss.

Source: Castañeda 2004.

The program was designed as a 15-year transition and is expected to be terminated in 2008.

PROCAMPO provides eligible agricultural producers with a fixed payment per hectare. Eligible producers are those who cultivated one or more of nine crops—barley, beans, cardamom, corn, cotton, rice, sorghum, soybeans, or wheat—in one of the three agricultural cycles (autumn/winter or spring/summer) *prior to* August 1993. Payment goes to whomever is cultivating the property, regardless of whether it is the owner, a renter, or a sharecropper. Producers with less than one hectare are paid for one hectare, and there is a maximum eligibility of 100 hectares for irrigated land and 200 hectares for rain-fed land. Because producers on irrigated land can cultivate for up to two seasons per year, they are eligible for payments up to twice a year; producers on rain-fed land are eligible for only one payment per year.[20]

Payments are decoupled from current cultivation, although PROCAMPO does impose a restriction that land must either be used in crops, livestock, or forestry, or be part of an approved environmental program (beneficiaries are free to choose among these options).

In addition to conforming to WTO rules, decoupled transfer payments have the benefit of addressing specifically the income shock resulting from liberalization of sensitive agricultural commodities. If implemented for a limited time period, in principle decoupled transfers also provide a clear and predictable timeframe under which producers can make the necessary economic adjustments (as under the phased liberalization negotiated under DR-CAFTA). Recent impact evaluation of PROCAMPO in Mexico also indicates that the program has conferred a number of positive effects—protecting recipients against negative income effects, generating positive income multipliers for many farm families, and raising household consumption and nutritional status. These, in turn, have contributed to lower poverty rates among *ejido* sector households (box 5.5).

At the same time, the evidence suggests that PROCAMPO has not contributed to significant improvements in farm sector efficiency (World Bank 2003d), nor has it been particularly effective in inducing farmers—at least smallholders and producers of rain-fed crops—to make the necessary economic transition to more remunerative means of production. This appears to result in part from the fact that the poorest recipients have tended to use transfers disproportionately for consumption purposes rather than for investment. The relative lack of impact on the pattern of rural production also appears to result from insufficient reforms and investments in complementary factors of production (such as energy, transportation infrastructure, and so forth) that affect the cost structure and competitiveness of the rural sector more broadly (World Bank 2003d).

Conditional Cash Transfers

Among the fastest growing and most successful categories of rural poverty alleviation programs in Latin America (and elsewhere) are conditional cash transfers. CCTs provide cash transfers to poor families residing in selected rural areas, on the condition that these families make specific investments in their children's human development—for example, sending school-age children to school, obtaining regular health checkups, ensuring that children under five years of age are vaccinated, and the like. The rationale for this is that

Box 5.5

PROCAMPO: Positive Impacts on Income, Consumption, and Poverty

Recent impact analysis of PROCAMPO indicates that the program has had a number of positive benefits—from increasing household incomes and protecting recipients from negative income shocks, to increasing household consumption, to contributing to poverty reduction among rural agricultural households. What follows is a list of examples:

- *Income effects:* PROCAMPO payments appear to have generated income multiplier effects among many of its recipients, apparently as a result of its effect on increasing liquidity among agricultural producers. The analysis indicates that, on average, for every peso received, households generate incomes that are 1.5 to 2.6 times higher (Sadoulet, de Janvry, and Davis 2001; Cord and Wodon 2001). Multipliers are highest among households with medium and large farms, nonindigenous households, households with fewer adults, and those farming on irrigated land. PROCAMPO also appears to provide a good countercyclical tool in the face of economic downturns. In 1994, for instance, incomes of PROCAMPO recipients increased by about 18 percent, whereas incomes of otherwise similar households that did not receive PROCAMPO declined by about 4 percent (Sadoulet, de Janvry, and Davis 2001).
- *Poverty and income distribution:* Given its special acreage provisions, PROCAMPO appears to provide relatively larger benefits to poor farmers—as a percentage of household income (Cord and Wodon 2001). Although in 1997 transfers represented 8 percent of household income in the *ejido* sector as a whole, they represented 40 percent of household income among those in the poorest decile. Moreover, analysis of panel data indicate that PROCAMPO payments reduced the probably of being poor among the *ejido* population by 10 percent (Cord and Wodon 2001). A recent World Bank Poverty Assessment for Mexico found, as well, that despite high land concentration there, the benefit-incidence of PROCAMPO is slightly progressive overall (World Bank 2003e).
- *Food consumption and nutrition:* Evidence also indicates that PROCAMPO has contributed to increased food consumption among recipients, raising households' calorie intake and nutritional diversity (Ruiz et al. 2002; Davis et al. 2002).

even if *poor rural* families recognize the long-term benefits of education and preventive health measures, they do not have the resources to cover the costs of school (such as books and uniforms) or health care or cannot afford the opportunity cost of schooling for school-age children. Cash transfers thus have the dual objectives of providing immediate short-term assistance to families to improve their basic consumption, health, and nutrition *and* of supporting long-term human development for children to reduce the chances of the intergenerational transmission of poverty.

Although CCT-related programs focus on *consumption* and *human capital investment* rather than on *production* support for rural families, they may be appropriate for compensating rural households for loss of employment or income resulting from tariff reductions and the loss of trade protection associated with DR-CAFTA. Decoupled payments, such as those provided under PROCAMPO, compensate farm managers, but not necessarily hired labor, who may also be affected by the loss of trade protection. Moreover, decoupled producer supports function best where there are good records of land ownership or use (Baffes and de Gorter 2003; Castañeda 2004). Where hired labors as well as self-employed farmers are affected by trade liberalization, or where records regarding ownership or use of land are weak or nonexistent, appropriately targeted CCTs may provide a viable alternative approach to supporting affected households. Furthermore, in the case of DR-CAFTA countries, CCT programs already exist: Honduras and Nicaragua already have targeted programs operating and El Salvador is in the process of developing one. In this context, using CCTs to compensate DR-CAFTA-affected households might have the additional benefit of building on existing programs, rather than requiring development from scratch of a new transfer program (and related institution).

As with PROCAMPO, recent impact evaluations undertaken for CCT programs in Mexico and Nicaragua show that they have important benefits to recipient families: increasing families' consumption and nutrition, increasing children's school enrollments, and improving preventive health care outcomes (box 5.6).

As is true of PROCAMPO, the extent to which CCTs are well suited to support the economic transition that will be necessary under DR-CAFTA is not clear. A recent evaluation of the impacts of the social safety net program *Red de Protección Social* (RPS) during the recent coffee crisis in Central America suggests that the effects of such programs in promoting structural change in rural production may be limited. Although evaluation of the RPS did show that the program has performed like a crisis safety net, there is a more mixed body of evidence on whether the RPS enabled coffee households to reallocate their resources in ways that are consistent with the historical downward trends in coffee prices (Maluccio 2004). Program beneficiaries who worked in the coffee sector as laborers were more likely to exit the industry, but self-employed coffee producers were less likely to leave. At the same time, although program beneficiaries living in coffee-growing regions reduced total hours worked in agriculture, they increased the role of agriculture in their portfolio—to the detriment of nonagricultural activities.

As in the case of decoupled income support payments, it would be important that in the context of DR-CAFTA, program benefits to affected households be made only along a limited and clearly specified time horizon, to en-

Box 5.6

Conditional Cash Transfer Programs: Strengthening Education, Health, and Nutrition Outcomes among the Poor

Recent evaluation results from two conditional cash transfer programs in Latin America—PROGRESA/Oportunidades in Mexico and the *Red de Protección Social* in Nicaragua—show that CCTs are an effective instrument for improving and protecting consumption while increasing the human capital of poor people in poor households. Specifically, CCTs provide the following benefits:

- *Increasing and protecting consumption:* Evidence indicates that consumption has grown faster for households participating in CCT programs than for similar households that did not participate. In Mexico, for example, the average consumption level in PROGRESA households increased rapidly (14 percent); after more than a year of program operation, median food expenditure was 11 percent higher in program participant households than in control group households. In Nicaragua, control households experienced a sharp decline in consumption partly as a result of low coffee prices and a drought, whereas the RPS provided some measure of protection in the face of a shock; average per capita household expenditures in RPS areas did not change over the same period.
- *Improving education:* CCT programs have raised enrollment rates for both boys and girls. In Mexico, primary school enrollment rates increased approximately 1 per-

Box 5.6, *continued*

centage point from a high pre-program level of about 90 percent. At the secondary school level, enrollment rates rose 7.2–9.3 percentage points for girls from baseline enrollment rates of 67 percent and rose 3.5–5.8 percentage points for boys from a baseline of 73 percent. In Nicaragua, program impacts are even more impressive. Average enrollment rates of children ages 7–13 in grades 1 to 4 in treatment areas increased nearly 22 percentage points as a result of the program—from a low starting point of around 70 percent. Program impact on attendance rates is more mixed. In Nicaragua, the RPS produced an increase of 30 percentage points in the share of children who had fewer than six unexcused absences during a two-month period.

- *Strengthening child health and nutrition:* Evaluations show improvement in health and nutrition also. Growth-monitoring visits of PROGRESA beneficiaries up to age 3 have increased between 30 and 60 percent, and beneficiaries up to age 6 have a 12 percent lower incidence of illness, compared with control group children. In Nicaragua, around 60 percent of children under age 3 participated in nutrition monitoring before the RPS was implemented. After a few months of program operation, more than 90 percent of children in RPS areas benefited from nutrition monitoring, compared with 67 percent in control areas. Among children age 12–23 months, the RPS increased timely immunization by 18 percentage points.

Source: World Bank 2005b.

sure the greatest possible incentives for households to make the necessary economic adjustments. Moreover, as in the case of decoupled income supports, to be maximally effective it would be important for CCTs to be accompanied by a complementary set of policies and investments that will enable affected families and their children to take the best advantage of new opportunities arising out of DR-CAFTA.[21]

Potential Fiscal Costs of Compensating Those Adversely Affected by DR-CAFTA

If it were possible to identify net producer households and the extent of their losses and to target compensation perfectly, then the fiscal costs of compensating those who are negatively affected would not be high. Indeed, estimates of the aggregate annual value of losses to net producers in El Salvador, Guatemala, and Nicaragua range from 0.01 percent of GDP (El Salvador) to 0.13 percent of GDP (Guatemala). These relatively low figures reflect two main factors: first, the share of net producers in each country is relatively small (from 4.1 percent in El Salvador to 15.7 percent in Guatemala; table 5.4), and, second, the average value of losses by net producers in each country is relatively low (from 0.8 percent in Nicaragua to 2.3 percent in Guatemala; table 5.5).

The actual fiscal costs of implementing a compensatory transfer program are likely to be considerably higher than 0.13 percent of GDP, however, at least if it entails creating a new program. This is the result of several factors, including (1) the practical impossibility of identifying and targeting program beneficiaries perfectly (that is, without "leakage" of resources to recipients who are not intended beneficiaries); and (2) the experience from recent programs that suggests the size of the program benefits may be larger than the average losses of net producers, at least if regional norms are followed. In addition, any new program entails at least some administrative costs.

There is a variety of data-related and administrative reasons why net producers cannot be identified and targeted perfectly. Indeed, targeted programs commonly make important errors of exclusion and inclusion; some people are excluded from the program who rightfully deserve to receive benefits, and others are included who are not part of the intended beneficiary population. In practice, when efforts are made to minimize errors of exclusion, errors of inclusion tend to increase, raising the costs of a program. Targeted programs often risk transferring considerable resources to people outside the group of intended recipients, especially when the targeted group is geographically disbursed or the targeting criteria are hard to observe, as is the case with net producers of sensitive agricultural commodities in Central America. To illustrate leakage in a targeted program, consider the Mexican experience. The benefits of the PROGRESA/Oportunidades program, which uses a combination of geographic and household criteria for targeting poor households, are highly progressive, and the program is considered well targeted. Nonetheless, in 2002, 28 percent of households receiving benefits were outside the bottom three income deciles, the program's target population (World Bank 2005a).[22]

Although average losses among net producers are estimated at no more than 2.3 percent of per capita consumption/income in the three countries analyzed, regional norms regarding benefits from decoupled income support and CCT programs are generally larger. In 1997, for example, transfers from PROCAMPO in Mexico averaged 8 percent of household per capita income in the target population as a whole (table 5.7; box 5.5). As can be seen in table 5.7, the size of conditional cash transfers relative to household consumption (income) varies considerably across programs and countries. Whereas transfers average less than 5 percent of per capita income in the case of the PRAF program in Honduras, they are as high as 21 percent of per capita expenditure in Mexico's PROGRESA/Oportunidades.

What might this imply for the fiscal costs of a program to compensate net producers adversely affected by DR-CAFTA in El Salvador, Guatemala, and Nicaragua? On one level, this question is impossible to answer because the costs of a program are dictated by any number of political and institutional factors, including decisions about the size of the transfer, the country's capacity to target, its tolerance for program leakage (errors of both exclusion and inclusion), and whether the government wants to launch a new program or build on an existing initiative. Nonetheless, recent experience in the region can provide some guidance on the costs of these types of programs, giv-

Table 5.7. Size of Transfers in Selected Transfer Programs—Decoupled Income Support and Conditional Cash Transfers—in Latin America

Program (country)	*Number of beneficiaries (000s)*	*Annual subsidy per family (US$)*	*Transfer (% of household per capita spending)*	*Program budget (US$ and % of GDP)*
Decoupled Income Supports				
PROCAMPO	3,000	367	8	$1.1 billion (0.17%, 2001)
Conditional Cash Transfer				
PROGRESA/ Oportunidades (Mexico)	4,200	380	21	$2.3 billion (0.32%, 2001)
Familias en Acción (Colombia)	315	260	15 (of MW)	$83 million (0.12%)
Red de Protección Social (Nicaragua)	10	236	18	$5 million (0.02%)
PRAF (Honduras)	51	110	< 5	$8 million (0.2%)

Source: Adapted from Castañeda 2004.
MW = minimum wage.

en program size, benefits size, and so on (table 5.7). Moreover, building on this guidance and on some assumptions about benefit sizes and leakages, it is possible to undertake illustrative calculations regarding the possible fiscal costs of a transfer program to compensate those adversely affected by DR-CAFTA. For example, if program benefits were set at 10 percent of household per capita consumption/income (roughly the middle of the range of benefits of programs listed in table 5.7), all households that were adversely affected by DR-CAFTA received benefits, and there was no program leakage, then the estimated annual fiscal costs of the transfer program would be roughly 0.03 percent of GDP in El Salvador, 0.55 percent of GDP in Guatemala, and 0.66 percent of GDP in Nicaragua. If program benefits were set at 10 percent of household per capita consumption/income; all adversely affected households received benefits; and, for reasons of targeting error, 28 percent of all program beneficiaries had not been adversely affected by DR-CAFTA (that is, levels of program leakage were similar to those found in PROGRESA/Oportunidades), then the estimated fiscal costs would reach about 0.05 percent of GDP in El Salvador, 0.76 percent of GDP in Guatemala, and 0.92 percent of GDP in Nicaragua.[23]

Decoupled Income Support Versus CCTs: Does One Approach Dominate the Other?

The choice of one or the other type of transfer program would depend on a number of factors that are both economic and institutional in nature, and that may differ across countries. Decoupled programs have the benefit of being designed specifically as producer-side interventions, providing income support directly in response to expected income losses associated with trade liberalization. Given the nature of the sensitive agricultural commodities to be liberalized under DR-CAFTA, and the fact that these commodities are commonly produced by self-employed farmers (as opposed to wage laborers), decoupled transfers are also likely to be appropriate and potentially effective in reaching their target constituency. Nonetheless, implementation (targeting) of decoupled programs requires good cadastral records; and if such records do not exist, then efforts would need to be undertaken to establish them, while the transfer program itself would provide incentives in favor of land titling.[24] Also, in spite of the evidence on the positive impacts of PROCAMPO on beneficiary-household incomes, the track record on implementation in Mexico and elsewhere is mixed (Baffes and de Gorter 2003;

Castañeda 2004). One issue is that decoupled programs by themselves do not appear to have contributed significantly to economic adjustment among agricultural producers in line with trade-related or other economic changes. This suggests that decoupled programs, if implemented, ought to be undertaken along with other measures—whether technical assistance or complementary investments—that would help to diversify income sources among DR-CAFTA-affected producers.

In contrast, CCTs have not traditionally been used to support trade adjustment or in response to terms of trade shocks. Rather, they have been implemented to foster household investments in human capital among the poor and, through that, to foster long-term poverty reduction. Nonetheless, although CCTs have not been designed to provide assistance to poor farmers during transitory adjustments, recent evidence suggests that these programs can be effective in protecting households from the worst effects of terms-of-trade or related income shocks, including negative effects on household consumption and investments in children's education, health, and nutrition (World Bank 2005a). As is well documented in the literature, short-term shocks to children's human capital development can have detrimental long-run impacts on their well-being, their productivity as adults, and on poverty. Moreover, because CCTs are currently or soon to be implemented in several Central American countries, they may have the advantage of providing an existing programmatic and institutional infrastructure upon which policymakers can build. Indeed, to the extent that net producers of basic grains are already targeted by existing CCTs, it would likely be efficient to build on those programs, both in terms of the targeting mechanisms and the fiscal costs of the program.[25]

In short, each type of program has its own particular strengths and weaknesses in the context of DR-CAFTA. Should the DR-CAFTA countries choose to pursue an approach of quick trade liberalization, the choice between a decoupled transfer program and a conditional cash transfer would likely hinge in part on very practical considerations—that is, on the specific institutional environments in each country and the preexisting administrative capacity to implement one type of program or another. Does the country have good cadastral records of land ownership and/or usage, or can they be developed in a reasonable period of time? Does it have or can it quickly develop the capacity and systems to target the programs to DR-CAFTA-affected households in a way that minimizes exclusion or inclusion targeting errors? In El Salvador, Honduras, and Nicaragua, where CCTs are being operated or are under development, can building on the existing programs provide the basis for effective intervention while containing the marginal fiscal costs of efforts to assist DR-CAFTA-affected households?

Policies and Investments to Ensure That Poor People Can Benefit from DR-CAFTA

Whether DR-CAFTA countries do or do not choose to pursue quick liberalization coupled with compensatory transfers, it will be important for the Central American governments to implement a core set of complementary policies and investments if they are to ensure that people adversely affected by liberalizing sensitive agricultural commodities—and especially those among the poor—are able to benefit from emerging opportunities arising out of DR-CAFTA. These policies and investments mirror closely the complementary agenda outlined elsewhere in this report, although here the focus is on more deliberate policies and investments that are targeted to households and regions that are either expected to be particularly affected by the agreement or that are particularly poor at its outset. These policies and investments would focus on facilitating greater economic progress in poor regions and greater economic mobility among poor or adversely affected households, including

- strengthening access to and quality of basic education
- targeting investments in economic infrastructure to poor areas in a way that lowers households' transaction costs and increases poor people's economic competitiveness and access to markets
- deepening rural financial services (both savings and credit) to enable investments in rural enterprises
- providing technical assistance to promote innovation and higher productivity in agriculture as well as diversification of rural enterprises
- implementing public information campaigns to promote widespread understanding of DR-CAFTA-related reforms and to create greater certainty in the investment climate.

These areas of emphasis are highlighted by several recent World Bank studies on poverty reduction and on trade. For example, a recent World Bank study of the effects of NAFTA in Mexico found that the poorer, less developed southern states of Mexico have not benefited to the same degree as the more developed northern and central states (Lederman, Maloney, and Servén 2005). Empirical analysis of the reasons behind these regional differences in benefits suggests that the southern states of Mexico have been less prepared to benefit because of the relatively low levels of education and economic infrastructure, and the low quality of local institutions. These findings for Mexico mirror in important ways the findings of recent World Bank Poverty Assessments that examine why the poorest Central Americans are often not able to benefit from economic progress in the region. Poor families commonly lack the education necessary to take advantage of new or emerging economic opportunities (World Bank 2004d, 2005c). Moreover, poor rural families often lack sufficient access to markets as well as to rural financial services, either because of great physical distances or a relative paucity of economic infrastructure in poor areas.

However, investments in quality education for the poor and in basic economic infrastructure, along with efforts to deepen rural financial services in poor, rural areas, would go far to strengthen the capacity of poor people to take advantage of new and emerging opportunities arising out of DR-CAFTA—through increasing their capabilities, by reducing transaction costs, and by increasing economic competitiveness of poor people's enterprises in rural areas. In addition, it will be important for the region's governments to carry out information and communication campaigns to promote widespread understanding of DR-CAFTA-related reforms, especially among the poor populations and those people who are likely to be adversely affected by the agreement in the short term. Making clear the nature of the forthcoming economic changes and the timeline for implementation would help enormously to create greater certainty in the investment climate as well as to establish a known timeframe and appropriate expectations for undertaking the inevitable economic adjustments.

Summary and Conclusion

Although the vast majority of Central Americans are expected to benefit from DR-CAFTA in the medium to long term, some households are at risk of bearing the short-term costs of trade-related adjustments. More specifically, these households are likely to be those who are net producers of agricultural commodities that still enjoy high levels of protection against imports. Chapter 5 has focused on quantifying the size of the potentially affected population and the magnitude of the potential effects. It additionally examined alternative policy approaches on how best to assist vulnerable groups to ensure that they can benefit from emerging opportunities arising out of the trade agreement.

Given current levels of protection, the introduction of more trade competition for sensitive agricultural commodities under DR-CAFTA can be expected to lead to lower domestic prices on sensitive commodities in each country—in some cases, significantly lower prices. DR-CAFTA consequently includes specific provisions for dealing with sensitive goods, including grace periods, extended tariff-phase-out periods, quotas and/or phase-downs of tariff-rate quotas, as well as special safeguards. Indeed, the agreement includes extended timetables for reducing protection on sensitive agricultural crops. These provisions represent important protections for producers of sensitive crops, giving them an extended timeframe over which to undertake the necessary economic adjustments.

Given this, what might policymakers expect to be the effects of removing barriers to trade in sensitive crops under the trade agreement? Three new empirical studies using nationally representative household survey data from El Salvador, Guatemala, and Nicaragua help shed light on this and related policy issues. All three studies apply a common analytical framework to assess the potential first-order effects of tariff elimination for sensitive agricultural products, including maize, beans, milk, poultry meat, bovine meat, apples, pork, wheat, and rice. Despite the phasing out of trade protection negotiated under DR-CAFTA, these analyses examine expected impacts *as if* all tariffs and quotas were going to be removed completely and immediately under the agreement. Such an approach provides useful insights into the first-order impacts of introducing more competition in the markets for sensitive commodities. It also provides a useful baseline from which to examine policy options, including some important policy trade-offs implicit in the gradual approach to easing trade barriers negotiated under the agreement.

This analysis on El Salvador, Guatemala, and Nicaragua indicates that the vast majority of households in these countries are net consumers of the sensitive commodities and thus are likely to experience welfare gains from the removal of trade barriers. As mentioned earlier, this is the case in 90 percent of Nicaraguan households, 84 percent of Guatemalan households, and 68 percent of Salvadoran households, respectively. In El Salvador, a further 27 percent of households remain unaffected because they experience essentially negligible gains or losses. Even though potential losers are thus small minorities, appropriate attention is needed to ensure that anticipated losses do not harm the poorest and most vulnerable groups. For people who may suffer significant welfare losses, targeted programs losses may be justified.

Built into the agreement are considerable grace periods and extended trade restrictions phase-out periods that provide reasonable protection to producers of sensitive crops over a prolonged adjustment period, but this approach is not without its own economic and social trade-offs. Although gradual reforms provide producers an extended period to make the necessary economic adjustments, it also deprives consumers of the benefits associated with lower prices for important agricultural staples for that same time period. In this context, an alternative (and some could argue more efficient) approach might involve a shorter liberalization period for the sensitive commodities, coupled with transfers targeted to those adversely affected in the short term. In principle, a shorter liberalization period combined with targeted transfers is more efficient economically than phased removal of barriers because consumers can reap the full benefits of lower prices more quickly. Coupling well-targeted transfer programs with quick easing of trade restrictions could thus enhance households' welfare in the short term on the consumption side while it provides producers with a reasonable period of support to make the economic transition.

Regardless of whether the DR-CAFTA countries in Central America choose to pursue this alternative approach, it is important to understand the broad options that policymakers can use to mitigate potential income losses arising from declines in commodity prices if extended phase-outs and safeguards are deemed insufficient: (1) decoupled income support payments to farmers of sensitive crops; (2) technical assistance programs to farmers of such crops; (3) CCTs to rural families, effective only as poor families make investments in their children's education, health, and nutrition; and (4) provision of public goods such as economic infrastructure, basic education, rural financial services, and technical assistance targeted to households and/or regions that are likely to be hard hit by the agreement.

These options can be considered from two different perspectives. The first perspective concerns the institutional sophistication required to implement support programs. This criterion recognizes that effective programs will require, inter alia, a viable method of targeting vulnerable populations, a minimum degree of know-how among the civil servants of the implementing public-sector agency, the creation of new government organizations (or transformation of old ones), and a minimum amount of independence for these agencies to ensure the application of technical criteria and avoid polit-

Figure 5.5. Options for Support Programs for Populations Potentially Affected by DR-CAFTA

international capacity	incentives/support for production diversificaton: low	incentives/support for production diversificaton: high
low	decoupled transfers	public goods
high	technical assistance	conditional cash transfers

Source: Authors' calculations.

ical interference. The second perspective is related to whether the program provides incentives (or other support) for production diversification, including strengthening the capacity of families to exploit new income opportunities for off-farm and/or nonagricultural activities—which may be critical to ensure greater economic mobility among poor households.

The two perspectives are useful to assess the requirements and objectives that may be relevant in each country, because the choice of the more appropriate type of support program should be made on the basis of country-specific factors (see figure 5.5). Decoupled transfers require relatively low institutional sophistication but offer few incentives for farmers to seek new income opportunities. Technical assistance programs place a greater burden on the capacities of government agencies while they give incentives for productive diversification or upgrading (but only within agriculture). Public goods programs require less institutional sophistication by relying on existing institutions for program delivery while they create conditions for rural inhabitants to diversify economic activities—although programs of this type may require a strong regional concentration of potentially affected poor households to make economic sense. CCTs require relatively sophisticated new institutional capacity (especially in countries where programs of this type are not currently being implemented), although by strengthening families' human capital, they offer broad support for production diversification.

Annex: Effective Tariff Rates Used in Ex Ante Impact Analyses for El Salvador, Guatemala, and Nicaragua

Table 5A.1. Nominal and Effective Tariffs for Sensitive Commodities in Nicaragua
percent

Product	*Nominal tariff*	*Effective tariff*	*Product*	*Nominal tariff*	*Effective tariff*
Milk	20	20	White maize	10	10
Rice	62	38	Bovine meat	15	15
Beans	10	10	Poultry meat	170	170

Source: Monge, Castro, and Saavedra (2004), based on tariff and trade data from the Nicaraguan Ministry of Industrial Development and Trade.

Table 5A.2. Tariff Rates and Levels of Imports of Sensitive Crops in Guatemala, 2001

	Tariff rate (%)				
Sensitive crop	*Within quota*	*Out of quota*	*Global quota (MTs)*	*Imports (MTs)*	*Weighted average tariff*
Apples	12.0	25.0	9,100	8,481	12.0
Beans	15.0	15.0	n.a.	n.a.	15.0
Bovine meat	0.0	30.0	1,595	10,595	25.5
Maize (yellow)	5.0	35.0	501,820	515,912	5.8
Milk	15.0	15.0	n.a.	n.a.	15.0
Pork	15.0	15.0	n.a.	n.a.	15.0
Poultry meat	15.0	45.0	7,000	14,915	30.9
Rice	6.0	36.0	33,435	42,165	12.2
Wheat	1.2	6.0	391,322	407,470	1.4

Source: Pörtner 2003.
n.a. = not applicable; MTs = metric tons.

Table 5A.3. Effective Tariff Reduction in El Salvador, 2003

			Tariff		*Import volume*		
Products	*SAC*[a]	*Quota (MTs)*	*Within quota*	*Out of quota*	*Origin*	*MTs*	*Effective tariff rate*
Wheat[b]	1001100	n.a.	0	0	Total	254,587	0
					U.S.	229,698	
					Other	24,889	
					CA	0	
White corn	10059030	36,288	15		Total	10,419	6.5
				20	U.S.	4,499	
				20	Other	0	
				0	CA	5,920	
Beans	713	n.a.	n.a.		Total	1,161	3.3
				20	U.S.	147	
				20	Other	44	
				0	CA	970	
Rice, rough	10061090	83,915	0		Total	86,810	0.8
				40	U.S.	85,676	
				40	Other	0	
				0	CA	1,134	
Rice, milled	10062000	n.a.	n.a.		Total	3,651	
	10063010			40	U.S.	0	
	10063090			40	Other	0	
	10064000			0	CA	3,651	
Poultry	020713- 020714-	n.a.	n.a.		Total	1,934	19.3
				164.4	U.S.	33	
				20	Other	1,593	
				0	CA	308	

Pork	0203-	955	0		Total	1,399	6.9
				40	U.S.	967	
				40	Other	229	
				0	CA	203	
Bovine meat	0201-	n.a.	n.a.		Total	15,030	0.3
				30	U.S.	99	
				30	Other	29	
				0	CA	14,902	
Milk, liquid	040110000-	n.a.	n.a.		Total	5,514	11.2
	040120000-			40	U.S.	18	
	040130000-			40	Other	6	
				0	CA	5,490	
Milk, powder	04021000/2111	n.a.	n.a.		Total	11,405	
	04022112/2121			20	U.S.	47	
	04022122/2900			20	Other	9,350	
				0	CA	2,008	
Cheese	04062010-	750	15		Total	9,669	8.6
	04061000/2090			40	U.S.	897	
	04063000/9010			40	Other	1,650	
	04069020/9090			0	CA	7,122	

Source: Marques 2005.

CA = Central America; n.a. = not applicable.

a. Central America Tariff Classification.

b. In 2003 wheat flour was imported from Costa Rica (20 MTs), Guatemala (19,558 MTs), Honduras (44 MTs), and Nicaragua (4,763 MTs), at zero tariff. The 10 percent tariff on U.S. imports will be eliminated during a five-year period under DR-CAFTA.

Notes

1. This is true at least for trade outside the Central American Common Market. Within the CACM, imports generally carry lower and often zero percent tariff levels.
2. See Monge, Loría, and González-Vega (2003), p. 46, table (Cuadro) 33.
3. In turn, these price reductions would reflect themselves in a fall in national consumer price indexes, which would depend on the level of tariff and nontariff barriers and on the share of these sensitive commodities in the bundle of consumption goods used to calculate such price indexes. Such an exercise is difficult to undertake because of problems in predicting the exact magnitude of the domestic price reductions, especially when quotas are in place and when the price-transmission between border price changes and producer prices within countries is imperfect.
4. See Hertel and Reimer (2004), as cited in Marques (2005).
5. These quintile averages conceal potentially important variations in the shares of sensitive agricultural commodities in total income of specific households within a quintile. Nonetheless, even the least diversified households tend to have multiple sources of income, both in terms of crops and in terms of a mix of wage and self-employed income within and outside of agriculture. Although not shown in figure 5.1, the share of income derived from self-employed agriculture (and thus from sensitive agricultural commodities) is much lower among urban households than among rural households in Nicaragua.
6. See Deaton (1997).
7. This net consumer–net producer framework is extended to all the sensitive agricultural commodities and used (below) to estimate the potential welfare impacts of liberalizing these goods in El Salvador, Guatemala, and Nicaragua.
8. In none of these cases does the percentage of net consumers and net producers of maize add up to 100 because in each category at least a small proportion of households consume and produce exactly the same quantities of maize, according to the 2000 ENCOVI data set.
9. In cases where long geographic distances or lack of communication or transport infrastructure result in high transaction costs, households may not be well connected to markets and thus may not experience very strong price signals to which they must adjust. In such cases, infrastructure and other investments to reduce transaction costs and strengthen poor farmers' ability to benefit from markets represent important long-run challenges for policymakers. It should be noted, however, that such a lack of connection to the market would mean that households would not experience very strong price signals—either positive or nega-

tive—from the type of domestic price changes that will likely be induced by DR-CAFTA. This relative absence of price signals appears to have been the case for some households in southern Mexico following NAFTA. Largely self-sufficient farmers in remote rural areas appear not to have been significantly affected—either for better or for worse—by NAFTA-related changes in commodity prices (De Ferranti et al. 2004).

10. Several approaches to providing social protection as a means to manage the short-term adjustment costs as well as the economic transition associated with DR-CAFTA are outlined below.
11. For Nicaragua, Monge, Castro, and Saavedra (2004) used the 2001 EMNV; for Guatemala, Pörtner (2003) used the 2000 ENCOVI; for El Salvador, Marques (2005) used the 2003 *Encuesta de Hogares para Propósitos Múltiples* (EHPM).
12. For additional technical detail on the methodology, see Deaton (1997), McCulloch (2002), Pörtner (2003), Monge, Castro, and Saavedra (2004), and Marques (2005).
13. As will be discussed further below, El Salvador is a less rural country, with less of its economy based on agriculture than either Guatemala or Nicaragua. Because urban areas in Guatemala and Nicaragua have higher concentrations of net consumers than do rural areas, one would expect a higher proportion of net consumers in El Salvador than in the other two countries, all other things being equal. This, too, provides some confidence that the El Salvador analysis does not grossly overstate the likely beneficiaries or understate those who may be adversely affected by price changes under the trade agreement.
14. It is possible that in remote areas such as Peten the transmission of price effects may be extremely weak because of high transaction costs and relatively weak integration with markets. In the case of Peten, some analysts have also argued that because of its proximity to Mexico, households may have already experienced some (or all) of the impact they will feel from liberalization, through the effects of NAFTA and informal cross-border trade of staple crops.
15. The Salvadoran statistical agency, DIGESTYC, estimates that approximately 55 percent of El Salvador's population is now urban, based on their population projections and using traditional administrative definitions of *rural* versus *urban*. In contrast, a new World Bank study on rural development in Latin America and the Caribbean (De Ferranti 2005) (which notes that the European Union's definition of *rural* and *urban*, based on population density and geographic distance from major urban centers) estimates that roughly 80 percent of the Salvadoran population could be classified as urban.
16. Monge, Castro, and Saavedra (2004) presented estimated gains to net consumers and losses to net producers at the national level, as well as for rural and urban areas. They did not, however, report expected gains and losses by quintile.

17. See Pörtner (2003); Monge, Castro, and Saavedra (2004); and Marques (2005) for details.
18. As noted above, the extent to which similarities in benefit patterns in rural and urban El Salvador are the result of actual similarities on the ground as opposed to limitations of the data set and the current administrative definitions of *urban* and *rural* is not clear.
19. World Bank 2005d.
20. In 1997 payments averaged US$67 per hectare and US$317 per recipient (Cord and Wodon 2001).
21. See the section titled "Policies and Investments to Ensure That Poor People Can Benefit from DR-CAFTA" below.
22. Consistent with this finding, a recent study on targeting transfers in developing countries found that 62.6 percent of program transfers went to the poorest 40 percent of the population, and 37.4 percent went to the wealthiest 60 percent.
23. These calculations do not include the administrative costs of such a program. Moreover, they assume the implementation of new programs rather than the expansion of existing ones, such as the *Red de Protección Social* in Nicaragua.
24. Strengthening a country's land rights and landholding records may be an important development objective in its own right, and production-decoupled transfers can provide incentives for farmers and other agents to formalize their property titles because such transfers would require proof of sensitive-crop cultivation in the past.
25. To the extent that countries in the region do not currently operate CCTs, but would benefit from them in terms of their long-run impacts, DR-CAFTA may provide a window of opportunity for putting in place a conditional cash transfer program that focuses first on DR-CAFTA-affected households, and then scales up over time to meet its longer-term objectives of reducing structural poverty.

CHAPTER 6

Macroeconomic Policy Implications of DR-CAFTA

It is common knowledge that trade reforms can have important implications for macroeconomic policies in developing countries, and DR-CAFTA is not an exception. Such reforms entail the reduction of trade taxes (especially import tariffs) that are often an important source of financing for the public sector, especially in countries with limited capacity to raise revenues through direct domestic taxes, such as income and property taxes. In fact, this concern has been long recognized by the welfare theory of commercial policies as one of the exceptions to the idea that freer trade is always superior to the imposition of trade taxes (Corden 1974).

A second policy issue is related to the long-term consequences of trade liberalization in general and to DR-CAFTA in particular. Because these policies will probably affect the structure of production within the beneficiary countries, especially those economies in Central America that are small in relation to the United States, how the economies change over time will affect the costs and benefits of pursuing the coordination of macroeconomic policies. That is, if the economies of Central America become more similar to each other, then the probability that they will face common macroeconomic shocks will increase and thus the benefits of having independent monetary policies will decline. The same logic applies with respect to coordinating monetary policies with the United States, which in this case can be narrowed to the possibility of adopting the U.S. dollar, as El Salvador has already done. In a previous publication, Lederman, Perry, and Suescún (2004) concluded that DR-CAFTA might lead to further business cycle synchronization and thus to the need to coordinate monetary policies, thereby leaving fiscal policy as the main shock-adjustment policy tool available to Central American countries in the long run.

This chapter revisits relevant empirical evidence that addresses both macroeconomic policy issues. The next section focuses on the potential implications of the trade agreement in terms of its impact on fiscal revenues. The third section turns to the issue of how the structure of trade affects business cycle synchronization across countries, reviews the evidence on cycle synchronization across Central America and with respect to the United States, and provides new evidence on the role of intra- versus inter-industry trade in affecting the extent of business cycle synchronization across countries. The last section summarizes the main findings and policy implications.

Potential Fiscal Revenue Losses from DR-CAFTA

The implementation of DR-CAFTA will lower fiscal revenues in Central American countries. Because of the sharp reduction of tariffs that has taken place in the region since the late 1980s (see chapter 2) and the associated reduced importance of trade taxes, fiscal losses associated with further tariff reductions should not pose as large a cost as in other liberalization experiences. For the case of Central America, revenues from trade taxes fell from a range of 3–6 percent of GDP in the 1980s to only 0.5–2.0 percent of GDP in the early 2000s (Barreix et al. 2004). In 2000–1, trade taxes accounted for an average 1.6 percent of GDP in Central America, somewhat above the Latin America and Caribbean regional average of 0.9 percent, with the share of total tax revenues ranging from a low of 8 percent in Costa Rica to a high of 14 percent in Honduras (table 6.1).

Estimates of the permanent direct fiscal loss that would be incurred once all tariffs on imports from the United States are eliminated suggest that, under most scenarios, it should not surpass 1 percent of GDP. Four recent estimates (including one commissioned for this report) suggest a range from 0.5 to 0.8 percent of GDP for the Central American average (table 6.2). The estimates reported in table 6.2 take into account the effect of lower tariffs on a constant volume of imports (direct effect) and the effect on revenues from

Table 6.1. Import Tax Revenues, 2000–1

Country	*Share of GDP (%)*	*Share of total tax revenues (%)*
Costa Rica	1.03	8
El Salvador	1.07	10
Guatemala	1.23	12
Honduras	2.37	14
Nicaragua	1.38	10
Central America average	1.55	11
Latin America and the Caribbean average	0.90	5

Source: Barreix, Villela. amd Roca 2004.

Table 6.2. Alternative Estimates of Fiscal Losses from DR-CAFTA
percent of GDP

Country	*Estimate 1*	*Estimate 2*	*Estimate 3*	*Estimate 4*
Costa Rica	0.65	0.33	0.30	0.38
El Salvador	0.39	0.32	0.41	0.78
Guatemala	0.39	0.50	0.46	0.60
Honduras	1.59	0.85	0.86	1.47
Nicaragua	0.39	0.39	0.47	0.57
Average	0.68	0.48	0.50	0.76

Sources: Estimate 1, Barreix, Villela, and Roca 2005; estimate 2, Bronchi and Chua 2005; estimate 3, Paunovic 2004; and estimate 4, authors' calculations.

value-added or excise taxes (indirect effect), which incorporate tariff-modified prices as part of the tax base. These are the only potential effects that do not require strong assumptions about potential responses in the economy to the lowering of tariffs, such as the effect of potential changes in volumes resulting from tariff changes, the effect of changes in tariff and other revenues from third-country imports, and the change in overall revenues from general equilibrium changes in production and consumption structures. Although there is significant heterogeneity among countries, results from different sources are also different. Most studies suggest that Honduras would suffer the largest losses (0.9 to 1.6 percent of GDP), with other countries suffering losses ranging from 0.3 to 0.8 percent of GDP.

Fiscal losses for the first years will be lower than those incurred once the treaty is fully implemented, as a result of the gradual phase out of tariffs that Central American countries negotiated. On average, only 55 percent of all imports from the United States will become duty free in the first year of the treaty (Bronchi and Chua 2005). Results for the first year from studies reported in table 6.3 indicate that the average loss will range from 0.2 to 0.5 percent of GDP. In two studies, the first-year losses for El Salvador, Guatemala, and Nicaragua are very small (less than 0.16 percent of GDP). By contrast, Costa Rica's first-years losses tend to be closer to the full implementation losses because it will liberalize most of its trade with the United States in the first year.

A more comprehensive calculation of fiscal revenue changes resulting from DR-CAFTA would require an assessment of the changes in production and consumption structure that could be induced by the treaty, including the impact of greater investment levels and growth. Although such estimates are beyond any of the studies that have been made for the case of DR-CAFTA, table 6.4 reports results from two studies (including our own estimates) that have attempted to quantify the potential effects of greater growth on fiscal losses. As expected, the growth effect generates compensatory revenues that diminish the fiscal impact.

The study by Paunovic (2004) used estimates of the growth trajectories of the DR-CAFTA countries provided by Hinojosa-Ojeda (2003), who pre-

Table 6.3. Alternative Estimates of Fiscal Losses from DR-CAFTA in the First Year
percent of GDP

Country	*Estimate 1*	*Estimate 2*	*Estimate 3*
Costa Rica	0.39	0.32	0.28
El Salvador	0.15	0.09	0.38
Guatemala	0.15	0.16	0.43
Honduras	0.29	0.22	0.82
Nicaragua	0.11	0.05	0.42
Average	0.22	0.17	0.47

Sources: Estimate 1, Barreix, Villela, and Roca 200); estimate 2, Bronchi and Chua 2005; and estimate 3, Paunovic 2004.

Table 6.4. Alternative Estimates of Fiscal Losses from DR-CAFTA, Including Growth Effects
percent of GDP

Country	*Estimate 1*	*Estimate 2*
Costa Rica	0.21–0.26	0.00–0.15
El Salvador	0.22–0.32	0.43–0.59
Guatemala	0.27–0.37	0.25–0.40
Honduras	0.78–0.83	0.92–1.17
Nicaragua	0.31–0.40	0.09–0.31

Sources: Estimate 1, Paunovic 2004; estimate 2, authors' calculations.

dicts GDP growth due to DR-CAFTA will be 0.76 percent for Costa Rica, 1.59 percent for El Salvador, 2.32 percent for Guatemala, 0.89 percent for Honduras, and 1.49 percent for Nicaragua. In turn, Paunovic added these predicted growth rates (allegedly to be caused by DR-CAFTA) to his organization's (United Nations Economic Commission for Latin America and the Caribbean) growth projections, thus assuming that the growth effects of DR-CAFTA would come on top of the previous growth forecasts. The resulting growth rates were then multiplied times estimates of the elasticity of imports with respect to GDP growth, which yields the effect of economic growth on imports. Furthermore, these expected effects on the value of imports were then multiplied by the author's estimate of the gain in indirect taxes charged on imports (that is value-added taxes, or VAT). Consequently Paunovic (2004) contemplated a revenue recovery effect that is limited only to the potential effect of DR-CAFTA through growth on indirect taxes paid by rising imports.

Our calculations assume that the growth effect of DR-CAFTA will be approximately 0.6–0.8 percent a year, which is the range of the estimations provided by Gould and Gruben (2005) and discussed in chapter 4 of this volume. Moreover, we assume that the long-term relationship between GDP and fiscal revenues is exactly one. That is, we assume a unitary elasticity of revenues, so that when GDP grows by 1 percentage point, revenues rise proportionately by 1 percent as well. This assumption seems generous, considering the empirical evidence for various Latin American and Central American countries suggests that the correlation between short-term indicators of GDP and tax revenues per capita is less than one (see table 6.5). Moreover, tax revenues in Central American countries are heavily dependent on consumption-related taxes rather than on progressive income or property taxation (table 6.6). Economic logic dictates that more progressive tax systems can generate higher revenues for each improvement in GDP because the average marginal tax rate would tend to rise as people become richer. This revenue-augmenting effect would undoubtedly be small or nonexistent in economies where the structure of taxation is not progressive and focused on income or property taxes. This is not necessarily a critique of the Central American tax systems, but undoubtedly these are important elements in assessing the validity of our assumptions regarding the potential revenue recovery effect of DR-CAFTA. In any case, it should be acknowledged that the assumption of a unitary elasticity of revenues with respect to long-term GDP changes implies that the ratio of tax revenues to GDP will remain con-

Table 6.5. Correlations between Macroeconomic and Fiscal Variables and GDP in Latin American Countries

Country	*Disposable income*	*Consumption*	*Investment*	*Trade balance to GDP*	*Government spending*	*Tax revenue*	*Government debt to GDP*
Argentina	0.97	0.93	0.91	−0.88	0.68	0.59	−0.94
Bolivia	0.90	0.74	0.43	0.02	0.15	0.40	−0.48
Brazil	0.91	0.30	0.83	−0.64	0.38	0.51	−0.55
Chile	0.97	0.93	0.72	−0.90	0.51	0.60	−0.91
Colombia	0.96	0.84	0.68	−0.49	−0.01	0.18	−0.79
Costa Rica	0.97	0.83	0.87	−0.64	0.63	0.23	−0.87
Dominican Republic	0.91	0.53	0.69	−0.26	0.61	0.53	−0.67
Ecuador	0.91	0.86	0.68	−0.44	0.51	0.01	−0.92
El Salvador	0.98	0.89	0.84	−0.65	0.36	0.78	−0.59
Guatemala	0.95	0.98	0.67	−0.24	0.66	0.52	−0.88
Mexico	0.98	0.95	0.85	−0.66	0.62	0.76	−0.46
Nicaragua	0.88	0.27	0.59	−0.17	0.34	0.47	−0.48
Panama	0.98	0.51	0.83	−0.60	0.63	0.85	−0.88
Paraguay	0.98	0.64	0.92	−0.52	0.52	0.69	−0.94
Peru	0.97	0.95	0.70	−0.51	0.80	0.56	−0.71
Uruguay	0.95	0.92	0.91	−0.79	0.54	0.73	−0.86
Venezuela, R. B. de	Outlier	0.82	0.82	−0.55	0.56	−0.03	−0.81
Average	0.95	0.76	0.76	−0.52	0.50	0.49	−0.75
Median	0.96	0.84	0.77	−0.53	0.53	0.53	−0.80
Maximum	0.98	0.98	0.92	0.02	0.80	0.85	−0.46
Minimum	0.82	0.27	0.43	−0.90	−0.01	−0.03	−0.94

Source: Suescún 2005, Table 9.

Note: Disposable income = GDP tax revenue; consumption = household final consumption; investment = gross capital formation; trade balance = exports of goods and services − imports of goods and services. All variables except net exports and government debt are in per capita terms and in logarithms; all variables filtered with the Hodrick-Prescott filter. Output correlation is the contemporaneous correlation with GDP. Tax data are from the International Monetary Fund Government Finance Statistics database. Government debt figures are constructed as indicated in the text. The remaining data are taken from the World Bank World Development Indicators database.

Table 6.6. Revenue Composition of Latin American Tax Systems: Revenues by Source as Share of Total Revenues, Average 1990–2000

Country	*Consumption taxes*[a]	*Social security contributions*	*Taxes on income*	*Other taxes*
Argentina	46.7	36.9	11.5	4.9
Bolivia	65.6	13.1	8.2	13.1
Brazil	33.5	28.4	19.5	18.6
Chile	66.0	8.0	21.3	4.8
Colombia	56.4	0.0	41.8	1.8
Costa Rica	54.2	32.4	12.3	1.1
Dominican Republic	76.1	4.2	18.3	1.4
Ecuador	41.4	0.0	56.7	1.9
El Salvador	70.5	0.0	26.7	2.9
Guatemala	73.5	0.0	22.9	3.6
Mexico	56.0	11.9	30.2	1.9
Nicaragua	70.5	13.4	13.4	2.8
Panama	39.5	27.7	27.1	5.6
Paraguay	65.4	6.5	16.8	11.2
Peru	64.9	10.1	17.6	7.4
Uruguay	44.0	32.1	11.1	12.7
Venezuela, R. B. de	36.9	4.7	55.7	2.7
Mean	56.5	13.5	24.2	5.8
Median	56.4	10.1	19.5	3.6

Source: Authors' calculations based on International Monetary Fund Government Finance Statistics database and World Bank World Development Indicators, as cited in Suescún (2005).
a. Consumption taxes = taxes on goods and services + taxes on international trade.

stant after the DR-CAFTA tariff reductions. Thus, even these calculations imply a permanent reduction of the revenue-to-GDP ratio, despite the rise of revenues driven by DR-CAFTA's dynamic effects. This growth-related revenue compensation varies by country but can reach as much as 0.5 percent of GDP for Honduras.

DR-CAFTA, Business Cycle Synchronization, and Trade Structure

With deeper trade integration between Central America and the United States, it is expected that there will be closer links in business cycles among Central America and the United States. From a theoretical point of view, the impact of trade integration on business cycle synchronization is not clear because increased trade can lead business cycles to either convergence or divergence. On one hand, if trade integration leads to increased inter-industry trade as a part of a specialization process, then business cycles are likely to become less similar because shocks specific to particular industries will become responsible for shaping business cycles. On the other hand, if trade integration leads to a higher share of intra-industry trade, business cycles will become more similar, as industry-specific shocks would affect trading partners in a similar way.

Assessing business cycle synchronization between Central America and the United States is not only useful for gaining a better understanding of the influence of important trading partners on business cycle fluctuations in the domestic economies. Information about the degree of business cycle synchronization also helps assess the necessity of independent fiscal and monetary policy. If the business cycles are similar and shocks are common, then a coordination of macroeconomic policies can become desirable, with a common currency as the ultimate form of policy coordination. Conversely, if shocks are predominately country specific and so result in a low degree of business cycle synchronization, then the ability to conduct independent monetary and fiscal policy is generally seen as important in helping an economy adjust to a new equilibrium.

Business Cycle Synchronization: Data and Methodology

Given that shocks are not observed directly, empirical studies rely on econometric methods for their identification. Helg et al. (1995) and Bayoumi and Eichengreen (1993) adopted a structural vector autoregression (VAR) approach, whereas Artis and Zhang (1995) developed an identification scheme based on cyclical components. Rubin and Thygesen (1996), Beine and Hecq (1997) and Beine, Candelon, and Hecq (2000) used a codependence framework. Filardo and Gordon (1994), Beine, Candelon, and Sekkat (1999), and Krolzig (2001) used a Markov-switching VAR model. This empirical work demonstrates that it is important to distinguish between short- and long-run effects. Bayoumi and Eichengreen (1993), Helg et al. (1995), and Rubin and Thygesen (1996) used differenced variables in the VAR representation. However, such a specification does not allow for a long-run relationship among the variables. Beine, Candelon, and Hecq (2000) overcame this by investigating simultaneously common trends and common cycles, where evidence of a common European cycle is taken as evidence of perfect synchronization of shocks. Breitung and Candelon (2001) used a frequency domain common cycle test to analyze synchronization at different business cycle frequencies.

The key variable in our study is the degree of business cycle synchronization between countries *i* and *j*. To measure this variable, we follow Frankel and Rose (1998) and compute the correlation between the cyclical component of the output in countries *i* and *j*, where a higher correlation implies a higher degree of business cycle synchronization. The cyclical component of output is obtained using different detrending methods. Given the lack of consensus on the optimal procedure and the sensitivity of the cycle to the detrending method, this approach should provide a robustness check of our results. For annual data we use first-differencing and band-pass filtering (Baxter and King 1999). Spectral analysis is used to assess business cycle synchronization with monthly data.

Data availability for Central America seriously limits the scope for any econometric analysis. To provide some inference about the level of business cycle synchronization and the link between trade structure and business cycle synchronization in that region, we make use of annual data on GDP from 1965 to 2002 and monthly data on economic activity from 1995 to 2003.

Synchronization Results with Annual Data

Band-pass–filtered data, our preferred method for business cycle extraction in this section, show that business cycle synchronization in Central America is highest among Costa Rica, El Salvador, Guatemala, and Honduras. Nicaragua and Panama appear to follow a different cycle, as correlation across business cycles is in most cases even negative, though not statistically significant.[1] These results are reported in table 6.7.

It is interesting to note that the correlation with the U.S. business cycle is also high. In the case of Costa Rica, El Salvador, and Honduras, business cycle synchronization with the United States appears even higher than among regional neighbors, indicating that bilateral relationships with the United States through trade and remittances are more important than regional effects. Somewhat surprising is that business cycle synchronization between the United States and Panama, which adopted full dollarization in 1904, appears to be much lower than in the rest of Central America, with the exception of Nicaragua. Based on business cycle synchronization, it appears that the rest of Central America would be better candidates for a currency union with the United States than would Panama. In fact, synchronization be-

Table 6.7. Business Cycle Synchronization Using Band-Pass Filter, with Central American Economies Highlighted

	Central America					
Band Pass	*Costa Rica*	*El Salvador*	*Guatemala*	*Honduras*	*Nicaragua*	*Panama*
Costa Rica	1.000					
El Salvador	**0.604**	1.000				
Guatemala	**0.632**	0.238	1.000			
Honduras	**0.524**	**0.442**	**0.590**	1.000		
Nicaragua	–0.214	0.015	–0.142	–0.157	1.000	
Panama	–0.007	–0.062	–0.087	–0.011	0.088	1.000
Argentina	**0.354**	0.111	0.187	0.043	–0.086	0.148
Brazil	**0.350**	0.028	**0.407**	0.174	–0.162	–0.001
Mexico	0.151	–0.335	**0.395**	0.168	–0.255	0.323
Canada	**0.621**	0.276	**0.492**	**0.359**	–0.214	–0.336
United States	**0.687**	**0.506**	**0.463**	**0.679**	–0.163	–0.148
France	0.239	0.113	0.394	0.152	–0.170	–0.138
Germany	0.167	0.107	0.308	0.107	–0.138	0.280
Portugal	0.124	–0.088	**0.540**	**0.423**	–1.127	–0.085
Spain	0.175	0.136	**0.389**	0.057	0.167	–0.218
United Kingdom	**0.402**	**0.479**	0.241	**0.459**	–0.268	–0.323

Source: Authors' calculations.

Table 6.8. Business Cycle Synchronization, Orthogonal to U.S. Business Cycle

	Costa Rica	*El Salvador*	*Guatemala*	*Honduras*	*Nicaragua*
Costa Rica	1.000				
El Salvador	**0.409**	1.000			
Guatemala	**0.488**	0.006	1.000		
Honduras	0.104	0.157	**0.421**	1.000	
Nicaragua	−0.141	0.115	−0.076	−0.063	1.000
Panama	0.134	0.014	−0.021	0.118	0.065

Source: Authors' calculations.

tween the United States and Costa Rica, El Salvador, Guatemala, and Honduras is even higher than the EU average (0.43).

Business cycle synchronization in the two countries of the *Mercado Común del Sur* (MERCOSUR), Argentina and Brazil, is below the levels of Costa Rica, El Salvador, and Guatemala. Although synchronization is also substantial between Canada and the United States, it is surprisingly low between Mexico and the United States. The finding of low synchronization between Mexico and the United States, as well as between Brazil and Argentina, is partly explained by the long time period being considered (1965–2002), but the next section shows that there has been a substantial increase in business cycle synchronization in the more recent past.

Table 6.8 shows business cycle synchronization among Central American countries after controlling for common impact of the U.S. cycle.[2] When the common effect of the U.S. cycle is removed, it appears that only Costa Rica and Guatemala, Costa Rica and El Salvador, and Guatemala and Honduras are affected by common factors other than the U.S. cycle. Because these countries also account for the largest share of intraregional trade, this finding can be taken in support of the often-postulated positive relationship between trade intensity and business cycle symmetry.

Synchronization Results with Monthly Data

The business cycle is usually defined in the range of 6 to 32 quarters, and thus low-frequency annual data might be insufficient to fully assess the degree of business cycle synchronization. In this section we therefore complement our analysis from the previous section with an analysis of monthly data, where output is proxied by seasonally adjusted monthly indexes of industrial production and economic activity.

Table 6.9. Business Cycle Synchronization, Other FTAs, with Members Highlighted

	MERCOSUR		*NAFTA*			*EU*				
	Argentina	*Brazil*	*Mexico*	*Canada*	*U.S.*	*France*	*Germany*	*Portugal*	*Spain*	*U.K.*
Costa Rica	**0.354**	**0.350**	0.151	**0.621**	**0.687**	0.239	0.167	0.124	0.175	**0.402**
El Salvador	0.111	0.028	−0.335	0.276	**0.506**	0.113	0.107	−0.088	0.136	**0.479**
Guatemala	0.187	**0.407**	**0.395**	**0.492**	**0.463**	**0.394**	0.308	**0.540**	**0.389**	0.241
Honduras	0.043	0.174	0.168	**0.359**	**0.679**	0.152	0.107	**0.423**	0.057	**0.459**
Nicaragua	−0.086	−0.162	−0.255	−0.214	−0.163	−0.170	−0.138	−0.127	0.167	−0.268
Panama	0.148	−0.001	0.323	−0.336	−0.148	−0.138	0.280	−0.085	−0.218	−0.323
Argentina	1.000	0.202	0.093	−0.095	−0.033	−0.212	0.273	−0.091	−0.067	−0.100
Brazil		1.000	0.122	**0.514**	0.283	0.080	0.070	0.209	0.223	0.320
Mexico			1.000	0.161	0.086	−0.007	0.156	0.159	0.013	0.209
Canada				1.000	**0.771**	**0.338**	−0.088	0.170	0.370	**0.607**
United States					1.000	**0.338**	0.104	0.292	0.329	**0.727**
France						1.000	**0.372**	**0.656**	**0.711**	**0.482**
Germany							1.000	**0.328**	**0.348**	−0.044
Portugal								1.000	**0.559**	**0.431**
Spain									1.000	**0.429**
United Kingdom										1.000

Source: Authors' calculations.
EU = European Union; MERCOSUR = *Mercado Común del Sur;* NAFTA = North American Free Trade Agreement.

We use spectral analysis to estimate the correlation at different frequencies and use the average "coherence" at business cycle frequency (6 to 32 quarters) of year-over-year changes in economic activity as a summary measure of business cycle synchronization (Garnier 2003). The advantage of using cross-spectral densities over simple correlations in the analysis of business cycle synchronization is twofold. First, spectral analysis avoids possible cycle distortions resulting from filtering because it is well known that the cycles change with the detrending method (Canova 1998). Second, contemporaneous correlation is unable to take lagged co-movement into account. Because coherence measures the correlation between two series in the frequency domain (that is, within each time window) and provides information on leads and lags, it provides a richer analysis of business cycle dynamics. Whereas coherence measures the extent to which two business cycles are dominated by the same frequency, the phase lag shows how elements with the same frequency are related over time (lags). In sum, a high degree of business cycle synchronization implies a high coherence and a low phase lag.

Table 6.10 shows the average coherence at business cycle frequency between year-over-year growth rates of economic activity during 1995 and 2003. The results broadly confirm the findings of the previous section.

Within Central America, cycle synchronization is again found to be highest between Costa Rica and El Salvador, El Salvador and Guatemala, El Salvador and Nicaragua, and Honduras and Nicaragua. With respect to the United States, synchronization is highest for Costa Rica, El Salvador, and Honduras, although at levels lower than those prevailing among members of NAFTA and MERCOSUR.[3]

Trade Structure, Exchange Rate Stability, and Business Cycle Synchronization

The impact of trade liberalization on cycle synchronization is theoretically ambiguous. Standard trade theory (Heckscher-Ohlin) predicts that the removal of trade barriers leads to an increasing specialization in production, which in turn leads to inter-industry trade patterns. As industry-specific specialization increases, industry-specific shocks (for example, a shock to commodity prices) will make business cycles more dissimilar and hence decrease the degree of synchronization.

Experience from industrial countries shows a trend toward intra- rather than inter-industry trade. If intra-industry trade is vertical (that is, if particular countries are specializing in different production stages of the same

Table 6.10. Average Coherence at Business Cycle Frequency, 1995 and 2003

	Costa Rica	*El Salvador*	*Guatemala*	*Honduras*	*Nicaragua*	*Argentina*	*Mexico*	*Canada*
Costa Rica			0.381					
El Salvador	**0.524**		0.534					
Guatemala	0.381	**0.534**						
Honduras	0.456	0.340	0.381					
Nicaragua	0.393	**0.510**	0.421	**0.554**				
Mexico	0.332	0.453	0.242	0.366	0.288	**0.537**	1.000	0.361
United States	0.454	0.427	0.336	0.421	0.322	0.486	0.468	**0.554**
Brazil	0.318	0.322	0.382	0.319	0.272	**0.500**	0.608	0.467

Source: Authors' calculations.

good), then industry-specific shocks will make business cycles more similar. The same results if intra-industry trade is horizontal (that is, if countries trade and compete with the same products). In that case, industry-specific shocks are also expected to increase business cycle synchronization.

Exchange rate stability is often considered important for trade integration. Whereas volatile exchange rates increase transaction costs, misaligned exchange rates create unfair competitive advantages for the trading partner with the undervalued currency and generate political backlash against free trade in the countries confronted with an import surge. Exchange rate stabilization and monetary coordination are therefore often seen as effective tools to contain the political pressure against further trade integration. However, as Eichengreen and Taylor (2003) pointed out, the vertical-versus-horizontal structure of trade is also decisive in shaping the competitive impact of bilateral exchange rate fluctuations. If trade and production are predominately vertical—as in the case of NAFTA, where Mexican producers provide inputs and assembly operations for manufacturers designed and marketed in the United States—the exchange rate fluctuations are less likely to increase competition. The case is reversed if intra-industry trade is predominately horizontal. In this case, the impact of undervalued exchange rates is likely to be much larger. This effect is amplified further if the goods in question cannot be relocated to a third market (regional goods, meaning they are uncompetitive outside the regional trade area). To summarize, intra-industry trade, vertical or horizontal, is expected to increase business cycle synchronization; exchange rate instability can become a concern for further trade integration if intra-industry trade is horizontal rather than vertical.

Tables 6.11 and 6.12 provide information about Central America's trade structure. Trade patterns of NAFTA and some countries in the EU and MERCOSUR are again provided for comparison. Unlike the situation for NAFTA, EU, and MERCOSUR members, trade measured as bilateral exports over total exports in Central America is not predominantly intra-regional. Even within the so-called Northern Triangle (El Salvador, Guatemala, and Honduras), and between El Salvador and Nicaragua, bilateral exports as a ratio of total exports barely exceed 10 percent. The United States is by far Central America's most important trading partner, although trade with the EU is also of some significance. Because there appears to be some underreporting of exports to the United States, imports from Central America to the United States as reported by the United States are provided as an alternative measure. These data indicate that exports to the United States account for more than 60 percent in the cases of Costa Rica, El Salvador, and Guatemala.

Table 6.11. Central America's Trade Structure: Ratio of Bilateral Exports to Total Exports, Average for 1995–2001

percent

	Costa Rica	*El Salvador*	*Guatemala*	*Honduras*	*Nicaragua*	*Argentina*	*Mexico*	*Canada*	*France*
Costa Rica		4.4	3.5	1.1	4.8	0.1	0.2	0.0	0.0
El Salvador	2.3		9.9	3.1	11.1	0.1	0.2	0.0	0.0
Guatemala	3.2	12.4		2.5	2.8	0.1	0.4	0.0	0.0
Honduras	1.7	6.8	2.0		5.3	0.0	0.1	0.0	0.0
Nicaragua	2.9	3.8	3.1	2.2		0.0	0.1	0.0	0.0
Mexico	1.1	0.7	2.3	0.3	2.8	1.2		0.5	0.4
Brazil	0.1	0.0	0.0	0.0	0.0	26.9	0.5	0.4	0.7
United States	21.3	11.1	50.7	61.1	38.0	9.4	87.1	85.3	7.3
Germany	3.6	6.1	3.3	3.8	9.9	2.3	0.9	0.9	15.7
European Union	16.0	10.7	10.4	12.2	23.1	18.5	3.6	4.9	61.6
Memo									
Free Trade Zone	39.1	54.5							
U.S. reported imports CIF	62.4	68.1	66.3						

Source: International Monetary Fund Direction of Trade Statistics.

Note: CIF = includes costs of customs, insurance, and freight. Interpretation of this table is as follows. The table should be read column-wise, where each row represents the share in total column-countries exports. As an example, the top-left figure indicates that exports from Costa Rica to El Salvador represent 2.3 percent of Costa Rica's total exports.

Table 6.12. Central America's Trade Structure: Ratio of Bilateral Exports to GDP, Average 1995–2001

percent

	Costa Rica	*El Salvador*	*Guatemala*	*Honduras*	*Nicaragua*	*Argentina*	*Mexico*	*Canada*	*France*
Costa Rica		0.8	0.7	0.6	1.2	0.01	0.05	0.01	0.01
El Salvador	0.8		1.8	1.5	2.9	0.01	0.05	0.00	0.01
Guatemala	1.1	2.3		1.2	0.7	0.01	0.11	0.01	0.00
Honduras	0.6	1.3	0.4		1.4	0.00	0.01	0.00	0.00
Nicaragua	1.0	0.7	0.6	1.1		0.00	0.01	0.00	0.00
Mexico	0.4	0.1	0.4	0.2	0.7	0.1		0.2	0.1
Brazil	0.0	0.0	0.0	0.0	0.0	2.4	0.1	0.1	0.1
United States	7.1	2.1	9.5	30.1	9.8	0.8	24.1	30.3	1.6
Germany	1.2	1.1	0.6	1.9	2.6	0.2	0.3	0.30	3.3
European Union	5.3	2.0	1.9	6.0	5.9	1.6	1.0	1.7	13.2
Memo									
Free Trade Zone (U.S.-Intel)	13.0	10.1							
U.S. reported imports CIF	19.4	11.8	11.7						

Source: International Monetary Fund Direction of Trade Statistics.

Note: CIF = includes costs of customs, insurance, and freight. To interpret this table, it should be read columnwise, where each row represents the share of bilateral exports in the column-countries' GDP. As an example, the top-left figure indicates that exports from Costa Rica to El Salvador represent 0.8 percent of Costa Rica's GDP.

Table 6.13 provides information on the importance of intra-industry trade in Central America based on the adjusted Grubel-Lloyd intra-industry trade index.[4] This index can take values between 0 (no intra-industry trade) and 1 (all trade is intra-industry). There appears to be some importance of intra-industry trade within Central America; however, with the exception of Costa Rica (0.3) there is virtually no evidence of intra-industry trade with the United States. For El Salvador and Guatemala, intra-industry trade appears to be quite high with Mexico and Brazil.

$$AIIT = \sum_{i}^{n}(X_i + M_i) - \sum_{i}^{n} | X_i - M_i | \qquad \text{(Eq. 6.1)}$$
$$\sum_{i}^{n}(X_i + M_i) - | \sum_{i}^{n} X_i - \sum_{i}^{n} M_i |$$

Trade and Business Cycle Synchronization

Empirical evidence on trade integration and business cycle synchronization is somewhat mixed. Whereas Frankel and Rose (1998), Calderón, Chong, and Stein (2002), and Calderón (2003) found that a higher trade intensity tends to increase synchronization, Shin and Wang (2004) reported that increasing trade itself does not necessarily lead to more synchronized cycles, and evidence for East Asia suggests that only the expansion of intra-industry trade had such an effect. However, Garnier (2003) found only weak or no relationship between intra-industry trade and cycle synchronization for 16 industrial countries, and conclude that intra-industry trade at most only partially explains business cycle transmission. The low correlations reported by Calderón, Chong, and Stein would suggest a similar interpretation for trade intensity and business cycle synchronization.

Using the statistics calculated in the previous section, we attempt to contribute to this debate. Figure 6.1 shows a cross-plot of bilateral export-to-GDP ratios and average coherence at business cycle frequency with respect to the United States.[5] We are able to identify a positive relationship between trade intensity and business cycle synchronization. We further find that the slope of the regression line is quite flat because most countries appear to fall into a relatively narrow range of synchronization (0.4–0.5), independent of their level of trade intensity. As an example, despite a big difference in trade intensity France and Mexico have similar degrees of business cycle synchronization with the United States.[6] This seems to support Shin and Wang's and Garnier's claims that cycle symmetry is only partly explained by trade inten-

Table 6.13. Intra-Industry Trade Index

Country	*Costa Rica*	*El Salvador*	*Guatemala*	*Honduras*	*Nicaragua*	*Argentina*	*Mexico*	*Canada*	*France*
El Salvador	0.36								
Guatemala	0.38	0.45							
Honduras	0.40	0.27	0.33						
Nicaragua	0.34	0.15	0.21	0.15					
Mexico	0.18	0.43	0.42	0.11	0.02	0.26		0.49	0.57
Brazil	0.08	0.43	0.51	0.03	0.28	0.39	0.51		0.11
United States	0.30	0.05	0.05	0.06	0.02	0.10	0.46	0.66	0.56
Germany	0.06	0.02	0.01	0.02	0.02	0.13	0.79	0.33	0.70

Source: Authors' calculations based on trade data from the UN Commodity Trade Statistics Database for the year 2001.

Note: A five-digit level of disaggregation is used for this exercise.

Figure 6.1. Business Cycle Synchronization and Trade with the United States

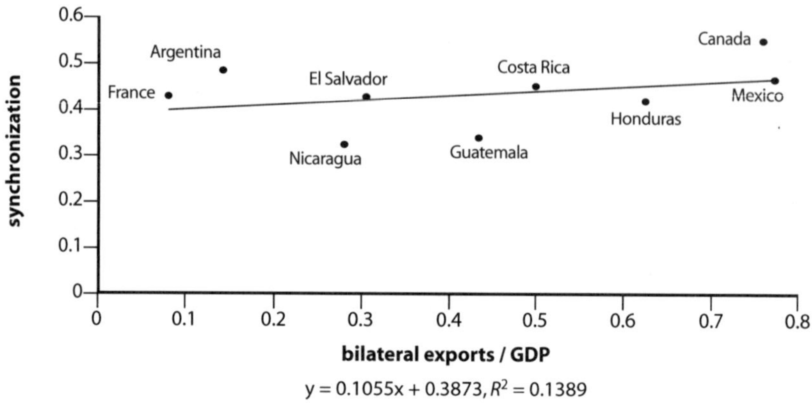

Source: Fiess 2005.

sity. In other words, for El Salvador to reach Mexico's level of synchronization with the United States—which is only slightly higher—in GDP terms El Salvador would have to more than double its exports to the United States. As in Shin and Wang and Garnier, the link between intra-industry trade and business synchronization is found to be stronger (figure 6.2).

Thus, the evidence suggests that the effects of DR-CAFTA on the structure of trade are unlikely to change the costs and benefits of macroeconomic policy coordination in the foreseeable future. Consequently, the choice of monetary and fiscal policies along the business cycle of these economies will continue to be driven by nontrade issues, such as the extent of financial asset and liability dollarization in the region.

The evidence discussed thus far on the structure of trade and cycle synchronization is less than conclusive. Other research by Calderón, Chong, and Stein and by Calderón looked at the relationship between bilateral-trade intensity across countries and over time for a sample of more than 100 countries during 1960–99. The econometric evidence discussed by those authors seems consistent with the ongoing discussion: They found that the positive relationship between synchronization and bilateral-trade intensity is higher among pairs of industrial (high-income) countries than among pairs of developing countries or developing-industrial countries. Inasmuch as the incidence of intra-industry trade among high-income countries is higher than among developing countries, this evidence is consistent with our findings

Figure 6.2. Business Cycle Synchronization and Intra-industry Trade

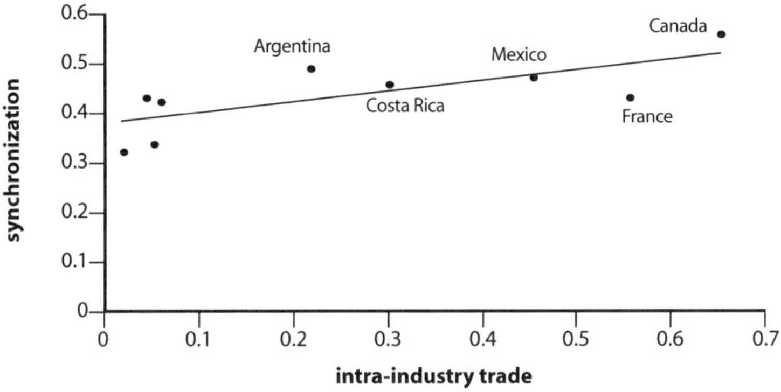

$y = 0.2164x + 0.376, R^2 = 0.5433$

Source: Fiess 2005.

that business cycle synchronization among Central American countries and with the United States is relatively low, but that it would tend to rise if intra-industry trade were to increase. Calderón (2003) also found that free trade agreements tend to increase the magnitude of the effect of bilateral-trade intensity on cycle synchronization across pairs of countries, but this effect is still lower for developing countries than for industrial economies.[7] Hence the international evidence suggests that DR-CAFTA could lead to more intra-industry trade with the United States and thus to higher synchronization, but these structural changes could be quite modest. Consequently, the potential effects of DR-CAFTA on the costs and benefits of dollarization or other forms of monetary policy coordination among the Central American and U.S. economies could be small relative to the relevance of other factors. Some of the most relevant factors are the extent of financial (asset and liability) dollarization that could lead countries to maintain stable dollar exchange rates to shield the financial system from sudden changes in the exchange rate (see Lederman, Perry, and Suescún 2004).

Summary and Policy Recommendations

This chapter reviews evidence related to two macroeconomic policy issues —the potential revenue losses that might be produced by DR-CAFTA's removal of import taxes and the treaty's potential effect on the patterns of business cycle synchronization that could be affected by changes in the structure of international trade.

The fiscal losses that DR-CAFTA is likely to create need to be compensated in all Central American countries to avoid further deterioration of public finances. At present, all Central American countries except Guatemala exhibit relatively high debt indicators and require tight fiscal stances to maintain or decrease indebtedness. However, relatively small anticipated losses in the first years allow for some flexibility in the timing of the fiscal response in some of the countries—particularly as some time may be needed for adequate political conditions to emerge.

A more comprehensive fiscal response to DR-CAFTA requires efforts to raise revenues above and beyond fiscal losses, inasmuch as some of the key measures needed to optimize its effect require increases in public investments (for example, in infrastructure, education, institutional strengthening, and transitional adjustment programs). Although some of these expenditures may be temporary and arguably could be financed by greater indebtedness, this may be difficult in practice because of high current debt levels.

The fiscal response to DR-CAFTA should be adapted to the fiscal situation of each country. For the cases of El Salvador and Guatemala, where tax revenue ratios are low (below 13 percent of GDP), the ideal fiscal response would be actions that go significantly beyond recovering direct losses in order to finance additional social and infrastructure investments that are needed to boost growth and that are made more urgent and productive by the opportunities of DR-CAFTA. In Costa Rica, where the tax ratio is higher but still short of the level needed to guarantee debt sustainability, the ideal response should also involve going beyond compensation for the relatively low projected losses, making improvements in the efficiency and allocation of public expenditures, as well as attracting private financing to fund some of the most significant infrastructural needs. Honduras and Nicaragua, which have benefited recently from the Heavily Indebted Poor Countries Initiative, will likely require additional fiscal revenues, improvements in expenditure efficiency, and attraction of private financing to respond to the opportunities of DR-CAFTA. In all countries, an essential element of efforts to improve fiscal performance should include the institutional strengthening of tax agencies and their collection capacity, as well as the elimination of exonerations from VAT and income taxes.

DR-CAFTA implementation should also be used to deepen regional coordination efforts in the realm of tax policy. Going forward, a regional coordination agenda should include gradual harmonization of VAT and excise rates, fiscal incentives for foreign investors, information exchange for tax enforcement efforts, double taxation treaties, and transference prices.

Regarding the prospects for macroeconomic policy coordination among Central American countries and perhaps with the United States, business cycle synchronization within Central America is quite low compared with that of NAFTA and the EU, but not when compared with MERCOSUR. In fact, synchronization in Central America is highest between Costa Rica and El Salvador, El Salvador and Guatemala, El Salvador and Nicaragua, and Honduras and Nicaragua. Costa Rica and Honduras have a higher degree of comovement with the United States than with any other Central American country. But synchronization with the United States is still below the levels among NAFTA and even MERCOSUR members.

Furthermore, unlike NAFTA, the EU, and MERCOSUR, trade in Central America is not predominantly intra-regional. Central America's most significant trading partner is certainly the United States. With the exception of Costa Rica, there is virtually no evidence of intra-industry trade between Central America and the United States. The level of intra-industry trade within Central America is comparable to that of MERCOSUR, but below the levels of NAFTA (Canada and the United States) and the EU (France and Germany). Finally, the degree of business cycle synchronization seems only weakly related to trade intensity and trade structure (intra-industry trade), although the relationship between intra-industry trade and synchronization is slightly stronger (which is consistent with existing international evidence). As such, the gain in synchronization through trade expansion could be modest.

In summary, at present neither Central America's trade structure nor its degree of business cycle synchronization makes a compelling case for macroeconomic coordination within Central America or between Central America and the United States. Clearly, trade integration is a dynamic process and as trade intensities and compositions of trade flows change, so will business cycle patterns. To fully assess the consequences of closer trade integration for the conduct of macroeconomic policies, information about the future evolution of trade structures in DR-CAFTA is needed. If trade becomes more intra-industry (vertical or horizontal), business cycles are expected to become more similar and the independence of macroeconomic policy will be less of a concern. However, if trade integration takes the form of higher inter-industry trade, then business cycles are likely to diverge from current levels and the ability to conduct independent macroeconomic policies will grow more important. In the meantime, other factors that are not directly related to the structure of international trade will remain more important considerations for the design of macroeconomic policies over the business cycle in Central America. One important consideration, for example, is the extent of dollarization of financial assets and liabilities. Hence, the macroeconomic agenda in the light of DR-CAFTA should remain focused on fiscal consolidation, at least in the short run.

Notes

1. Results based on first differences are not reported here, but are available in Fiess (2005).
2. Table 6.9 reports the correlation between the cyclical components of band-pass–filtered GDP series orthogonal to the U.S. business cycle.
3. We abstain from reporting the phase lag because it is very poorly estimated if the coherence is small, which is the case for most country pairings in table 6.10.
4. X and M are exports and imports of industry, respectively. The adjusted Grubel-Lloyd index makes an adjustment for trade imbalances.
5. We find similar results if bilateral exports/total exports are used as a measure of trade intensity.
6. Argentina's relatively high level of cycle synchronization despite low trade intensity appears to be linked to dollarization and capital flow integration.
7. Calderón (2003, p. 2) reported that a "one standard deviation increase in bilateral trade intensity will increase output correlation from 0.53 to 0.64 among industrial country pairs with FTA in the 1990s, from 0.21 to 0.29 among developing country pairs with FTAs."

CHAPTER 7

Obtaining the Payoff from DR-CAFTA

Priorities for the Complementary Agenda

The benefits from DR-CAFTA will depend on the ability of the Central American economies to pursue a complementary policy agenda, as was explained in chapter 4. By itself and without parallel efforts in certain key areas, the trade agreement is unlikely to lead to substantial developmental gains. This chapter presents a review of the remaining areas of the complementary agenda for DR-CAFTA—areas in addition to those related to the management of the transition presented in chapter 5 and the macroeconomic implications covered in chapter 6. The goal here is to provide a brief assessment of the key policy priorities for Central American countries.[1]

Although virtually all public policies in a sense can be complementary and can affect future economic development, this chapter focuses on three policy areas that have obvious interactions with international trade, some of which were highlighted in chapter 4. These policy areas are (1) trade facilitation infrastructure and institutions, such as ports, roads, and customs procedures; (2) other institutional and regulatory reforms that affect the ability of firms and workers to seek out new opportunities created by DR-CAFTA and the consequent expected increase in trade and investment flows; and (3) innovation and education policies, which will affect Central America's ability to adopt and adapt technologies embodied in imported goods and to introduce new export products and services.

The analyses contained in the following sections provide estimates of where the Central American economies stand relative to each other and to countries of similar levels of development in terms of their infrastructure, institutional, and innovation-related characteristics. Although admittedly this type of benchmarking does not say much about the potential social returns from specific policy interventions, it reveals where the different countries seem to be lagging behind expectations in terms of such intermediate development outcomes as the coverage and quality of infrastructure, regulations, and innovation. The purpose is to provoke public discussion about what each country can do to improve its performance in these policy areas that are most likely to determine the extent of the gains from DR-CAFTA in the long run.

We acknowledge that although the chapter tries to identify deficiencies and areas of weaknesses, virtually all Central American nations have made substantial strides in reforming their policies at least since the early 1990s. Details about the advances made in most areas can be found in the World Bank's recent country-specific studies on the challenges of the growth agenda.[2] However, here we focus on what remains to be done. At the end, we conclude the chapter by briefly stating what seem to be the most pressing future priorities for each Central American country, derived from the evidence reviewed in this chapter.

Trade Facilitation

As mentioned, a key area of the complementary agenda concerns the infrastructure and institutions that directly affect the capacity of economies to move traded merchandise within and outside their borders. The following paragraphs thus discuss where the Central American economies stand in terms of roads, ports, and customs procedures.

Roads

Despite progress in recent years, indicators of road access still show significant deficiencies in Guatemala, Honduras, and Nicaragua. In comparisons with countries of similar income per capita, road density is farthest from expected values for Guatemala (nearly 70 percent lower than expected),

Figure 7.1. Deviation from Predicted Levels of Road Access and Quality in Central America

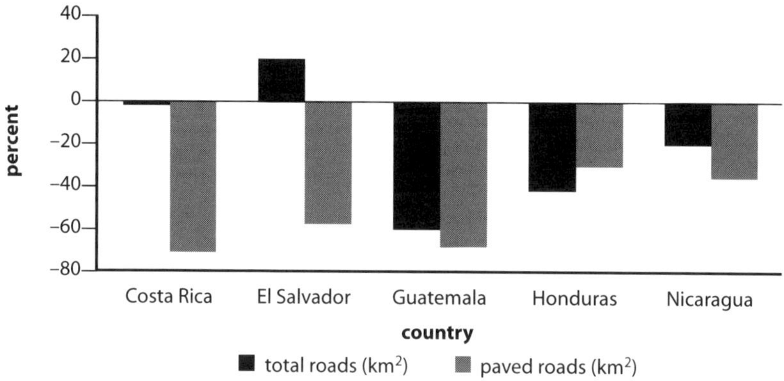

Source: Authors' calculations.

whereas Honduras and Nicaragua fall short by about 30 percent each. In contrast, El Salvador performs 20 percent beyond expectations because of the large investments of recent years, and Costa Rica comes out at the predicted level for its level of income (figure 7.1).[3]

Road quality indicators for Central American countries are lower than predicted by their levels of development. Costa Rica, El Salvador, and Guatemala exhibit the largest shortfalls in the share of paved roads with respect to GDP levels (figure 7.1). The overall poor quality of roads implies that mobility is low and costly and affects the potential competitiveness of goods produced in rural areas.

Scarce public resources and inadequacies in the legal framework for private-sector participation are key limitations to improvement in road coverage and quality. The low fiscal base in most Central American countries constrains investment in roads. Tight fiscal situations in recent years have led to contractions of public capital formation, which has contributed to a slowdown in construction and upkeep of regional infrastructure. Although there are examples of private-sector participation in all segments of transport activities (construction, rehabilitation and maintenance of infrastructures, and operation of transport services), the significant potential in this area has not been developed, mainly because of deficient and uncertain legal frameworks and poor institutional capacity of the entities in charge of regulations.

Improving access to roads and their quality to boost competitiveness and attract investment requires action on several fronts:

- Coverage of the road network should be extended selectively within a strategy that aims at strengthening rural–urban links, developing trade corridors, and incorporating a regional perspective, by strengthening the regional road network (*Red Internacional de Carreteras Mesoamericanas*), among other things. This effort is particularly important for reducing trade costs in countries such as El Salvador and Nicaragua, which rely on access to ports in neighboring countries for significant shares of their trade.
- Road quality needs to be improved by designing institutional mechanisms to assign funds for road maintenance.
- Regulatory frameworks need to be strengthened (especially concession legislation) as does the institutional capacity to attract private-sector participation in the construction, operation, and maintenance of transport infrastructure.
- Public investments in those areas where private financing is unlikely (for example, rural roads and rural telecommunications) must be protected.
- Planning capacity at both central and local levels must be reinforced; stronger coordination efforts are required for significant cross-country road developments with other Central American countries.

Ports

The quality and productivity of port services in Central America is low by international standards, according to a variety of sources. Figure 7.2 displays a benchmarking exercise using a port efficiency indicator designed to measure the quality of maritime and air ports facilities (Wilson, Mann, and Otsuki 2005).[4] All Central American countries perform at least 5 percent short of the benchmark, except El Salvador, which falls short only by 1 percent. Most notable are the deviations of more than 10 percent for Costa Rica, Guatemala, and Nicaragua. A parallel exercise in which the benchmarking uses the value of trade per capita yields similar results, with deviations of more than 15 percent for all countries except El Salvador.

High costs for Central American ports have been attributed to low volumes, poor management by public agencies, and lagging infrastructure. In many cases these difficulties have been compounded by slow customs procedures, security problems, and poor human resource management (Londoño-Kent and Kent 2003; World Bank 2004a, 2004c, 2004e). Puerto Cortés in Honduras exemplifies well many typical problems. In this port, container ships lie idle 22 percent of the time, compared with an international standard

Figure 7.2. Port Efficiency with Respect to GDP Per Capita

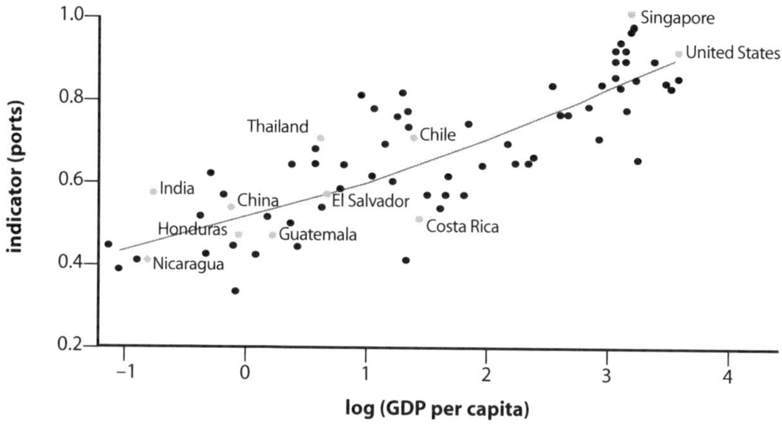

Source: Calculated from data compiled for Wilson, Mann, and Otsuki 2003.

of 5 percent. General cargo is moved at the rate of 24–55 tons per hour, substantially below the international standard of 90 tons per hour, and dry cargo in bags moves at 89 tons per hour versus the international standards of 1,000 tons per hour. As a result of these problems and relatively low volumes, shipping costs to major U.S. destinations are higher from Central American ports than from ports in South American competitors (figure 7.3).

Low quality and productivity in Central American ports contribute to higher maritime transport costs. According to U.S. Department of Transportation data for garment exports, maritime transport costs from Central American ports (except Acajutla, El Salvador) compare favorably with global competitors in shipments to the East Coast of the United States. However, Acajutla, Puerto Cortés (Honduras), and Santo Tomás (Guatemala) do not compare as well in shipments to the U.S. West Coast, even in relation to ports as far away as China, Thailand, and Turkey (figure 7.4). More evidence on this is provided in table 7.1, in which Central America's costs for shipping textiles and apparel to the United States are compared with those of other developing countries. Although most countries of the region have relatively low shipping costs because of their geographic proximity to the United States, it is notable that Colombia and even Mexico have highly competitive shipping costs. Port inefficiencies are likely to play a role in determining shipping costs, as are other factors that can raise freight values, such as the

Figure 7.3. Shipping Cost per 20-foot Container

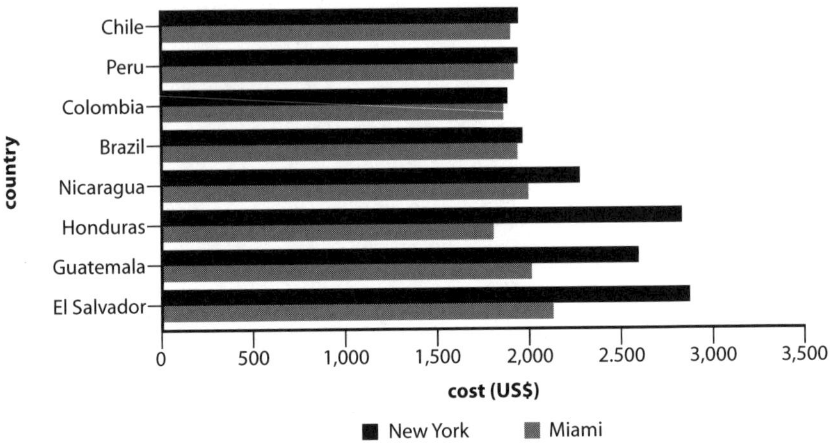

Source: Pizarro 2005.

size of the ships and containers used and higher fixed costs from lower trade volumes. More in-depth analysis in this area is needed to determine the relative weight of these factors in explaining higher maritime transport costs from ports in Central America.

Stagnant port development in recent years has resulted from outdated legal and institutional frameworks that have hindered trade expansion prospects in the region. Concessioning or privatization attempts have been limited, partly because of a lack of a stable regulatory environment (for example, lack of adequate concession legislation). Progress is under way in Costa Rica (Caldera) and El Salvador (Acajutla) where upcoming private participation is expected to improve infrastructure and port efficiency. In Guatemala, the only port in private hands (Puerto Barrios) is perceived by private users to be more efficient, whereas Santo Tomás, in which private-sector involvement has been minimal, is still considered by users to be the least efficient port (World Bank 2004c). At Santo Tomás, plans are now under way for private participation through the construction of a new private warehousing facility that is expected to improve the situation. More broadly for the region as a whole, in the absence of strong and efficient regulatory bodies, state-owned port operators (*empresas portuarias*) have become powerful and heavily politicized institutions, reducing opportunities for reform.

Key actions to improve the efficiency of ports in Central America include

Figure 7.4. Maritime Transport Costs from Selected Ports to the United States, as a Share of Export Value

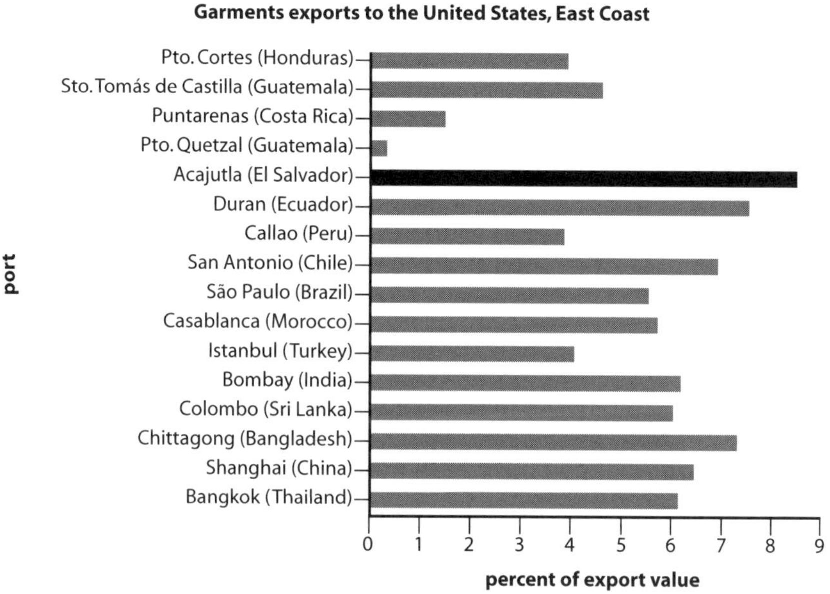

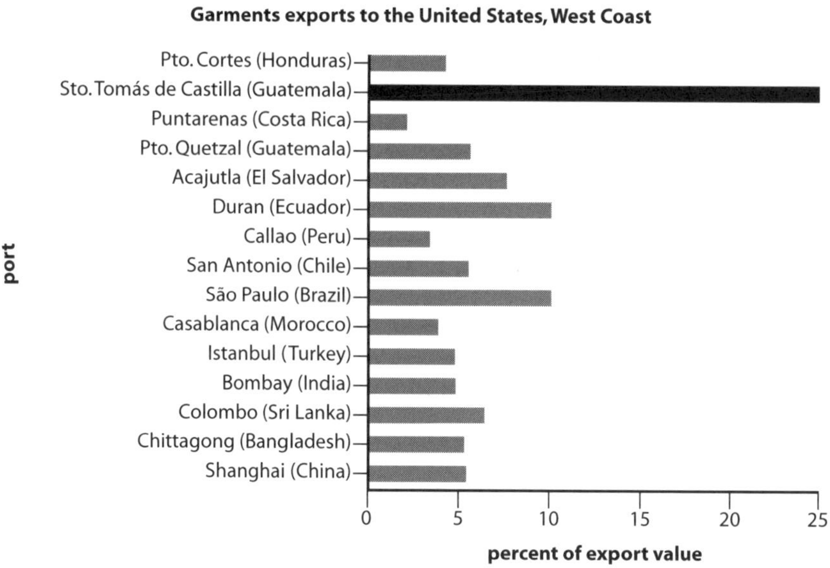

Source: U.S. Department of Transportation, as quoted in El Salvador Investment Climate Assessment.

Table 7.1. Use of Shipping Modes to the United States for the Textiles and Apparel Industry

	Average charge (% FOB)		
Economy	*Ocean*	*Air*	*Shipped by air (%)*
Central and South America			
El Salvador	2.0	5.9	6.5
Guatemala	2.5	8.1	10.0
Honduras	1.9	8.0	2.7
Nicaragua	2.8	4.8	11.1
Costa Rica	2.4	4.7	7.6
Argentina	6.9	11.8	33.4
Brazil	7.0	10.0	39.3
Colombia	1.6	4.3	56.3
Ecuador	5.0	15.3	36.3
Mexico	2.2	5.6	2.0
Peru	2.6	7.2	41.5
Asia			
Bangladesh	5.3	22.9	11.3
China	3.6	11.1	24.3
Hong Kong (China)	2.8	12.4	24.0
Indonesia	4.2	17.0	17.0
Africa			
Kenya	4.5	20.3	19.3
Lesotho	4.3	18.5	16.5
Mauritius	4.1	14.4	27.6
South Africa	5.1	17.1	18.3

Source: Londoño-Kent and Kent 2003.

- implementing regulatory and institutional reforms to facilitate private participation in ports, with the aim of upgrading infrastructure and improving administration.
- improving public administration where ports cannot be privatized, including actions to foster greater transparency, improved management (including human resources), reduction of political interference, greater participation by users on the executive boards, and stronger financial discipline.
- including port development in a coordinated regional transportation strategy for Central America, to ensure rational use of resources to facilitate trade within the region and with external partners. Reducing the costs and times at border crossings is imperative, particularly to resolve

bottlenecks faced by El Salvador and Nicaragua in reaching ports on the Atlantic Ocean.

Customs

Customs performance in the region traditionally has been considered deficient by international standards and custom procedures often have been considered a major obstacle for business operations in the region. Figure 7.5 displays a benchmarking exercise using a customs environment indicator designed to measure the administrative transparency of customs and border crossings (Wilson, Mann, and Otsuki 2005).[5] In this exercise, El Salvador and Nicaragua perform well, just above the benchmark value, whereas the remaining countries fall 10–13 percent short of the values predicted by their levels of income. The performance is less satisfactory for all countries (except El Salvador) in a similar benchmarking exercise using the value of trade per capita.

An alternative assessment of actual port operation delay times caused by customs procedures is given by the results of recent investment climate surveys. Figure 7.6 displays results on the average and longest delays reported by importers for a sample of countries. The Central American countries for which the information is available perform near the sample average (with the exception of Guatemala), better than Brazil, China, and Peru, but worse than Croatia, Hungary, Malaysia, Morocco, Poland, and Turkey. This is also

Figure 7.5. Benchmarking with Respect to GDP Per Capita

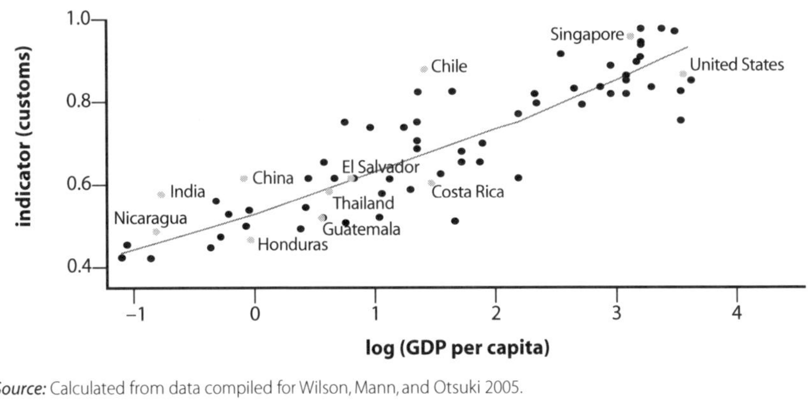

Source: Calculated from data compiled for Wilson, Mann, and Otsuki 2005.

Figure 7.6. Days Needed for Imports to Clear Customs, Selected Countries

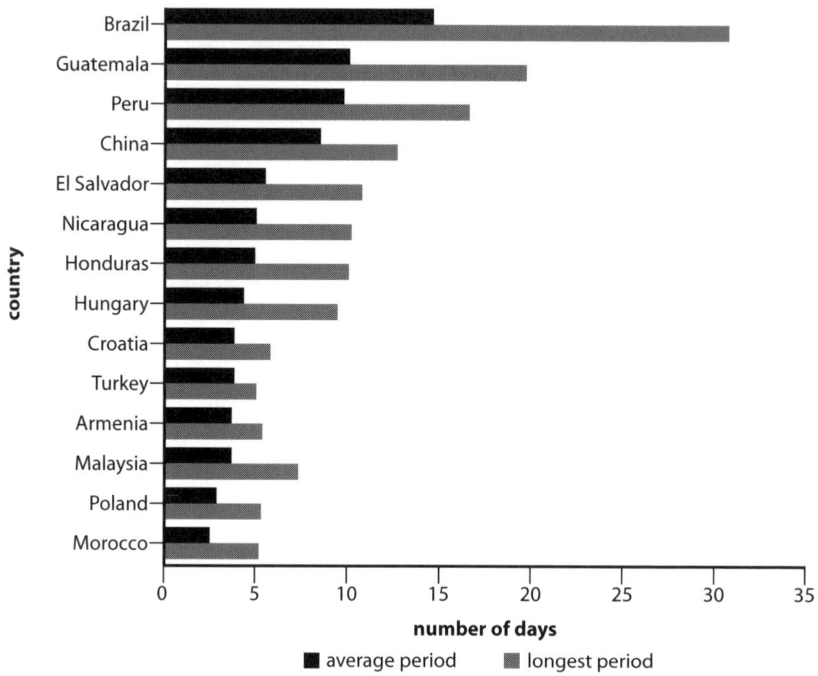

Source: World Bank Investment Climate Surveys.

confirmed in the case of delays faced by exporters (figure 7.7). This good performance is a likely reflection of recent modernization and simplification efforts. Despite the progress achieved, however, interviews with private customs agents and freight transporters reveal there is still room for improvement. The reduction in clearance times achieved with the Internet-based system is sometimes offset by the delays caused by security agencies' stringent physical controls aimed at fighting smuggling and drug trafficking. Other problems arise from the use of excessive discretion by officials, the lack of an adequate and enforceable code of conduct, the importance of the political affiliation of candidates when filling positions, and the lack of modern risk analysis techniques and appropriate equipment for nonintrusive inspections and faster turnaround in laboratory sample testing.

Customs-related constraints were a greater concern in Guatemala than in other Central American countries, and they tend to acquire much greater

Figure 7.7. Days Needed for Exports to Clear Customs, Selected Countries

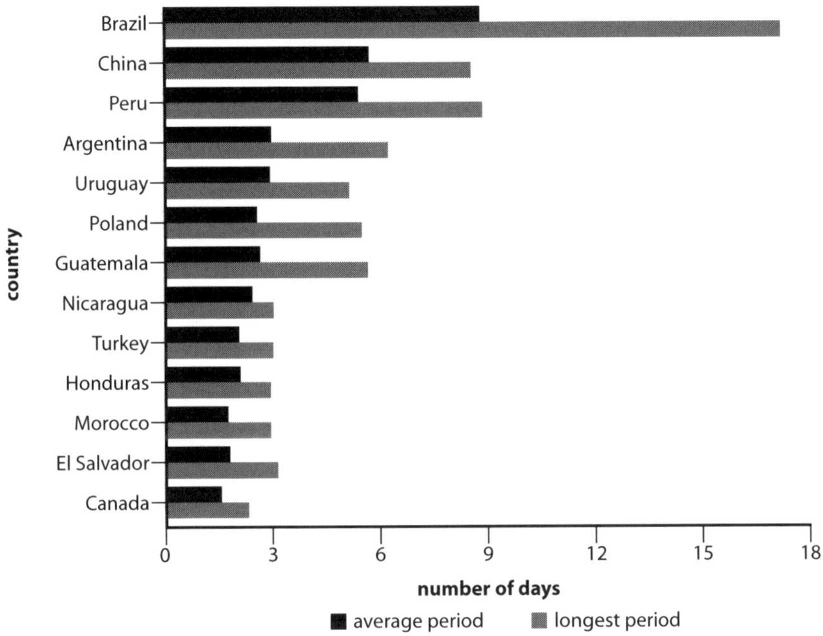

Source: World Bank Investment Climate Surveys.

importance in the context of DR-CAFTA. Although less than 10 percent of the firms surveyed in El Salvador, Honduras, and Nicaragua reported that they face major or very severe constraints in the area of customs (figure 7.8), this percentage is much higher for Guatemala (23.7 percent).[6] The concerns are significantly higher when firms are asked whether problems at customs could constrain their ability to benefit from DR-CAFTA: 51 percent of Guatemalan firms report major or very severe constraints, compared with approximately 37 percent for El Salvador, 35 percent for Nicaragua, and 25 percent for Honduras (figure 7.9). In addition, importers are more likely to report customs concerns than are exporters.

Implementing Central American customs unions is the key next step to facilitating trade in the region. Eliminating border crossings among countries would allow substantial reduction in transportation costs and times, and foster the economies of scale and greater efficiency that would be derived from a true regional market. Although important advances toward this goal have

Figure 7.8. Firms Constrained by Customs

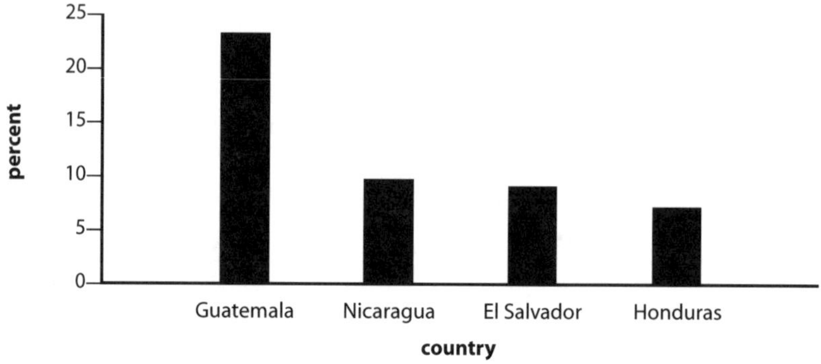

Source: World Bank Investment Climate Survey.

Figure 7.9. Percentage of Firms That Expect to Be Hampered by Customs Procedures When DR-CAFTA Is Implemented

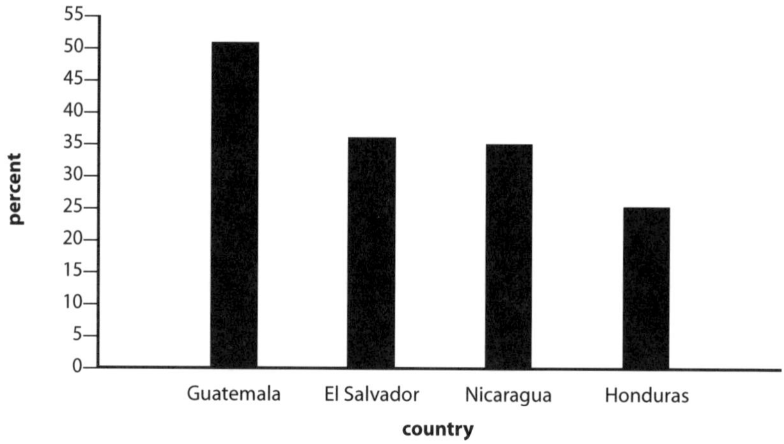

Source: World Bank Investment Climate Survey.

been made over the past year—including the preparation of a unified customs' regulatory agency (*Consejo Arancelario y Aduanero Centroamericano,* or CAUCA) and its *reglamento* (RECAUCA), and the creation of unified customs among El Salvador, Guatemala, and Honduras—Central American nations need to take the remaining steps to abolish all border controls among them. Key steps include elimination of tariffs on a few pending goods for intraregional trade, full agreement on the common external tariff schedule, and procedures to facilitate the distribution of VAT and tariff revenues among member nations. Temporary arrangements may be needed to deal with differential external tariffs arising from bilateral treaties that were signed by different CACM members with third countries, as well as with differences in DR-CAFTA tariff phase-out periods and excluded goods. In the short run, key actions are implementing the *manual unico de procedimientos de aduanas,* and fully integrating binational customs procedures in order to have only one control post at each border.

Central American countries should deepen modernization efforts, with a focus on reducing costs and delays faced by importers. This endeavor requires pressing forward with recent modernization processes, intensifying training, and implementing quality-based management. For example, one good initiative is that of the ISO 9,000 certifications in El Salvador. Remaining deficiencies in customs procedures and operations could be addressed by facilitating inspections through the incorporation of modern equipment and risk analysis techniques, and by increasing the professionalization of the customs agencies.

Institutions and Regulations

Certain institutions and regulations are essential to ensure that trade opportunities arising from DR-CAFTA materialize and eventually are translated into higher growth levels. As argued in chapter 4, most relevant for this connection are indicators of the ease with which firms and factors can be redeployed to take advantage of new productive opportunities. Other important areas that can create unnecessary costs to the reallocation of productive resources are those related to administrative corruption (which also affects the attractiveness to foreign investors) and those that reduce access to credit.

Excessive levels of regulation across Central American countries compared with those elsewhere in Latin America and among other developing countries suggest that regulatory reform should be a key priority in the complementary agenda. Using the labor and firm entry index of regulations constructed by Bolaky and Freund[7]—available for Costa Rica, Guatemala, Honduras, and Nicaragua—all Central American countries fall short of their expected levels by income, with Costa Rica and Honduras lagging farthest behind (see figure 7.10).

Figure 7.10. Regulations Index

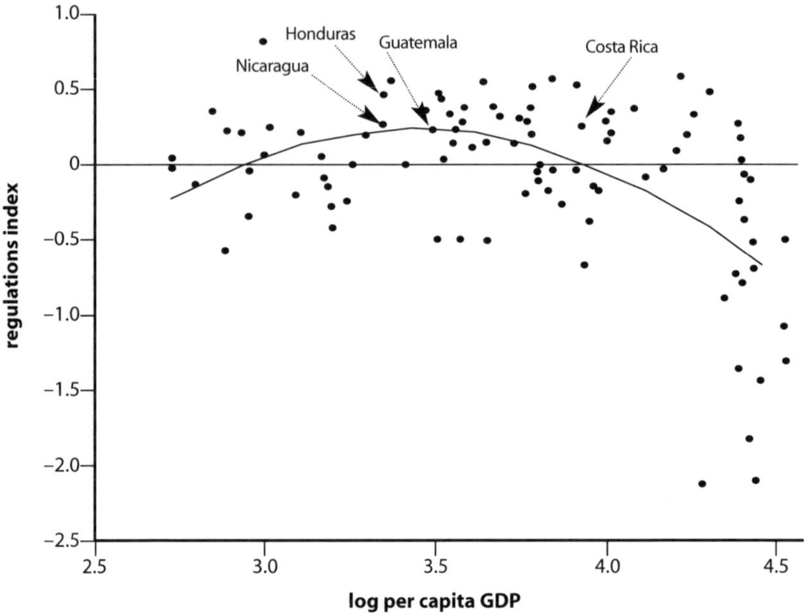

Source: Authors' calculations, based on Bolaky and Freund 2003.

Labor Regulations

An assessment of the labor regulations component of the regulations index of Bolaky and Freund (2003) reveals significant levels of underperformance for all Central American countries (6 percent to 11 percent of predicted values) with Guatemala and Nicaragua exhibiting the widest gaps.[8] Although this may be reflecting some excess regulations in formal norms, in economies in which the informal sector accounts for a large size of employment it is unknown how costly these regulations may be. The partial evidence available does not suggest that labor turnover rates—firing and hiring rates—are abnormally low in Central American countries, but more in-depth studies of labor markets in Central America are required.[9]

Firm Entry

Excessive regulations for firm entry are an issue in some countries in Central America, as measured by the number of days required by respondent manufacturing firms to register for the first time. According to the World Bank's (2003a) *Doing Business* survey series, a typical firm in Nicaragua takes 29 days to register compared with 46 days in El Salvador, 56 days in Guatemala, and 83 days in Honduras (figure 7.11). Summing up the average number of days required to go through six different types of registration procedure leads to 74 days in El Salvador, 251 in Guatemala, 215 in Honduras, and 82 in Nicaragua.[10] Figure 7.11 compares the available data on registration times from the investment climate surveys and the World Bank's Doing Business database.[11] A benchmarking exercise using the firm entry component of the regulations index of Bolaky and Freund (2003) finds that Honduras exhibits the largest lag with respect to the predicted value for its level of income per capita (entry procedures take almost three times longer to be completed than in the rest of the world). Costa Rica exhibits only a modest gap, and Guatemala and Nicaragua are near the levels predicted for their respective levels of income.[12]

Administrative Corruption

The prevalence of corruption is a significant issue of concern in several Central American countries. Administrative corruption can have a deleterious effect on the costs faced by private firms in doing business and can affect the

Figure 7.11. Number of Days to Register a Firm

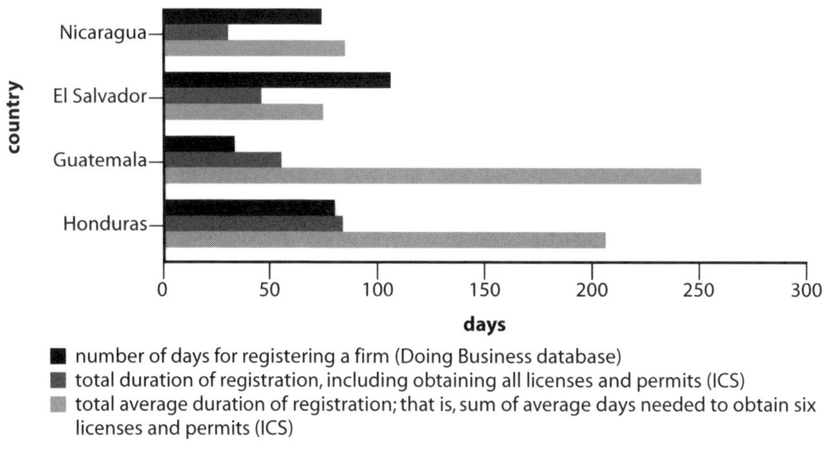

Sources: World Bank Investment Climate Surveys (ICS) and World Bank 2003 Doing Business database.

country's attractiveness to foreign investors. Moreover, corruption and weak rule of law can make any regulatory environment exert unintended consequences when legal norms and regulations are not applied accordingly.

Transparency International's Corruption Perceptions Index (CPI) places Costa Rica and El Salvador, respectively, in the 72nd and 66th percentiles of a sample of 145 countries, compared with the 24th percentile (on average) for Guatemala, Honduras, and Nicaragua. A similar ordering can be derived from the World Bank Institute's 2004 indicator of the control of corruption, although El Salvador falls farther behind Costa Rica and is actually surpassed by Nicaragua (figure 7.12).[13]

Similar rankings with respect to Central American countries are obtained for other governance indexes covering the prevalence of the rule of law, government effectiveness, and regulatory quality. Indeed, as seen in figure 7.13, El Salvador systematically ranks below Costa Rica, but above Guatemala, Honduras, and except for the index for corruption, above Nicaragua.

Honduran firms lead the region in the perception that bribes are required "to get things done" (figure 7.14). In 2003, Guatemalan firms were more likely than their peers to describe the government as inefficient and to state that government regulations are interpreted in an inconsistent and unpredictable way—although this result may be partly attributable to the intense conflict that existed between the private sector and the government under the Portillo administration. At the other end, Salvadoran firms have more confidence in public officials than do their counterparts from other Central

Figure 7.12. International Corruption Rankings of Central American Countries

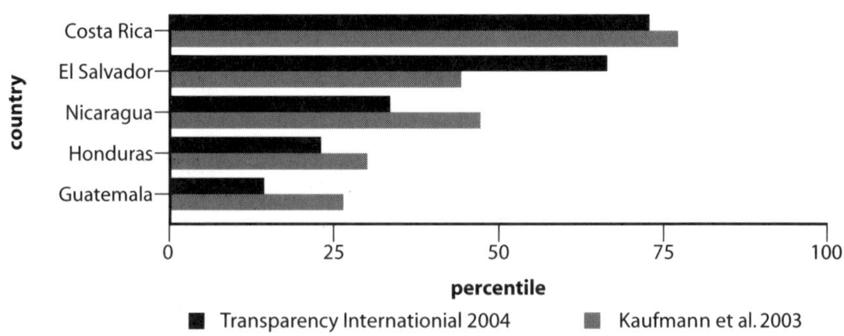

Source: Data from Transparency International, available at www.transparency.org.

Figure 7.13. WBI Governance Indicators for Central America, 2004

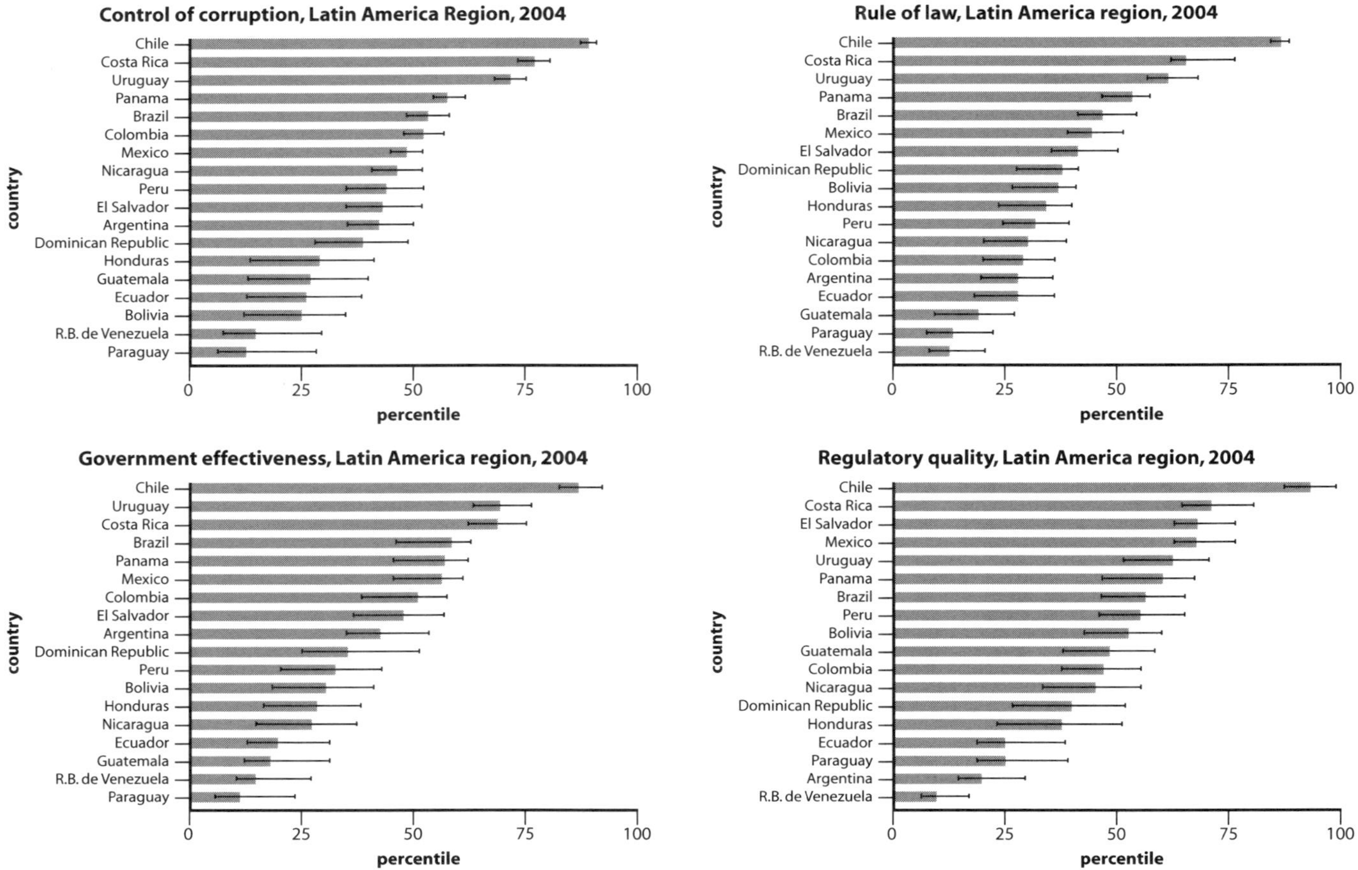

Source: Kaufmann, Kraay, and Mastruzzi 2005.

Figure 7.14. Inconsistency and Unpredictability of Regulations, Government Inefficiency, and Bribery

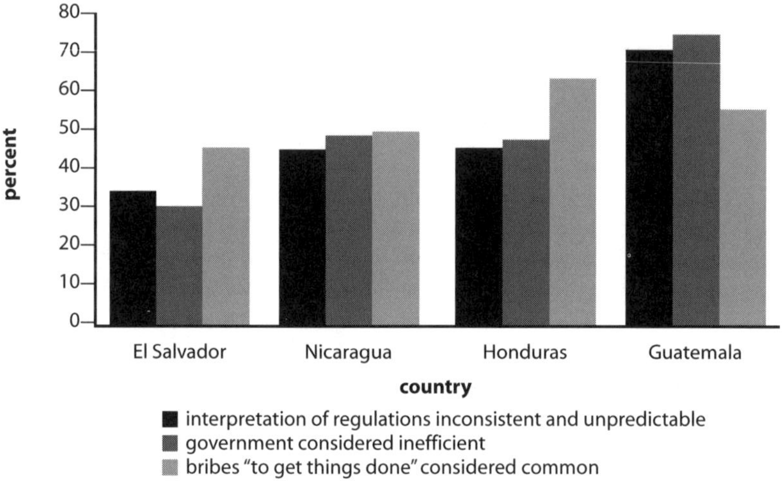

Source: World Bank Investment Climate Surveys.

American countries: only 35 percent of the firms state that public officials do not interpret government regulations in a consistent and predictable way, compared with about 45 percent in Honduras and Nicaragua, and 71 percent in Guatemala. Although to an extent lower than in neighboring countries, administrative corruption seems to affect almost half of the firms surveyed in El Salvador.

Regulations and Access to Credit

Sufficient access to credit is important for firms to respond to new investment opportunities arising from DR-CAFTA. The level of access to credit varies across Central American countries, but firms seem to face significant credit constraints in all of them. One sign of credit constraints is the intensive use of retained earnings to fund new investments. This source supplies more than half of the funds for firms in Guatemala, Honduras, and Nicaragua (figure 7.15). Credit constraints may be much higher than in global competitors: according to investment climate survey data from the early years of this century, the share of firms with access to loans in Central America ranged between 43 percent and 63 percent, in comparison with 87 percent for countries like Thailand and Malaysia (figure 7.16). Within Central America the share of firms facing constraints is lower in El Salvador (17 percent) than in Guatemala (28.1 percent) and Honduras (27.8 percent), with Nicaragua lagging behind (36.2 percent).

Figure 7.15. Main Sources of Finance for Investment Capital, by Country

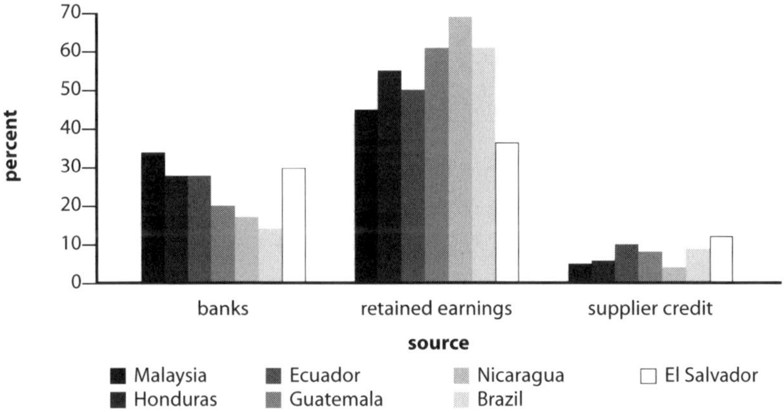

Source: World Bank Investment Climate Surveys.

Figure 7.16. Share of Firms with Loans, International Comparison

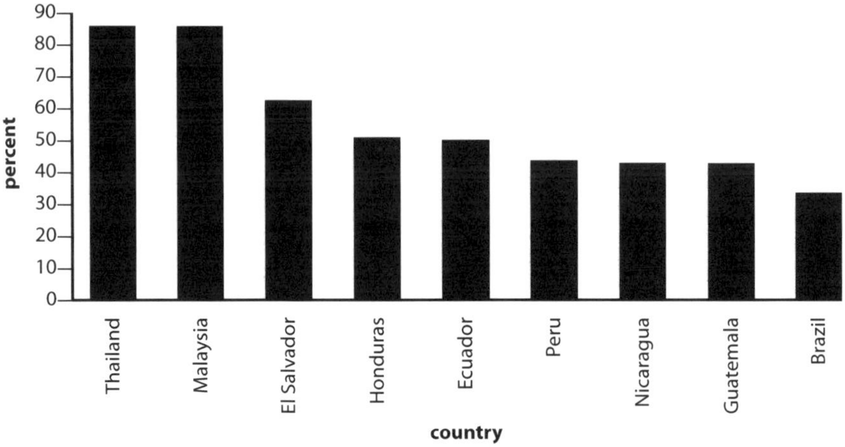

Source: World Bank Investment Climate Survey.

Smaller firms face more restrictions in accessing credit than do larger firms. Within El Salvador, for example, the fraction of credit-constrained enterprises decreases with firm size: only 6 percent of large and 10 percent of medium-size firms are credit constrained, compared with 30 percent and 23 percent, respectively, for micro and small firms (figure 7.17).[14] The low share of finance-constrained firms among large enterprises is explained by their overall easier access, including access to external finance. In addition, access to formal credit in rural areas tends to be low, despite high repressed demand (World Bank 2005b).

Measured by broader indexes of financial depth, Costa Rica and Guatemala underperform their peers relative to their level of development. By contrast, El Salvador, Honduras, and Nicaragua perform above expected levels, using private-sector credit as a share of GDP.[15] Furthermore, interest rate spreads are very low in El Salvador because of its dollarized regime and a more efficient banking sector, whereas rates in Costa Rica are among the highest in Latin America (see table 7.2).

Credit access limitations in Central America are linked to key institutional and regulatory weaknesses, such as weak enforcement of creditor rights, slow and politicized judiciaries, inoperative bankruptcy procedures, and poor registry systems for property rights, as well as weaknesses in banking supervision and regulation. Key actions of an agenda aimed at improving access to credit should include these:

Figure 7.17. El Salvador Firms Reporting Major or Severe Obstacles Related to Finance, by Size of Firm

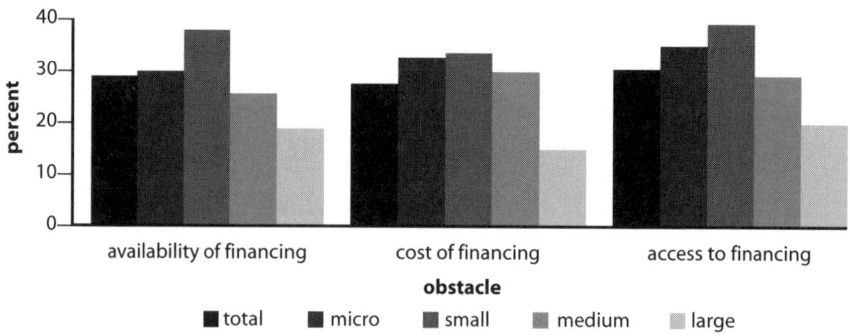

Source: World Bank Investment Climate Survey.

Table 7.2. Banking Systems in Central America, End of 2003

percent, unless otherwise indicated

Country	*Assets (US$ billions)*[a]	*Assets relative to GDP*	*Credit to private sector relative to GDP*	*Deposits relative to GDP*	*Real lending rate*[b]	*Interest rate spreads*
Costa Rica	8.2	56.9	36.0	43.4	16.1	15.2
El Salvador	9.8	68.7	49.6	42.7	4.4	3.2
Guatemala	6.5	26.6	18.0	22.1	9.5	10.2
Honduras	4.0	59.3	37.6	43.1	13.1	9.3
Nicaragua[c]	2.1	56.9	26.4	41.0	9.2	9.9
Average	6.1	53.7	33.5	38.5	10.5	9.6

Source: Nicaragua Development Policy Review (World Bank, 2004).

a. The real lending rate is calculated as the average lending rate reduced by consumer price index inflation.

b. Data for Costa Rica, El Salvador, and Nicaragua relative to GDP are for 2002.

c. Total of claims excluding fixed and other assets.

- strengthening creditors' rights by making enforcement procedures of secured and unsecured claims shorter and more efficient
- improving the efficiency and independence of the judiciary, including judges' experience with and knowledge of commercial law, in order to bring more certainty to the resolution of commercial disputes
- modernizing and unifying registry systems for both movable and immovable assets, and continuing efforts to clarify property rights for real estate and their formal registration
- upgrading bankruptcy and reorganization procedures to facilitate the speedy reorganization of viable insolvent enterprises and the efficient liquidation of nonviable ones
- developing credit information systems to reduce the high operational costs of microfinance institutions
- strengthening banking regulations and supervision.

To cope with the increasing integration of Central America's financial sectors, which is likely to speed up with DR-CAFTA, action should be taken to consolidate supervision. The increasing regional nature of most financial groups in Central America allows for the quick cross-border transmission of shocks originating in any one country. DR-CAFTA is also likely to make industrial and commercial operations more regionalized in Central America. Although many commercial banks have quickly adjusted by organizing themselves on a regional basis, the region's supervisory authorities have not. Efforts to develop a coordinated strategy for effective regional consolidated supervision and regulation are required to avoid the limitations of the current individual country approach.[16]

Innovation and Education

As explained in chapter 4, DR-CAFTA offers opportunities for Central American countries to boost their long-term productivity by increasing imports of capital goods and adapting foreign technology to the local context. However, adopting existing technology is not without cost, and an enabling environment requires a well-functioning national innovation system and complementary actions on the education front (De Ferranti et al. 2003). This section of the chapter provides a preliminary assessment of how Central American countries perform in these areas by concentrating on three themes. First, we benchmark some Central American countries on their enabling environments for innovation by reporting data on innovation outcomes, inputs, and the efficiency of R&D. Second, we assess the recent performance of Central American countries with respect to discoveries of new export products, a key outcome that has been linked in the recent literature to growth and productive investments (Hausmann and Rodrik 2003b). Third, we provide a quick assessment of educational performance in Central America, with special emphasis on those areas that are required for the functioning of a successful NIS. At the end, we offer some recommendations.

Innovation: Outputs, Inputs, and R&D Efficiency

Central America's success in intermediate innovation outcomes across time can be tracked by following two common measures: the number of patents granted by the U.S. patenting authority and the number of scientific publications. Figure 7.18 benchmarks performance in each dimension by researchers residing in Costa Rica and El Salvador, comparing them with the average of researchers in countries with the same levels of GDP, labor forces of the same size, and the same value of merchandise exports to the United States since the 1960s.[17] The graph shows how far these countries are from the average of similar economies (the zero line). A negative number on the vertical axis is evidence of underperformance. Because the predicted number of patents is relatively small (one or two), the performance of Costa Rica in terms of patents appears to be erratic. Nonetheless, one could say that Costa Rica does not seem to underperform systematically. Conversely, the outcome of scientific publications is approximately 50 percent below average. El Salvador has historically underperformed in scientific publications by about 95 percent, although this can only be taken as suggestive because absolute numbers are quite small. The picture for patents is ambiguous, again as a result of the small absolute numbers, although figure 7.18 suggests certain deficiencies in patent achievement in El Salvador.

Similar benchmarking can be made with two indicators of innovation inputs: expenditures on research and development and payments for licensing of new foreign technologies, again with respect to GDP and size of the labor force. The former indicator extends beyond investment in cutting-edge technologies to include most expenditures in adoption and adaptation of technologies. Not only does the share of GDP dedicated to R&D in the average country increase with income per capita, but several high-growth comparator countries—Finland, the Republic of Korea, and Israel—also had dramatic take-offs relative to this benchmark, a path that China and India appear to be

Figure 7.18. Do Costa Rica and El Salvador Underperform in Innovation Outputs?

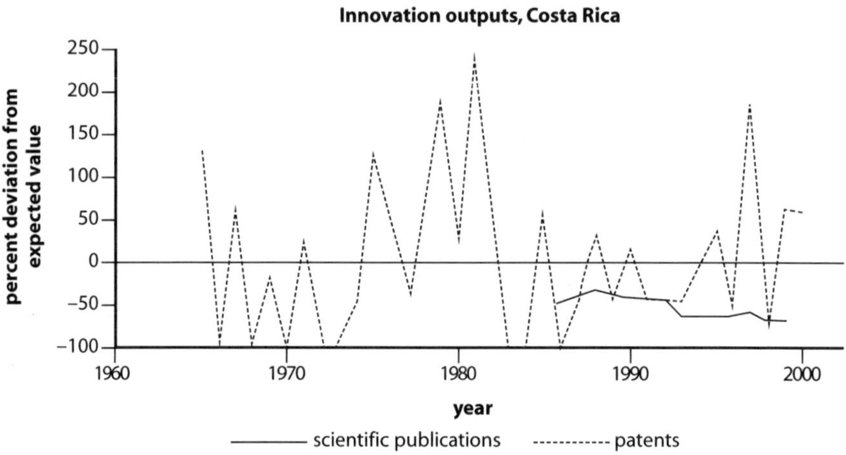

Decade	Scientific publications	Patents
1990s	2	0
1980s	3	0
1970s	—	1
1960s	—	2

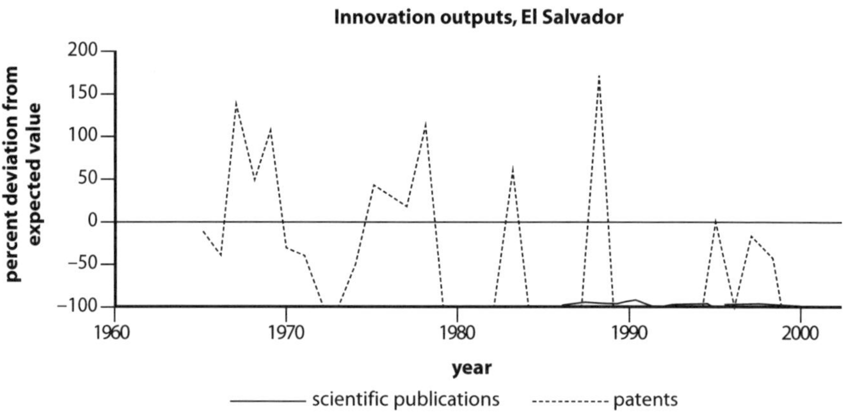

Decade	Scientific publications	Patents
1990s	62	3
1980s	50	2
1970s	—	1
1960s	—	1

Source: Calculations by Daniel Lederman and William F. Maloney (World Bank) based on data from Lederman and Saenz (2005).

trying to follow (Lederman and Maloney 2003a). It is disappointing that the average efforts of five Latin American countries for which data exist (Argentina, Brazil, Chile, Costa Rica, and Mexico) are substantially below trend.

Costa Rica's underperformance in the outcomes of innovation is partly the result of lackluster performance in innovation investments, at least in R&D expenditures. Costa Rica's R&D effort has been weak compared with countries of similar size. The share of GDP that Costa Rica devoted to licensing, however, does not show significant gaps with respect to the proper benchmark. This is not because of low private and social returns to R&D because Lederman and Maloney (2003a) have estimated that the economic returns to R&D and to licensing for countries of Costa Rica's level of income are high (around 65 percent). More likely, Costa Rica's low investments in this area are probably linked to deficiencies in the areas of financial depth, protection of intellectual property rights, ability to mobilize government resources, and quality of research institutions, all of which have been shown to be key determinants of R&D effort across countries. As a result, not only is Costa Rica not experiencing a take-off in innovation effort such as those seen in dynamic economies like Finland, Korea, and Israel, but it also is below the "average" performer.

Low levels of innovation outcomes may also arise from inefficiencies in the way in which existing innovation-related resources are used through the NIS. One way of estimating the efficiency of an NIS is to examine how R&D investments translate into commercial patents and how the "elasticity" of patents with respect to R&D investment compares to the world average.[18] Figure 7.19 shows the elasticity or sensitivity of patents with respect to R&D in Costa Rica, El Salvador, and several comparator countries. Costa Rica's positive value can be seen to indicate the extent to which the country performs in patenting efficiency relative to the OECD average. In fact, Costa Rica and the República Bolivariana de Venezuela are the only two Latin American and Caribbean countries that perform better than the OECD average. Additional statistical exercises show that Costa Rica's privileged position compared with the rest of the Latin American and Caribbean countries results from the higher quality of its research institutions and greater collaboration with private firms.

El Salvador is more inefficient in innovation outcomes than the average of countries in Latin America and the Caribbean. A good share of this inefficiency is likely related to the lack of collaboration between the private sector and research organizations, such as universities, which is the main expla-

Figure 7.19. Efficiency of R&D Expenditures Compared with the OECD Countries

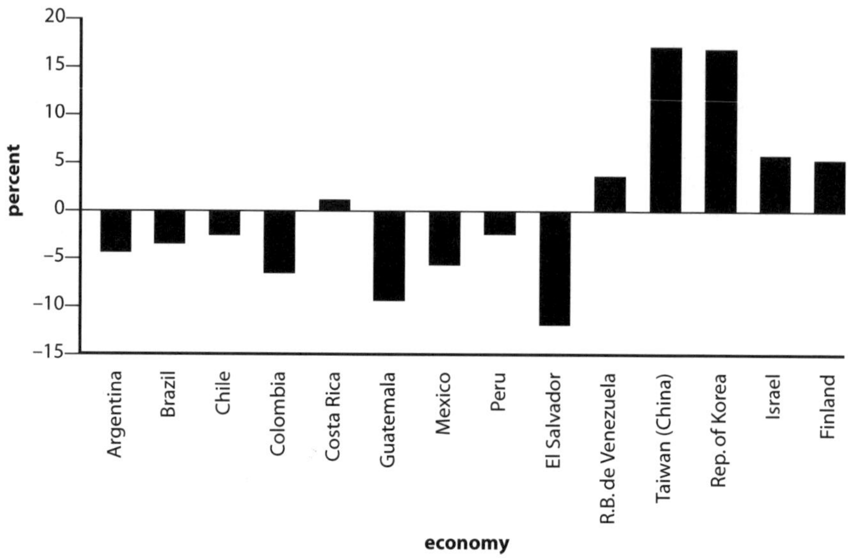

Source: Calculations by Daniel Lederman and William F. Maloney (World Bank , based on data from Lederman and Saenz (2005).
OECD = Organisation for Economic Co-operation and Development; R&D = research and development

nation found for the situation in Latin America and the Caribbean by Bosch, Lederman, and Maloney (2005).[19]

Discovering New Export Products

Recent attention has been given to the link between the appearance of new export products and economic growth. Some authors have argued that public sector policies are needed to provide incentives for entrepreneurs to invest in discovering new and potentially profitable businesses, because of problems with externalities and private appropriation of rents similar to those that hinder innovation and technology adaptation (Hausmann and Rodrik 2003b). In fact, for the case of El Salvador, Hausmann and Rodrik (2003a) argued that public-sector subsidies for the introduction of new products may be needed to revitalize economic growth. Furthermore, Klinger and Lederman (2004) do find evidence suggesting the market failures might in fact impede economic discovery, and Khan (2004) reported that the introduction of new products does affect economic growth by stimulating productive investment.

Among Central American countries, Guatemala has been the main underachiever in discovering new export products. Figure 7.20 shows the predicted and the observed numbers of export discoveries in the 1990s, which are a function of the level of development (GDP per capita) of each country.[20] El Salvador, Honduras, and Nicaragua show only slight levels of underperformance and Costa Rica is a strong overachiever. Given this evidence, policies to stimulate economic discoveries should not be a powerful priority over other policy needs, with the only possible exception of Guatemala.

Education for Innovation and Growth

Innovation and technological change require a strong education base. This is one of the important conclusions of a recent World Bank report on education and innovation in Latin America and the Caribbean (De Ferranti et al. 2003). This report highlighted how technological innovation and educational levels (particularly skills and ability to learn) are complementary and reinforce each other's contribution to economic growth. The study showed the need to coordinate and sequence both education and technology absorption policies. It also argued that there must be a sharp acceleration in educational attainment for a country to benefit from the knowledge economy and from the growth-enhancing potential of technology transfers through FDI and trade.

DR-CAFTA and the greater flows of foreign investment that should accompany its introduction are likely to increase the demand for secondary and

Figure 7.20. Discovery Curve and Central America, 1990s

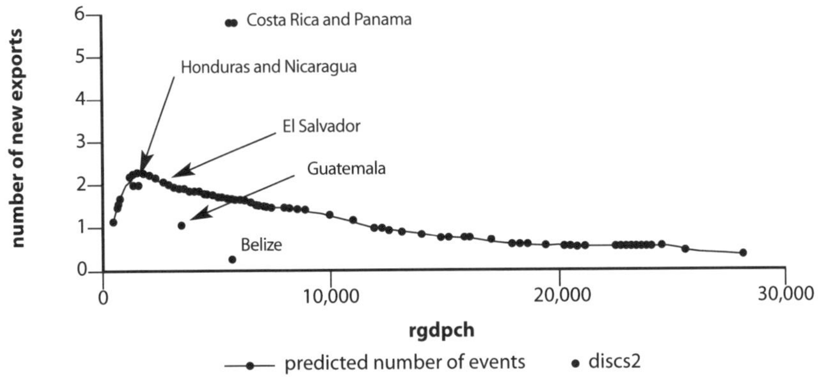

Sources: Authors' calculations, based on data from Klinger and Lederman 2004.
discs2 = actual number of new exports; rgdpch = real gross domestic product per capita.

skilled workers. Investors are likely to require higher skills (including bilingual skills) to function in an increasingly global market and to use new imported inputs. Local firms willing to take advantage of new DR-CAFTA-related opportunities also will likely demand new skills to adapt innovations and improve productivity levels. Most countries of Central America, with the only exception being Costa Rica, are likely to face shortages of appropriately skilled workers to meet these demands. The absence of a considerable mass of secondary-educated workers in most countries of Central America is the result of the slow expansion of educational opportunities and its unbalanced pattern. Most countries have not followed an orderly and sequential growth across educational levels, which is reflected in the fact that from 1960 to 2000 the ratio of workers with university education relative to those with secondary education almost quadrupled in El Salvador, Costa Rica, and Guatemala, and tripled in Honduras. The result is inequities in the labor market, where most workers only have minimum literacy and math skills; very few have skills in quantitative analysis, communication, and other basic competencies provided by secondary education, yet the percentage of workers with a university education has been rising. In other words, there is a curious trend where secondary enrollment has stagnated, whereas enrollment in tertiary education by those who finish secondary school is increasing. This tendency may be reversing in Costa Rica and El Salvador, given recent persistent increments in secondary education investment. Nevertheless, coverage and quality of secondary education are weaknesses in all Central American countries, although inefficiencies of resource use are more acute in Honduras and Nicaragua. This is a concern because higher levels of secondary schooling are crucial to facilitate the technological upgrading of local manufacturers, to attract foreign direct investment with high technological content, and to benefit from the potential spillovers of those investments to the rest of the economy. Coverage of the secondary cycle is low (around 56–61 percent) or very low (around 37–43 percent) in all countries (table 7.3). Quality is low at all educational levels, as illustrated by the still high repetition rates and the unsatisfactory results from the standardized national exams (di Gropello 2006). Inadequate curricula and textbooks combined with insufficient learning times and teacher quality are among the main contributing factors to low educational achievement in the region. Inefficiency of resource use is a problem in Honduras because of the excessive share of spending on salaries relative to nonsalary expenditures and the lack of effective teacher incentives. Inefficiencies in Nicaragua relate to excessive central administration costs.

Table 7.3. Gross Enrollment Rate at the Secondary Level, 2002–3
percent

Country	*Enrollment*	*Country*	*Enrollment*
Costa Rica	56	Honduras	37
El Salvador	59	Nicaragua	61
Guatemala	43		

Source: World Bank, World Development Indicators.

Central American firms use in-house and external skills training to upgrade and complement the educational profiles of their workforces. There may be some reasons to believe that markets may underprovide training relative to the social optimum (as a result of externalities associated with a more highly skilled workforce), but public provision of training has been characteristically inefficient and unresponsive to private-sector needs across Central America. For instance, returns to public training programs in Guatemala have been shown to be very low, whereas the returns are positive for privately provided and funded training (World Bank Guatemala CEM 2004b). Recent reforms to the *Instituto Salvadoreño de Formación Profesional* (Salvadoran Institute of Professional Development or INSAFORP) \have removed it from directly providing training, a key factor in the improvement of training services in that country (see box 7.1).

Areas for Action

For lower-income countries such as Honduras and Nicaragua, national innovation systems should focus primarily on facilitating technology absorption. Priority actions should include

- improving the capacity to absorb new technologies from the external stock of knowledge by simplifying processes to import capital goods and to license foreign technologies
- strengthening the institution in charge of innovation policy and its coordination with private-sector needs, and improving the quality of the information on R&D
- improving the efficiency of low R&D public spending by increasing links with the private sector, and increasing accountability for the use of these resources.

Box 7.1

The Positive Experience of Reform of the Value-Added Tax System in El Salvador

INSAFORP primarily finances training solicited by companies and provided by private training centers. Only when no private provider exists does INSAFORP provide direct training. This structure seems to avoid at least one of the two common pitfalls of many training systems in Latin America—(1) provision of irrelevant training with little impact on productivity and wages, and (2) inefficient public provision of training. Whether the creation of INSAFORP led to additional skill formation or it simply substituted for firm payment of training is uncertain. However, with the high levels of training achieved in 2001, it seems plausible that the introduction of the training levy raised the level of training beyond the pure market solution and thus successfully addressed some of the market failures involved in the provision of training.

The organization is facing issues of financial sustainability. The rapid increase in funded courses has outpaced revenue growth, and as a consequence INSAFORP used accumulated reserves during 2001 to accommodate high demand. Hence, the current high level of firm training is unsustainable in the medium to long run without additional funds or efficiency savings.

Source: World Bank 2004a.

For middle-income countries such as Costa Rica, El Salvador, and Guatemala, national innovation systems should support technology adaptation and generation. Priority actions include

- strengthening public–private partnerships by increasing links between public research centers and private firms, aligning incentives for research in universities, and improving the accountability of R&D performed with public resources
- promoting output-based/market-oriented R&D in public research institutes and universities by gradually reducing their access to earmarked funds and, at the same time, expanding their autonomy to look for new sources of funding, particularly through different partnerships with the private sector; and by introducing flexibility in the regulation ruling the assignment of property rights over inventions generated in these institu-

tions, possibly enabling main researchers and their institutions to benefit from their discoveries

- gradually increasing public R&D funding, preferably through an innovation fund to finance experimental development (as opposed to basic research), by matching grants and competitive subsidies directed to commercial applications
- strengthening the governance of technology policy by defining an explicit technology and innovation policy, enhancing the policymaking role of a public–private board, and simplifying the concessions of public funds for R&D
- enhancing institutional capacity to enforce intellectual property rights laws, possibly by upgrading the registries and investing in process simplification and staff training.

Sequencing education policies with the stage of development and innovation policies is important. For those countries farthest away from the technological frontier—such as Honduras and Nicaragua—the best technology policy is likely to be simply sound education policy. The agenda for countries that require educational improvements to adopt relatively simple technologies should be aimed at achieving completion of universal primary education, with gradual expansion of secondary education. In the more advanced settings of Costa Rica and El Salvador, where adaptation and creation of new technologies is more important, issues of education quality and completion of secondary schooling are more significant.

In vocational training policy, Central American countries should change the existing public–private balance toward greater in-service training and should introduce competition into the provision of training services. Training policy should be viewed not just as subsidizing or providing training, but also as increasing the demand for training through appropriate technology policy and increasing the trainability of workers through appropriate education policy. For this, it is important to build partnerships between the private sector and universities or technical schools, and to encourage apprenticeships.

Although it is important to ensure that an appropriate supply of tertiary education is available, the justification for public funding is weak because high private returns already create high demand. Public policies toward expansion of tertiary education should focus on facilitating private investment through regulation that would improve the functioning of the market for higher education. These initiatives could include (1) increasing the information available to students, (2) maintaining a flexible accreditation system, and (3) enabling greater cost recovery in public universities (Holm-Nielsen, Blom, and Garcia 2003).

Universal primary school completion remains a vital unfinished agenda in Guatemala, Honduras, and Nicaragua. To compete in a global economy, ensuring quality universal primary education for all boys and girls of all ethnicities and ensuring that they acquire basic cognitive skills of literacy and numeracy must be the top priorities in education in Central America. The trends for Honduras Nicaragua, and Guatemala indicate that they need to redouble efforts to achieve the Millennium Development Goal of universal primary school completion by 2015. Except for Guatemala, these countries are already spending a high proportion of their national budgets on education, so reforms and external support are essential for these countries to achieve the goal.

Summary of Priorities for Central American Countries

The chapter has reviewed recent evidence in the areas of trade facilitation, institutional and regulatory reforms, and innovation and education so as to identify key priorities for the complementary agenda for DR-CAFTA. The main challenges (and therefore the priorities) identified for Costa Rica include improving road quality and port and customs efficiency, boosting financial depth, and improving the quality and coverage of secondary education. For El Salvador, priorities focus around increasing road quality, reducing shipping costs, and tackling governance challenges, as well as improving the quality and coverage of secondary education. Both countries need to devote more public resources to R&D (with monitoring and evaluation efforts put in place to assess results over time), strengthen public–private partnerships for innovation, and enhance the institutional capacity to enforce intellectual property rights laws. In addition to shoring up weaknesses in the areas identified for Costa Rica and El Salvador, Guatemala also needs to continue to build on recent accomplishments in improving customs administration, coverage and quality of primary education, and road density, as well as to devote some attention to fostering the development of new export products.

The challenges for Honduras and Nicaragua are likely to encompass a broader set of policy issues because they face more limitations as a result of their lower development levels. Both countries need to address governance and to work on improving the coverage and quality of primary education. They must improve the operational efficiency of ports and increase the quality of roads and their density. And they have to improve their capacity to absorb knowledge from abroad, strengthen institutions in charge of innovation policy, and increase links between public R&D programs and the needs of the private sector. Honduras also must upgrade its customs administration and reduce the costs and time to establish new business ventures.

All Central American countries share a regional economic agenda that must focus urgently on achieving a customs union, which is critical to reducing transaction costs to trade within the region. In addition, efforts should be deepened to coordinate the development of infrastructure that benefits from a regional perspective, including major road networks, and the development of ports. Mechanisms to formulate a common regional trade policy should be strengthened to ensure coherence of future bilateral, regional, and global commitments with the new framework provided by DR-CAFTA. In addition, improved coordination of key regulatory policies (such as those concerning financial supervision, competition, and fiscal incentives) may be needed to establish the basis of a deeper and more integrated regional market in the future.

All of the elements of the complementary agenda mentioned here are also components of the broader agenda to boost economic growth in the region. Recent analytical work produced by the World Bank to prioritize actions for broad-based growth in the nations of Central America has highlighted the high return that would be obtained from improvements in the areas of infrastructure, education, and governance (World Bank 2004a–c, 2004e–f). DR-CAFTA enhances the social return to these actions and makes them more urgent. Hopefully, this important agreement will serve as a useful tool to rally support for consolidating the policy reforms of recent years and pushing forward with new energy in the areas in which weaknesses remain to boost the pace of growth and poverty reduction across Central America.

Notes

1. The assessment and recommendations summarized here draw from recent Country Economic Memorandum and Development Policy Review studies performed in El Salvador (2004), Honduras (2004), Nicaragua (2004), and Guatemala (2005), as well as Investment Climate (IC) Assessments in Honduras (2004), Guatemala (2004), Nicaragua (2004), and El Salvador (2005). IC comparisons do not include Costa Rica because data from this survey will not be available until 2006. Useful attempts to outline some of the challenges of the complementary agenda include Salazar-Xiriñachs and Granados (2004), González and Lizano (2003), and Rodlauer and Schipke (2005).

2. See, for example, the references included in the previous footnote.
3. In comparisons of road availability per inhabitant, El Salvador joins Guatemala and Honduras among lagging countries, whereas Nicaragua surpasses comparators because of its relatively low population.
4. The indicator is an average of three indexes concerning port efficiency, port facilities and inland waterways, and air transport, as discussed in Wilson, Mann, and Otsuki (2005).
5. The indicator is the average of five indexes concerning irregular payments, low import fees, hidden import barriers, bribery and corruption, and corruption perceptions, as discussed in Wilson, Mann, and Otsuki (2005).
6. The results of Guatemala's Investment Climate Assessment (World Bank 2004c) indicated that, among the infrastructure variables, customs regulations are the major obstacle to business operation and growth for large enterprises. These results may have reflected a deterioration in the business environment that had intensified toward the end of the Portillo administration. Prior to this period, Guatemala had made strong gains in the efficiency of customs procedures, when customs were integrated in the modern and autonomous *Superintendencia de Administracion Tributaria* (Superintendency of Tax Administration, or SAT), and computerization allowed streamlining 90 percent of customs declarations. These efforts are getting renewed impetus under the Berger administration.
7. The index of regulations is a weighted average of an index of labor regulations and an index of firm entry regulations, with weights determined by factor analysis (Bolaky and Freund 2003). Higher values of this index reflect a greater degree of regulation, both in the labor market and in the business sector. Because of delays in data collection, El Salvador is not included in this analysis.
8. The labor regulations index is the sum of an employment law index and an industrial relations law index. See Bolaky and Freund (2003) for further details.
9. Preliminary evidence from recent investment climate surveys suggests that Salvadoran firms appear to be the least constrained by labor regulations, whereas those from Guatemala are the most constrained within the Central American context. In addition, a larger percentage of (formal) firms in Honduras pointed to laws and regulations regarding dismissal of workers as a significant factor affecting employment levels.
10. The six registration processes are drafting the constitution of the firm, inscribing the firm in the Public Registry, registering with the tax authority, obtaining an operating license, registering with the Health Ministry, and securing environmental permits.
11. The Doing Business database of 2003 found that the registration of a limited liability company in San Salvador takes 115 days on average (or close to four

months), which seems to contradict data from the World Bank's investment climate survey of firms. This may be because *Doing Business* relates only to limited liability companies and reflects the answers of only one law firm, which supplies the data on duration of business registration. In contrast, the investment climate survey covers more than 400 firms of different legal status in each country, and the respondents are the firm managers.

12. The index of entry regulations uses data on the number of procedures and the time it takes to start a business in each country (Bolaky and Freund 2003).
13. In the larger sample of 195 countries used in the World Bank's indicator of control of corruption, El Salvador is placed only at the world's 34th percentile, compared with the 77th percentile for Costa Rica, and the average 34th percentile for Guatemala, Honduras, and Nicaragua. This may be related to poor perceptions in the areas of judicial independence and organized crime, according to results from the World Economic Forum's Growth Competitiveness Index, inasmuch as El Salvador performs quite well in the indexes of corruption in public services, corruption in foreign trade, and corruption in tax collection.
14. Credit constraints are prevalent when firms with viable investment projects do not have access to credit. This means that it is difficult to conclude that firms are constrained when they report obstacles to access finance. This is particularly important when assessing the constraints by firm size. If scale matters for profitability of investment projects, then naturally small firms will be less likely to access credit than will large firms—not because there is something wrong in the credit market, but because their investment projects might not be profitable. Thus, the analyses reported here and in other studies need to be complemented with subsequent analyses that directly assess credit constraints in a more rigorous fashion.
15. These results are from a benchmarking exercise of private-sector credit as share of GDP against log GDP per capita and a squared term. Results for Honduras may be affected by a potential undervaluation of its true GDP.
16. This is the subject of important recent studies by the International Monetary Fund, including those of Morales and Schipke (2005) and Canales-Kriljenko, Khandelwal, and Lehmann (2003).
17. To answer this question we use data collected by Lederman and Saenz (2005) on patents granted by the U.S. Patent Office to innovators residing around the globe and the number of scientific publications as provided by the U.S. National Research Foundation. The series plotted are the residuals from a regression on GDP and population and their squares. See Bosch, Lederman, and Maloney (2005) for technical details about the methodologies and data.
18. Bosch, Lederman, and Maloney (2005) discussed in detail how these elasticities are estimated and how they vary across regions of the world.

19. This result was derived by estimating a patenting function that includes the interaction between R&D investment and a dummy variable for Latin American and Caribbean countries. In turn, the same function was estimated including additional explanatory variables. Among these, the private sector's perception of the quality of research institutions and the extent of collaboration between private firms and universities were the ones that eliminated the statistical significance of the Latin American and Caribbean variable interacted with R&D. See Bosch, Lederman, and Maloney (2005) for details.
20. A *discovery* is defined as a good exported for less than US$10,000 in 1995, but for more than $1,000,000 in 2000, 2001, and 2002, based on disaggregated export data classified at the six-digit level of the Harmonized System of tariff codes. See Klinger and Lederman (2004).

Bibliography

Acemoglu, D., S. Johnson, and J. A. Robinson. 2001. "The Colonial Origins of Comparative Development: An Empirical Investigation." *American Economic Review* 91 (5): 1369–401.

Albuquerque, Rui, Norman Loayza, and Luis Servén. 2005. "World Market Integration through the Lens of Foreign Direct Investors." *Journal of International Economics* 66 (2): 267–95.

Anderson, K. 2004. "Agricultural Trade Reform and Poverty Reduction in Developing Countries." Policy Research Working Paper 3396, World Bank, Washington, DC.

Arce, Carlos, and C. Felipe Jaramillo. 2005. "El CAFTA y la agricultura centroamericana." Photocopy. World Bank, Washington, DC. http://www.worldbank.org/cafta.

Arellano, M., and S.R. Bond. 1991. "Some Tests of Specifications for Panel Data: Monte Carlo Evidence and an Application to Employment Equations." *Review of Economic Studies* 58: 277–97.

Arias, Omar. 2004. "Poverty in El Salvador During the 1990s: Evolution and Characteristics." Draft. Poverty Reduction and Economic Management Unit, Latin America and the Caribbean Region, World Bank, Washington, DC.

Armington, Paul. 1969. "A Theory of Demand for Products Distinguished by Place of Production." *IMF Staff Papers* 16: 159–78.

Artis, M., and W. Zhang. 1995. "International Business Cycles and the ERM: Is There a European Business Cycle?" *Oxford Economic Papers* 51: 120–32.

Baffes, John, and Harry de Gorter. 2003. "Decoupling Support to Agriculture: An Economic Analysis of Recent Experience." Draft. World Bank, Washington, DC.

Baldwin, R., J. Francois, and R. Portes. 1997. "The Costs and Benefits of Eastern Enlargement: The Impact on the EU and Central Europe." *Economic Policy: A European Forum* 24: 125–76.

Barreix, A., L. Villela, and J. Roca. 2004. "Fiscal Impact of Trade Liberalization in the Americas." Periodic Note, Inter-American Development Bank, Washington, DC.

Barro, Robert. 2000. "Inequality and Growth in a Panel of Countries." *Journal of Economic Growth* 5 (1): 5–32.

Baumol, William J., Richard R. Nelson, and Edward N. Wolff, eds. 1994. *The Convergence of Productivity, Its Significance, and Its Varied Connotations.* Oxford: Oxford University Press.

Bayoumi, T., and B. Eichengreen. 1993. "Shocking Aspects of European Monetary Unification." In *Adjustment and Growth in the European Monetary Union*, ed. F. Torres and G. Giavazzi, 193–221. New York: Cambridge University Press.

Baxter, M., and R. G. King. 1999. "Measuring Business Cycles: Approximate Band-Pass Filters for Economic Time Series." *Review of Economics and Statistics* 81: 575–93.

Beine, M., B. Candelon, and A. Hecq. 2000. "Assessing a Perfect European Optimal Currency Area: A Common Cycle Approach." *Empirica* 27: 115–32.

Beine, M., B. Candelon, and K. Sekkat. 1999. "Stabilization Policy and the Business Cycle Phases in Europe: A Markov Switching VAR Analysis." SFB 373, Working Paper 91/1999, Humboldt-Universität zu Berlin.

Beine, M., and A. Hecq. 1997. "Asymmetric Shocks inside Future EMU." *Journal of Economic Integration* 12: 131–40.

Beneke de Sanfelíu, Margarita, and Mauricio Shi. 2004. "Dinámica del ingreso rural en El Salvador." Photocopy. Fundación Salvadoreña para el Desarrollo Económico y Social, San Salvador, El Salvador.

Berthelon, Matías. 2004. "Growth Effects of Regional Integration Arrangements." Photocopy. Catholic University of Valparaiso, Chile, and University of Maryland, College Park.

Bliss, C., and R. Di Tella. 1997. "Does Competition Kill Corruption?" *Journal of Political Economy* 105: 1001–23.

Blomstrom, Magnus, and Edward N. Wolff. 1994. "Multinational Corporations and Productivity Convergence in Mexico." In *Convergence of Productivity: Cross-National Studies and Historical Evidence*, ed. W. J. Baumol, R. Nelson, and E. N. Wolff. New York: Oxford University Press.

Bolaky, Bineswaree, and Caroline Freund, 2003. "Trade, Regulations, and Growth." World Bank. http://www.worldbank.org/cafta.

Bosch, Mariano, Daniel Lederman, and William F. Maloney. 2005. "Patenting and Efficiency: A Global View." Photocopy. Office of the Chief Economist for Latin America and the Caribbean Region, World Bank, Washington, DC.

Bravo-Ortega, Claudio, and Daniel Lederman. 2005. "Agriculture and National Welfare around the World." Policy Research Working Paper 3499, World Bank, Washington, DC.

Breitung, J., and B. Candelon. 2001. "Is There a European Business Cycle? New Insights from a Frequency Domain Analysis." *Vierteljahrshaefte zur Wirtschaftsforschung* 70 (3): 331–38.

Bronchi, Chiara, and Dale Chua. 2005. "Trade Liberalization and Tax Coordination." In *Central America: Global and Regional Cooperation*, ed. M. Rodlauer and A. Schipke. Occasional Paper 243. Washington, DC: International Monetary Fund.

Brown, Drusilla, Alan V. Deardorff, and Robert Stern. 2004. "The Effects of Multinational Production on Wages and Working Conditions in Developing Countries." In *Challenges to Globalization*, ed. R. E. Baldwin and L. A. Winters. Chicago: University of Chicago Press.

Bruehlhart, M., and M. Thorpe. 2001. "Export Growth of NAFTA Members, Intraindustry Trade and Adjustment." *Global Business and Economics Review* 3 (1): 94–110.

Burfisher, M. E., S. Robinson, and K. Thierfielder. 2001. "The Impact of NAFTA on the United States." *Journal of Economic Perspectives* 15: 125–44.

Busse, Mathias. 2002. "Do Labor Standards Affect Comparative Advantage in Developing Countries?" *World Development* 30 (11): 1921–32.

———. 2004. "On the Determinants of Core Labour Standards: The Case of Developing Countries." *Economics Letters* 83: 211–17.

Bussolo, Maurizio, and Yoko Niimi. 2005. "Do the Poor Benefit from Regional Trade Pacts? An Illustration from the Central American Free Trade Agreement in Nicaragua." Photocopy. World Bank, Washington, DC.

Calderón, C. 2003. "Do Free Trade Agreements Enhance the Transmission of Shocks across Countries." Working Paper 213, Central Bank of Chile, Santiago.

Calderón, C., A. Chong, and E. Stein. 2002. "Trade Intensity and Business Cycle Synchronization: Are Developing Countries Any Different?" Working Paper 195. Central Bank of Chile, Santiago.

Canales-Kriljenko, Jorge I., Padamja Khandelwal, and Alexander Lehmann. 2003. "Financial Integration in Central America: Prospects and Adjustment Needs." Policy Discussion Paper 03/3, International Monetary Fund, Washington, DC.

Canova, F. 1998. "Detrending and Business Cycle Facts." *Journal of Monetary Economics* 41: 475–512.

Carkovic, M., and R. Levine. 2005. "Does Foreign Direct Investment Accelerate Economic Growth?" In *Does Foreign Investment Promote Development*, ed. T. H. Moran, E. M. Graham, and M. Blomstrom. Washington, DC: Institute for International Economics and Center for Global Development.

Caselli, Francesco, Gerardo Esquivel, and Fernando Lefort. 1996. "Revisiting the Convergence Debate." *Journal of Economic Growth* 1 (3): 363–89.

Castañeda, Tarcisio. 2004. "Compensation for Trade Reforms in Agriculture in Latin America and the Caribbean: Policy Options and Design and Implementation Issues." Draft. World Bank, Washington, DC.

CEPAL (Comisión Económica para América Latina y el Caribe). 2004. "El tratado de libre comercio Centroamérica-Estados Unidos: Resultados de la negociación y características principales." Mexico DF: CEPAL.

Chen, Shaohua, and Martin Ravallion. 2003. "Household Welfare Impacts of China's Accession to the WTO." Policy Research Working Paper 3040, World Bank, Washington, DC.

Choe, J. 2001. "An Impact of Economic Integration through Trade on Business Cycles for 10 East Asian Countries." *Journal of Asian Economics* 12 (4): 569–86.

Coady, David, Pedro Olinto, and Natalia Caldes. 2003. "Coping with the Coffee Crisis in Central America: The Role of Social Safety Nets in Honduras." Draft. International Food Policy Research Institute, Washington, DC.

Cohen, Wesley M., and Daniel A. Levinthal. 1989. "Innovation and Learning: The Two Faces of R&D." *Economic Journal* 99: 569–96.

Copeland, Brian R., and M. Scott Taylor. 2003. "Trade, Growth, and the Environment." Working Paper 9823, National Bureau of Economic Research, Cambridge, MA.

Cord, L., and Q. Wodon. 2001. "Do Agricultural Programs in Mexico Alleviate Poverty? Evidence from the Ejido Sector." *Cuadernos de Economía* 38 (special issue): 239–56.

Corden, W. M. 1974. *Trade Policy and Economic Welfare.* Oxford, UK: Clarendon Press.

Costa Rica, Ministerio de Comercio Exterior. 2004. "Tratado de libre comercio: Documento explicativo." San José.

Cox-Edwards, Alejandra, and Sebastian Edwards. 1994. "Labor Market Distortions and Structural Adjustment in Developing Countries." In *Labor Markets in an Era of Adjustment*, ed. S. Horton, R. Kanbur, and D. Mazumdar. Washington, DC: World Bank.

Cuevas, A., M. Messmacher, and A. Werner. 2002. "Macroeconomic Synchronization between Mexico and Its NAFTA Partners." Photocopy. World Bank, Washington, DC.

Davis, B., S. Handa, M. Ruiz, M. Stampini, and P. Winters. 2002. "Conditionality and the Impact of Program Design on Household Welfare: Comparing Two Diverse Cash Transfer Programs in Rural Mexico." Working Paper 7, Agricultural and Development Economics Division, Food and Agriculture Organization of the United Nations. http://www.fao.org/es/ESA/work-e.htm.

Dean, Judith. 2002. "Does Trade Harm the Environment? A New Test." *Canadian Journal of Economics* 35 (4): 819–42.

Deardorff, Alan V. 2003. "Ricardian Comparative Advantage with Intermediate Inputs." Unpublished paper. University of Michigan, Ann Arbor.

Deaton, Angus. 1997. "The Analysis of Household Surveys." Baltimore: Johns Hopkins University Press.

De Ferranti, David, Guillermo Perry, Daniel Lederman, William Foster, and Alberto Valdés. 2005. *Beyond the City: The Rural Contribution to Development.* Washington, DC: World Bank.

De Ferranti, David, Guillermo Perry, Francisco Fereira, and Michael Walton. 2004. *Inequality in Latin America and the Caribbean: Breaking with History?* Washington, DC: World Bank.

De Ferranti, David, Guillermo Perry, Indermit Gill, J. Luis Guasch, William F. Maloney, Carolina Sánchez-Páramo, and Norbert Schady. 2003. *Closing the Gap in Education and Technology.* Washington, DC: World Bank.

De Ferranti, David, Guillermo Perry, Daniel Lederman, and William F. Maloney. 2002. *From Natural Resources to the Knowledge Economy: Trade and Job Quality.* Washington, DC: World Bank.

Di Gropello, E. 2006. *A Comparative Analysis of School-Based Management in Central America.* Washington, DC: World Bank.

Dollar, David, and Aart Kraay. 2002. "Growth Is Good for the Poor." *Journal of Economic Growth* 7 (3): 195–225.

Dutt, P. 2005. "Trade Protection and Bureaucratic Corruption: An Empirical Investigation." Photocopy. INSEAD, Singapore.

Easterly, W., and R. Levine. 2003. "Tropics, Germs, and Crops: How Endowments Influence Economic Development." *Journal of Monetary Economics* 50 (1): 3–47.

Easton, J., and S. Kortum. 2002. "Technology, Geography, and Trade." *Econometrica* 70 (5): 1741–79.

Eichengreen, B., and A. B. Taylor. 2003. "The Monetary Consequences of a Free Trade Area of the Americas." Working Paper 9666, National Bureau for Economic Research, Cambridge, MA.

El Salvador, Ministerio de Economía y Comercio. 2004. "Tratado de libre comercio: Documento explicativo." San Salvador.

FAOSTAT (Food and Agriculture Organization Statistics). 2004. http://faostat.fao.org/.

Fiess, Norbert. 2005. "Business Cycle Synchronization and Integration: A Case Study for Central America." Policy Research Working Paper 3584, World Bank, Washington, DC.

Filardo, A. J., and S. F. Gordon. 1994. "International Co-Movements of Business Cycles." RWP 94-11, Federal Reserve Bank of Kansas, Kansas City.

Fink, Carsten, and Keith Maskus. 2004. *Intellectual Property and Development: Lessons from Recent Economic Research*. Washington, DC: World Bank.

Fink, Carsten, and Patrick Reichenmiller. 2005. "Tightening TRIPS: The Intellectual Property Provisions of Recent US Free Trade Agreements." Trade Note. World Bank, Washington, DC.

Forbes, N., and D. Wield. 2000. "Managing R&D in Technology Followers." *Research Policy* 29: 1095–109.

Frankel J. A., and A. Rose. 1998. "The Endogeneity of the Optimum Currency Area Criteria." *Economic Journal* 108: 1009–25.

———. 2005. "Is Trade Good or Bad for the Environment? Sorting Out the Causality." *Review of Economics and Statistics* 87 (1): 85–91.

Frankel, J. A., and S. Wei. 1998. "Regionalization of World Trade and Currencies: Economics and Politics." In *The Regionalization of the World Economy*, ed. J. A. Frankel. Chicago: University of Chicago Press.

Garnier, J. 2003. "How Much Does Intra-industry Trade Matter in Business Cycle Transmission?" European University Institute. http://www.iue.it/Personal/Researchers/JulienGarnier/Julien Garnier 3YF II.pdf.

Glewwe, P., and G. Hall. 1998. "Are Some Groups More Vulnerable to Macroeconomic Shocks Than Others? Hypotheses Tests Using Panel Data from Peru." *Journal of Development Economics* 56 (1): 181–206.

González, Anabel. 2005. "The Application of the Dominican Republic–Central America–United States Free Trade Agreement." Office of Trade, Growth, and Competitiveness, Organization of American States, Washington, DC.

González, Anabel, and Eduardo Lizano. 2003. "El tratado de libre comercio entre el Istmo Centroamericano y los Estados Unidos de América—oportunidades, desafíos y riesgos." Documento diseminación 9, Instituto para la Integración de América Latina y el Caribe, Buenos Aires, Argentina.

Gould, David, and William Gruben. 2005. "The Impact of DR-CAFTA on Economic Growth." Photocopy. Central America Country Management Unit, World Bank, Washington, DC.

Government of Honduras. 2003. "Honduras: Tratado de libre comercio con Estados Unidos: informe final de negociación." Tegucigalpa.

———. 2004. "Informe final de la negociacion." Tegucigalpa.

Greene, William H. 2000. Econometric Analysis. New York: Prentice Hall.

Griffith, R., S. Redding, and J. Van Reenen. 2003. "R&D and Absorptive Capacity: From Theory to Data." Working Paper 01/03, Institute for Fiscal Studies, London.

Hall, Robert, and Charles I. Jones. 1999. "Why Do Some Countries Produce So Much More Output Per Worker Than Others?" *Quarterly Journal of Economics* 114 (1): 83–116.

Hausmann, Ricardo, and Dani Rodrik. 2003a. "Discovering El Salvador's Production Potential." Photocopy. Kennedy School of Government, Harvard University, Cambridge, MA.

———. 2003b. "Economic Development As Self-discovery." *Journal of Development Economics* 72: 603–33.

Heckman, James. 1979. "Sample Selection Bias As a Specification Error." *Econometrica* 47: 153–61.

Helg, R., P. Manassa, T. Monacelli, and R. Rovelli. 1995. "How Much (A)symmetry in Europe? Evidence from Industrial Sectors." *European Economic Review* 39: 1017–41.

Hertel, T., and J. Reimer. 2005. "Predicting the Poverty Impacts of Trade Reform." *Journal of International Trade and Economic Development* 14 (4): 377–405.

Hilaire, Alvin, and Yongzheng Yang. 2003. "The United States and the New Regionalism/Bilateralism." Working Paper WP/03/206, International Monetary Fund, Washington, DC.

Hinojosa-Ojeda, R. A. 2003. "Regional Integration among the Unequal: A CGE Model of USCAFTA,NAFTA, and the Central American Common Market." Photocopy. University of California, Los Angeles.

Holm-Nielsen, Lauritz, Andreas Blom, and Patricia Garcia. 2003. "The World Bank in Tertiary Education in LAC." In Spanish. Report 26906, World Bank, Washington, DC.

IADB (Inter-American Development Bank). 2002. *Beyond Borders: The New Regionalism in Latin America.* Washington, DC: Inter-American Development Bank.

Jalan, J., and M. Ravallion. 1999. "Are the Poor Less Well Insured? Evidence on Vulnerability to Income Risk in Rural China." *Journal of Development Economics* 58: 61–81.

Jones, R. W. 2000. *Globalization and the Theory of Input Trade.* Cambridge, MA: MIT Press.

Kehoe, Timothy. 2003. "An Evaluation of the Performance of Applied General Equilibrium Models of the Impact of NAFTA." Research Department Staff Report 320, Federal Reserve Bank of Minneapolis, MN.

Keller, Wolfgang. 2002. "Geographic Localization of International Technology Diffusion." *American Economic Review* 92 (1): 120–42.

Khan, Faruk. 2004. "New Product Technology and Factor Accumulation." Photocopy. Department of Economics, Williams College, Williamstown, MA.

Klinger, Bailey, and Daniel Lederman. 2004. "Discovery and Development: An Empirical Exploration of 'New' Products." Policy Research Working Paper 3450, World Bank, Washington, DC.

Klugman, Jeni, Diana Kruger, and Kate Withers. 2003."Consumption Risk and Smoothing during Disasters: The Case of Hurricane Mitch in Nicaragua." Draft. World Bank, Washington, DC.

Kraay, A. 2003. "When Is Growth Pro-Poor? Cross-Country Evidence." Policy Research Working Paper 3225, World Bank, Washington, DC.

Krolzig, H. M. 2001. "Business Cycle Measurement in the Presence of Structural Change: International Evidence." *International Journal of Forecasting* 17: 349–68.

Krueger, A. O. 1974. "The Political Economy of the Rent-Seeking Society." *American Economic Review* 64: 291–303.

Lederman, Daniel. 2005. *The Political Economy of Protection: Theory and the Chilean Experience.* Palo Alto, CA: Stanford University Press.

Lederman, Daniel, Norman Loayza, and Rodrigo Soares. 2005. "Corruption and Accountability: Political Institutions Matter." *Economics and Politics* 17 (1): 1–35.

Lederman, Daniel, and William F. Maloney. 2003a. "R&D and Development." Photocopy. Office of the Chief Economist for Latin America and the Caribbean Region, World Bank, Washington, DC.

———. 2003b. "Trade Structure and Growth." Policy Research Working Paper 3025, World Bank, Washington, DC.

Lederman, Daniel, William F. Maloney, and Luis Servén. 2005. *Lessons from NAFTA for Latin American and Caribbean Countries.* Palo Alto, CA: Stanford University Press.

Lederman, Daniel, and Caglar Ozden. 2005. "Geopolitical Interests and Preferential Access to U.S. Markets." Policy Research Working Paper 3531, World Bank, Washington, DC.

Lederman, Daniel, Guillermo Perry, and Rodrigo Suescún. 2004. "Trade Structure and Policy in Central America." In *The Macroeconomy of Central America,* ed. R. Rennhack and E. Offerdal. New York: Palgrave Macmillan.

Lederman, Daniel, and Laura Saenz. 2005. "Innovation and Development around the World, 1960–2000." Policy Research Working Paper 3774, World Bank, Washington, DC.

Levy-Yeyati, E., E. Stein, and C. Daude. 2002. "Regional Integration and the Location of FDI." Photocopy. Inter-American Development Bank, Washington, DC.

Lipsey, R. 2002. "Home and Host Country Effects of FDI." Working Paper 9293, National Bureau of Economic Research, Cambridge, MA.

Loayza, Norman, Pablo Fajnzylber, and Ricardo Calderón. 2005. *Economic Growth in Latin America and the Caribbean: Stylized Facts, Explanations, and Forecasts.* Washington, DC: World Bank.

Londoño-Kent, M., and P. Kent. 2003. "A Tale of Two Ports: The Costs of Inefficiency." Photocopy. World Bank, Washington, DC. http://www.worldbank.org/cafta.

López, J. Humberto. 2004. "Pro-growth, Pro-poor: Is There a Tradeoff?" Policy Research Working Paper 3378, World Bank, Washington, DC.

López, J. Humberto, and Luis Servén. 2005. "A Normal Relationship? Poverty, Growth, and Inequality." Photocopy. World Bank, Washington, DC.

López, Ramón. 2003. "Trade Policy and the Poor in Developing Countries." Unpublished paper. University of Maryland, College Park.

López-Córdova, Ernesto. 2003. "NAFTA and Manufacturing Productivity in Mexico." *Economía* 4 (1): 55–89.

Lora, Eduardo. 2001. "Las reformas estructurales en America Latina: Que se ha reformado y como medirlo," Working Paper 462, Inter-American Development Bank, Washington, DC.

Lundberg, M., and L. Squire. 2003. "The Simultaneous Evolution of Growth and Inequality." Photocopy. World Bank, Washington, DC.

Maluccio, John. 2004. "Coping with the Coffee Crisis: in Central America: The Role of the Nicaraguan Social Safety Nets Program." International Food Policy Research Institute background paper for *Shocks and Social Protection: Lessons from the Central American Coffee Crisis.* Washington, DC: World Bank.

Marques, Jose. 2005. "El Salvador: A Partial Equilibrium Estimate of the DR-CAFTA's Welfare Impact." Draft. World Bank, Washington, DC.

Martin, William, and Devashish Mitra. 2001. "Productivity Growth and Convergence in Agriculture and Manufacturing." *Economic Development and Cultural Change* 49 (2): 403–22.

Mason, Andrew D. 2005. "Ensuring That the Poor Can Benefit from DR-CAFTA: Policy Approaches for Managing the Economic Transition." Photocopy. Central America Country Management Unit, World Bank, Washington, DC.

McCulloch, Neil. 2002. "The Impact of Structural Reforms on Poverty: A Simple Methodology with Extensions." Photocopy. Institute of Development Studies, University of Sussex, UK.

Milanovic, Branco. 2003. "Income Convergence during the Disintegration of the World Economy, 1919–39." Policy Research Working Paper 2941, World Bank, Washington, DC.

Monge, R., F. Castro, and D. Saavedra. 2004. "La agricultura Nicaragüense ante el DR-CAFTA." Draft. World Bank, Washington, DC.

Monge, R., M. Loría, and C. González-Vega. 2003. "Retos y oportunidades para los sectores agropecuario y agroindustrial de Centro América ante un tratado de libre comercio con los Estados Unidos" Report prepared for the World Bank DR-CAFTA Studies Program. www.worldbank.org/cafta.

Morales, R. Armando, and Alfred Schipke. 2005. "Regional Integration and Financial Systems Issues." In *Central America: Global and Regional Cooperation*, ed. M. Rodlauer and A. Schipke. Occasional Paper 243. Washington, DC: International Monetary Fund.

Paunovic, Igor. 2004. "The United States-Central American Free Trade Agreement: Fiscal Implications for Central American Countries." Working paper LC/MEX/L.616, United Nations Economic Commission for Latin America and the Caribbean, Mexico City.

Pavitt, Keith. 2001. "Public Policies to Support Basic Research: What Can the Rest of the World Learn from U.S. Theory and Practice? (And What They Should Not Learn)." *Industrial and Corporate Change* 10: 761–79.

Pörtner, Claus C. 2003. "The Expected Impacts of DR-CAFTA in Guatemala." World Bank. www.worldbank.org/cafta.

Ravallion, Martin. 2001. "Growth, Inequality, and Poverty." World Bank, Washington, DC.

Rodlauer, Markus, and Alfred Schipke, eds. 2005. *Central America: Global and Regional Cooperation*. Occasional Paper 243. Washington, DC: International Monetary Fund.

Rodríguez, Francisco, and Dani Rodrik. 2000. "Trade Policy and Economic Growth: A Skeptic's Guide to the Cross-National Evidence." *NBER Macro Annual*. Cambridge, MA.

Rubin, J., and N. Thygesen. 1996. "Monetary Union and the Outsiders: A Cointegration-Codependence Analysis of Business Cycles in Europe." *Economie Appliquée* 49 (3): 123–71.

Ruiz, M., M. Stampini, B. Davis, P. Winters, and S. Handa. 2002. "More Calories or Food Diversity: The Impact of PROGRESA and PROCAMPO on Food Security in Rural Mexico." Working Paper 6, Agricultural and Development Economics Division, Food and Agriculture Organization of the United Nations. http://www.fao.org/es/ESA/work-e.htm.

Sadoulet, E., A. de Janvry, and B. Davis. 2001. "Cash Transfer Programs with Income Multipliers: PROCAMPO in Mexico." Discussion Paper 99, International Food Policy Research Institute, Washington, DC.

Salazar-Xiriñachs, José Manuel. 2002. "Proliferation of Sub-regional Trade Agreements in the Americas: An Assessment of Key Analytical and Policy Issues." *Journal of Asian Economics* 13: 181–212.

Salazar-Xiriñachs, José Manuel, and Jaime Granados. 2004. "The US-Central America Free Trade Agreement: Opportunities and Challenges." In *Free Trade Agreements: US Strategies and Priorities,* ed. Jeffrey Schott, 225–75. Washington, DC: Institute for International Economics.

Salazar-Xiriñachs, José Manuel, Theresa Wetter, Karsten Steinfatt, and Daniela Ivascanu. 2001. "Customs Unions in the Western Hemisphere." Trade Unit, Organization of American States, Washington, DC.

Schiff, Maurice, and Yangling Wang. 2003. "Regional Integration and North-South Technology Diffusion: The Case of NAFTA." Photocopy. Development Economics Research Group, World Bank, Washington, DC.

Shin, K., and Y. Wang Yunjong. 2004. "Trade Integration and Business Cycle Co-movements: Case of Korea with Other Asian Countries." *Japan and the World Economy* 16 (2): 213–230.

Stern, Robert M. 2003. "Labor Standards and Trade Agreements." Discussion Paper 496, University of Michigan, Ann Arbor.

Suescún, Rodrigo. 2005. "Size and Effectiveness of the Fiscal Automatic Stabilizers in Latin America." Photocopy. Office of the Chief Economist for Latin America and the Caribbean, World Bank, Washington, DC.

Tejada, Ricardo A., and C. Felipe Jaramillo. 2005. "Comparing Tariff Negotiations for Sensitive Crops in U.S. FTAs." World Bank, http://www.worldbank.org/cafta.

Trigueros, Alvaro, and Carolina Avalos. 2004. "Analysis of the Poverty and Social Impacts of the Coffee Crisis (Price Shock) in El Salvador." Draft. Fundación Salvadoreña para el Desarrollo Económico y Social, San Salvador, El Salvador.

USTR (United States Trade Representative). 2004. "Free Trade with Central America, Trade Facts." Washington, DC.

Vakis, Renos, Diana Kruger, and Andrew D. Mason. 2004. "Shocks and Coffee: Lessons from Nicaragua." Draft. Human Development Department, Latin America and the Caribbean Region, World Bank, Washington, DC.

Warcziag, Romain. 2001. "Measuring the Dynamic Gains from Trade." *World Bank Economic Review* 15 (3): 393–429.

Wilson, John S., and Tsunehiro Otsuki. 2003. "Trade Facilitation and the Central American Free Trade Agreement (DR-CAFTA)." Photocopy. Central America Country Management Unit, World Bank, Washington, DC.

Wilson, J. S., C. L. Mann, and T. Otsuki. 2005. "Assessing the Benefits of Trade Facilitation: A Global Perspective." *World Economy* 28 (6): 841–71.

Winters, Alan L., Neil McCulloch, and Andrew McKay. 2004. "Trade Liberalization and Poverty: The Evidence So Far." *Journal of Economic Literature* (U.S.) 42 (1): 72–115.

World Bank. 2001. "Nicaragua Poverty Assessment: Challenges and Opportunities for Poverty Reduction," Report 20488-NI, World Bank, Washington, DC.

———. 2002. *Global Economic Prospects and the Developing Countries: Making Trade Work for the World's Poor.* Washington, DC: World Bank.

———. 2003a. Doing Business. http://www.doingbusiness.org.

———. 2003b. "El Salvador Country Economic Memorandum." World Bank, Washington, DC.

———. 2003c. "Guatemala: Poverty Assessment." World Bank, Washington, DC.

———. 2003d. "Income Support Program in Turkey and Mexico and Agricultural Reform in New Zealand." Draft case studies. World Bank, Washington, DC.

———. 2003e. "Mexico: Poverty Assessment." World Bank, Washington, DC.

———. 2004a. "El Salvador: Country Economic Memorandum." World Bank, Washington, DC.

———. 2004b. "Guatemala: Country Economic Memorandum." World Bank, Washington, DC.

———. 2004c. "Guatemala: Investment Climate Assessment." World Bank, Washington, DC.

———. 2004d. "Honduras: Country Procurement Assessment Review." World Bank, Washington, DC.

———. 2004e. "Honduras: Development Policy Review." World Bank, Washington, DC.

———. 2004f. "Nicaragua: Development Policy Review." World Bank, Washington, DC.

———. 2004g. "Poverty in Mexico: An Assessment of Conditions, Trends, and Government Strategy." Report 28612-ME, World Bank, Washington, DC.

———. 2005a. "Assessing the Impact of the Investment Climate on Productivity Using Firm-level Data: Methodology and the Cases of Guatemala, Honduras, and Nicaragua." World Bank, Washington, DC.

———. 2005b, "Guatemala Country Economic Memorandum." World Bank, Washington, DC.

———. 2005c. "Mexico: Social Protection Study." Mexico Country Management Unit and Human Development Sector Management Units, Latin America and the Caribbean Region, World Bank, Washington, DC.

———. 2005d. "Shocks and Social Protection: Lessons from the Central American Coffee Crisis," Poverty Reduction and Economic Management and Human Development Sector Management Units, Latin America and the Caribbean Region, World Bank, Washington, DC.

Index

B

C

D

V

W